The Open
University

A207
From Enlightenment to Romanticism,
*c.*1780–1830

Block 6 New Conceptions of Art and the Artist

This publication forms part of an Open University course A207 *From Enlightenment to Romanticism, c.1780–1830*. Details of this and other Open University courses can be obtained from the Course Information and Advice Centre, PO Box 724, The Open University, Milton Keynes MK7 6ZS, United Kingdom: tel. +44 (0)1908 653231, e-mail general-enquiries@open.ac.uk

Alternatively, you may visit the Open University website at http://www.open.ac.uk where you can learn more about the wide range of courses and packs offered at all levels by The Open University.

To purchase a selection of Open University course materials visit the webshop at www.ouw.co.uk, or contact Open University Worldwide, Michael Young Building, Walton Hall, Milton Keynes MK7 6AA, United Kingdom for a brochure. tel. +44 (0)1908 858785; fax +44 (0)1908 858787; e-mail ouwenq@open.ac.uk

The Open University
Walton Hall, Milton Keynes
MK7 6AA

First published 2004

Edited, designed and typeset by The Open University.

Printed and bound in the United Kingdom by The Alden Group, Oxford.

ISBN 0 7492 9600 3

1.1

Contents

Introduction to Block 6

Prepared for the course team by Robert Wilkinson

In this block of the course, the focus turns very definitely to Romanticism and largely, though not exclusively, to the many states that made up Germany. It needs to be stressed from the start that the block does not aim to offer a *definition* of Romanticism: that is, it does not try to list qualities which *all* Romantic works are supposed to have, nor does it offer a neat set of ideas which can be labelled 'Romantic'. Historians of culture have tried to do this for the best part of two centuries with little success – the Romantic movement is much more elusive in this respect than the Enlightenment. (This is a theme that will be taken up again in the Course Conclusion.) Romanticism grew out of the confluence of a number of different sources, evolved so quickly, and shows such variations as it manifests itself in the context of the various cultures of Europe (even among near neighbours like France and Britain) that attempts to define it in any short or simple way have proved very difficult. (See, for instance, the classic discussion in Lovejoy, 1948.) This is not to say that the position is hopeless: just to point out that you need to be extremely wary of any one-line statements which claim to sum up the 'nature' or 'essence' of Romanticism. The best way to begin to appreciate the complexity of this very important change of direction in European culture is to look at some of its characteristic ideas and productions, and this block makes a start in that direction.

The first two units focus on ideas about art and on changes in the aesthetic beliefs of the period. A characteristic view of what art is and of the nature of artists was part of the world-view of the Enlightenment and was largely shared across Europe. The contrary view that was part of Romanticism was first made theoretically explicit by a group of young men in Germany in the last decade of the eighteenth century, and it is their ideas which are contrasted with those of the Enlightenment in Units 24–25. This is not to say that these men were 'the first Romantics': to put it more accurately, they were providing a theoretical statement of changes that had been gathering momentum for some time. Works of art which exhibited features that came to be regarded as characteristic of Romanticism had begun to appear (notably in Britain, as well as in Germany) before these theoretical works were written: the theory did not bring about the practice, as it were. Rather, the theory articulated and clarified, in general terms, changes in belief and practice which were already happening. Nor was it the case, of course, that all the artists in Europe suddenly changed direction once the new ideas became widely disseminated: the prime motivation of artists is rarely a desire to conform to a theory about art. The change in artistic practices and in ideas about art that are part of Romanticism came about gradually, and at different rates and with different emphases in different countries; but a change there certainly was, and a very deep one, reflecting changes in the entire world-views of which these ideas form a part.

It is to be noted that these ideas were enthusiastically taken up and developed in Germany. It has to be stressed at once that to refer to 'Germany' as if it were a state in any sense like that in which Britain or France were states at this time is quite misleading: the geographical area which was eventually to become a unified country in the late nineteenth century was in the period covered by this course composed of approximately 400 states, some tiny, others (like Prussia or Bavaria) larger and more influential. These states were nominally independent, though in theory all owed allegiance to the Holy Roman Empire. The mutual political relations of these states defy summary in a short compass: the point to fix on is that such unity as 'Germany' had at the time was a result of a common language and culture rather than political structure. (For more detail, see Holborn, 1965.) What is true is that Germany, thus understood, cannot be said to have been in the intellectual driving seat, as it were, during the Enlightenment. The German states had been subjected to the most appalling devastation, both economically and culturally, by the Thirty Years' War (1618–48), a particularly grim episode in the protracted power struggle between the kings of France, the Habsburg dynasty and Spain which occupied Europe intermittently from 1491 to 1715. It was said at the time that in Germany there were only dogs left for the dogs to feed on, so terrible was the depopulation of the country. The effects of this war were felt in Germany for almost a century, and the development of German cultural life (in most respects) was, unsurprisingly, slowed down. Equally unsurprisingly, German intellectuals and artists spent much of the eighteenth century feeling that they had ground to make up by comparison with their neighbours, a feeling the French (and Francophile rulers such as Frederick the Great of Prussia) were only too pleased to reinforce. By the end of the century this had begun to change. German intellectuals were ready to show that they could take the lead in the development of European culture, and Romantic aesthetic theory was one manifestation of this growing confidence.

The complexity of the Romantic period and its productions could hardly be better illustrated than by the case of Goethe and his major work *Faust*. The Faust legend from which Goethe began has at its core the story of a scholar who sells his soul to the devil for various worldly goods and duly pays the price of damnation when the bargain falls due. In Goethe's hands, however, this potentially trite morality story is transformed into something much deeper, more ramified and complex, as Carmen Lavin makes clear in Units 26–27. Yet, as is also made clear, the relationship of this play both to its creator and to its times is by no means straightforward. Faust (the character) is not damned in Goethe's version of the story, despite having been involved in actions by no means acceptable by the standards of orthodox Christian morality. He is not damned because he accepts and tries to live by one of the key tenets of a morality which coincides with thoroughgoing Romanticism: he never accepts that he has reached a stage of moral development which is *final,* for there was held to be no such state. Perfection is unattainable: the nearest we can come to it is never to cease to strive for it, and it is Faust's perpetual striving to reach yet another stage of development which causes the Lord, in this version of the legend, to grant him salvation at the end of the play. However, despite this apparent presence of Romantic morality in the play, it would be a mistake to assume that *Faust* neatly reflects its times, or that Goethe can be simply categorized as a Romantic, since neither of these ideas is true in any straightforward way.

Of all the arts it was music that the Romantic theorists held in highest regard, since it seemed the art best able to embody the striving to express something deep and infinite which haunted so many of them. Unit 28 discusses some songs by Schubert. Schubert developed his own unique musical voice, and this is shown nowhere more clearly than in the settings of poems by Goethe considered in the unit. It is instructive to compare them with the arias in *Don Giovanni,* which you studied at the start of the course. As Robert Philip notes, Schubert's 'Ganymed' is far freer in structure than anything written by Mozart, seeming to be guided 'solely by imaginative recreation of a developing psychological situation' (p.190). The difference (in this case) between Mozart and Schubert in their approach to musical structure is an instance of the change in artistic practice that Romanticism brought with it. However, as in the case of Goethe, it is necessary to resist the temptation to try to make artists fit the neat categories invented by theorists: Schubert had by no means abandoned all the musical practices of the Classical period, and would use Classical musical vocabulary if he judged that the material he was using demanded it.

The block ends with a study of Canto III of Byron's *Childe Harold's Pilgrimage,* a work which again in its own way also illustrates the dangers of trying to sum up Romanticism too neatly. Byron would have accepted relatively few of the ideas of the German Romantic theorists discussed in the two opening units of the block, yet equally this poem is undeniably Romantic. Interestingly, it was regarded by contemporaries as gloomy and sublime, characteristics they regarded as Germanic. Again, the poem made fashionable a character type (the Byronic hero) and certain attitudes to the world which became hugely influential in the years after its publication. The Byronic attitudes described by Nicola Watson became essential attributes for anyone at the time who wished to be considered as part of the cultural avant-garde.

What all these similarities and differences might indicate about Romanticism is a theme we return to at the end of the block.

References

Holborn, H. (1965) *A History of Modern Germany 1648–1840*, London, Eyre and Spottiswoode.

Lovejoy, A.O. (1948) *Essays in the History of Ideas*, Baltimore, Johns Hopkins University Press.

Units 24–25
Two conceptions of art

Prepared for the course team by Robert Wilkinson

Contents

Study components

Weeks of study	Supplementary material	Audio-visual	Anthologies and set books
2	AV Notes Illustrations Book	Audio 5	Anthology II

Important note: most of the reading associated with these units concerns the Romantic conception of art. The balance of work is not designed to be 50 per cent on the Romantics and 50 per cent on the eighteenth-century conception of art. You should aim to devote one-third of your study time for these units to the latter, and two-thirds to the sections on Romanticism.

Aims

Units 24–25 and their associated components are designed:

- to introduce you, via the reading of selected primary source texts, to the Romantic conception of art;
- to introduce you to the eighteenth-century conception of art which preceded it;
- to indicate briefly how these conceptions of art were embedded in contrasting views of the world;
- to indicate how Romanticism spread, and was variously interpreted, throughout Europe.

Objectives

By the end of your work on these units you should:
- have an understanding of the main features of eighteenth-century and Romantic conceptions of art;
- be able to compare and contrast the two;
- be familiar with the ideas of a number of important German theorists of Romanticism;
- be aware in broad terms of what Romanticism meant in artistic practice.

1 Introduction

This part of the course is an example of how the philosophical discipline of aesthetics – which you have already met briefly in your study of picturesque tourism in the Lake District – can be used to provide an understanding of the arts of a given period by investigating the *concepts and beliefs* in terms of which those living at the time thought about the aesthetic dimension of life. By the term 'art' in the title of these units, I mean all the arts, not simply the visual arts, although they are of course included.

By using the techniques of aesthetics my aim is to introduce you to one of the most dramatic changes that has yet occurred in the history of European thought about the arts and about the aesthetic dimension of life in general, a change which occurred at around the end of the eighteenth century. Whether their ideas on the subject are explicitly formulated or not, it is always the case that the artists, critics, philosophers and art-lovers of a given time and place have some basic notions about what art *is* (put another way: about the nature of art) and about what it is fundamentally *for* – what it does for us, what its role is in our life, how its purposes are to be achieved, and what skills or special qualities an artist must have if these goals are to be attained. It happens that the views on these questions which characterized European thought in the eighteenth century, on the one hand, and the Romantic period, on the other, are close to being polar opposites. They were also explicitly formulated and debated by major figures of the time, and in these units we will investigate them via a close reading of some important selected primary source texts.

For most of the time, to make matters memorable, I will set out what will appear to be a bold and clear contrast of views. At the end of these units, however, I will introduce a few important qualifications. One thing the history of humanity is not is neat and tidy, and this applies as much to the history of aesthetic beliefs as it does anywhere else. It is not the case that what I am going to call the eighteenth-century view of art was accepted in every detail by all the artists alive at the time when this theory was most widely canvassed. Equally, even among the members of so close-knit a group as that of the early German Romantics whose ideas we will study in detail, there were differences. What is to be set out in these units, therefore, is really a statement of two opposed points of view about the arts, which would have been signed up to in differing degrees by the thinkers adhering to each of the outlooks we are going to consider. Moreover, while it is quite certain that these views of art are not compatible in theory, it is to be stressed that – then as now – practising artists are rarely as bothered about the considerations of logical consistency which so exercise theorists and philosophers as are these latter. Broadly speaking, the primary goal of an artist is to produce a work that articulates an experience that has intrigued or interested them and that they find significant enough to want to convey to us. In the pursuit of this goal they will use whatever selection of techniques and theoretical ideas are appropriate, whether they are neatly consistent or not.

Further, each of these outlooks about art is logically grounded in other beliefs held at the time, and the change in opinion about art is in a formal sense a logical consequence of a contrast in beliefs at a deeper level. A change in the understanding of art of the magnitude we are going to look at could not rationally come about unless there was also a more widespread change in the dominant way of looking at the world as a whole, a change in what philosophers and historians of ideas call a world-view, and this is precisely what happened. Accordingly, in the case of both of the views of art we are going to study, that of most of the eighteenth century and that of the early Romantic movement, a few pages will be devoted to outlining this background of more general beliefs. To repeat, serious changes in beliefs about aesthetic matters do not come out of the air, but are always coherent with other changes in the culture in question. We have seen an example of this in the aesthetic domain already, on a smaller scale, in our investigation of the phenomenon of picturesque tourism, and of the development of views about the sublime and the beautiful. In the present case, we are going to look at a much larger-scale example of the same thing.

We will begin, then, by looking at the conception of art, and to some extent of the entire aesthetic dimension of life, which was dominant in Europe in the eighteenth century prior to Romanticism. You will find this point of view variously referred to in books about the different arts, sometimes as classicism or based on classical models or as Augustan or sometimes (confusingly) as Neoclassicism. These labels have their justifications and uses as a shorthand, and we will look at the reasons for them as we go along, together with some other important terms (such as '**rationalism**') which you need to master if you are to understand the history of European culture. For the moment, let us just call it the eighteenth-century conception of art (in Europe, of course, but we can drop this qualification from now on, and take it as read).

2   The eighteenth-century conception of art

As stated above, the eighteenth-century view of art is grounded in some more general features of the world-view of that time, and in a quite direct way. Accordingly, we need to spend a short time looking at these more basic beliefs, before moving on to the point of view about aesthetic issues that they invite and support.

The order of things

The most general of the beliefs underpinning the eighteenth-century view of art is the belief that the universe or 'what there is', as philosophers like to put it, has a fixed order. This order is something we discover: nature is out there, independent of us, not created by us. At the time, this would have been expressed in terms of a Latin phrase: there is a *rerum natura*, a nature of things. This belief is not, of course, peculiar to the eighteenth century, having been part of European thought since ancient times, but it had been reinforced in the most spectacular way around the start of the century by the discoveries of Sir Isaac Newton. Newton's laws of motion and associated theory of gravitation seemed for the first time in history to have rendered the operation of the cosmos on the largest scale intelligible. What had hitherto been a mystery was revealed as understandable (and predictable) in terms of mathematically-formulable laws. The well-known couplet by Alexander Pope (1688–1744) sums up without hyperbole the attitude of the time:

> Nature, and Nature's Laws lay hid in Night:
> God said, *Let Newton be!* and All was *Light.*

(Quoted in Butt, 1963, p.808; italics in original)

After Newton, it seemed, the reach of science was effectively coextensive with the universe. He had found the key to understanding how the entire cosmos worked, a key unavailable to all preceding generations.

It was also assumed (quite reasonably, since there was no good reason at the time to doubt it) that this order of things was, as has been said, fixed: it had always been so and always would be so. Additionally, this assumption was made in other areas: for example, it was assumed that the species of living beings of all kinds were fixed and immutable, and in the absence of any knowledge of natural selection, this is not an irrational belief (though it turned out to be false). It was reasonable in the eighteenth century to believe that many basic features of the universe are invariant and static, not dynamic and liable to change. (This point is worth stressing because such an assumption manifests itself in other ways that bear directly on beliefs about art, as we will see presently.) The universe, it seemed, was an orderly, static system. When such systems are made by humans, we call them machines, and this is precisely how the universe was conceived of at the time. Now a machine has a nature which a human being can in principle get to the bottom of, can understand. Even though it may be ever so complex and take centuries for human beings to work out, yet there was assumed to be no reason to doubt that in the fullness of time human beings could answer all properly-posed questions about the nature of things.

Summary point: those alive at the time had good reason to believe that they lived in a universe with an immutable and intelligible nature, and this nature was that of a mechanism (not,

importantly, an organism): the favourite analogy of the time was that with a watch or clock. It is important to bear in mind a point about this image which is not made explicit but which matters: a machine does not, like an organism, develop over time. A machine has a fixed and invariant nature, not a dynamic one. The universe was thought of on the analogy of a giant clock, and for most it seemed that there had to be a clockmaker to bring it into being. This artificer was God.

Rationalism and empiricism

These two terms are among the most important used in descriptions not only of eighteenth-century thought but of human thought in general, and it is necessary to see how they apply in the present context. Newton had arrived at his revolutionary discoveries by using an empiricist method and by reasoning about the data thus gathered. One consequence of this was that the empiricist method and its assumptions were regarded at the time as having been entirely vindicated. You have already been introduced to the term 'empiricism' in Units 4–5, and so here I will concentrate on only one element of the empiricist view (concerning the imagination) which is important in the present context. Before coming to that, however, it is appropriate to say what is meant by the term 'rationalism' as it will be used in these units.

Rationalism can be defined as the belief that human reason is capable of discovering the ultimate truth about what there is. That is: there is nothing about the entire order of things that is in principle beyond rational comprehension. Rationalism is generally contrasted with the thesis that certain truths are beyond our intellectual capacity to discover unaided. These truths are usually theological, and it has often been contended that they can be known to human beings only if they are *revealed* to us by a divinity. Such truths of revelation, it has been held, can be found only in certain sacred books (of which the Christian Bible is of course one) or sometimes in the words of avatars or prophets. Interestingly, Newton himself was not a pure rationalist, and spent much of his time thinking and writing about theology. However, many of the most important figures in eighteenth-century Europe were rationalists, and believed that if we but applied our reason to all the problems of the human condition, at the same time following a strict empiricist method, then these problems would eventually succumb to our efforts. This is an optimistic outlook, and underlies many of the great intellectual enterprises of the period before Romanticism.

There is a further component to the rationalist outlook which we need to notice, and it is this: truths discovered by the use of reason are universally true: not just true of me, or my tribe, or my family, or my country or my period in history, but just true. It seemed to those at the time inescapably the case that if by rational means they could discover an ideal form of political association, or set of religious, moral or aesthetic beliefs, then these ideas would be of universal application. To us now, steeped in awareness of deep differences between cultures, this may seem odd; but that should not be allowed to cloud understanding of how deep this universalist strain was in the thought of the time. Again, this may seem abstract, but it has a direct bearing on the aesthetic ideas of the time, as will be seen presently.

Summary point: in the period preceding Romanticism, it was generally assumed that the human faculty which is our means for attaining to the truth about anything is reason. This is an assumption of great profundity, and to deny it is to make a very major philosophical claim indeed. (We will come back to this issue later.)

We can return now to the notion of empiricism and in particular to its view of the imagination. As has been mentioned earlier in the course, one of the central assertions of the philosophical approach called empiricism is that the mind of a human being at birth is a blank slate (*tabula rasa*): all the contents of the mind (so to speak) are the results of experiences we have had, either sense experiences of the world outside us, or sensations from within our own body, or our mental life: the elements making up our inner awareness of ourselves – thoughts, emotions, volitions, and so forth. However (to repeat another point made earlier in the course), empiricists do have to admit that the mind has certain capacities which are built-in and are prior to our experience, or as philosophers put it, are innate. These are, for instance, the capacity to notice sameness and difference within our experience, to compare and contrast, and this capacity itself presupposes that we have memory, since you can only compare what you can recall (if the items to be compared are not simultaneous, as often they are not). Again, it was accepted that we can abstract common elements from different experiences, and it was this capacity which was supposed to allow us to form general concepts: for example, we have the concept 'cat' (it was held) because we can abstract from all our experiences of cats those things which all cats have in common.

Human beings also have the mental capacity of imagination, and empiricist philosophers had to give an account of what it is and how they claim that it works. The first reading associated with these units is an extract from one of the major classics of empiricist thought, *A Treatise of Human Nature* (1739 and 1740) by the Scottish philosopher David Hume.

EXERCISE   Read the passage from Hume's *Treatise* (Anthology II, extract 1, pp.206–7), and write short answers to the following questions:

1   What difference does Hume assert there is between ideas of the memory and ideas of the imagination?

2   What is the essential activity of the imagination which distinguishes it from the memory?

Note on Hume's terminology: you will notice that Hume makes a distinction between impressions and ideas. By an 'impression' he means a sensation of some kind, either of our own bodily workings or of an object in the outside world, or occurrences of our emotions; by an 'idea' he means, as he puts it, 'the faint images of these in thinking and reasoning' (1978, p.1). He claims that impressions are always much more vivid than ideas.

DISCUSSION   1   The ideas of the memory are always *more* vivid than those of the imagination; or in other words, memories are always more vivid than imaginings. (You may like to ask yourself whether you think Hume has the right to be quite so confident about this as he is.)

2   The imagination reorganizes our ideas as it pleases. The memory retains its ideas in the order of the corresponding impressions; the imagination can recombine them as we please.

This is a typical (and very influential) empiricist account of what the imagination can do, and it is worth dwelling on it for a moment. Granted the assumption of the truth of rationalism, and the view of the nature of the mind and its powers which is part of the empiricist view, a view of the imagination of this sort is logically the most likely outcome. The activity of the imagination is restricted, in effect, to recombining memories into complex ideas that have no counterpart in real life. Hume's example makes this quite clear:

> The fables we meet with in poems and romances put this entirely out of question [i.e. beyond doubt]. Nature there is totally confounded, and nothing mentioned but winged horses, fiery dragons, and monstrous giants.

> (Anthology II, p.207)

Notice also the unarticulated but clearly present assumption that this activity is not of particular importance: we can indeed alter and combine our memories into these pleasing fancies, but that is all they are: fancies or mental toys arrived at by 'confounding' (i.e. mixing up) the truth of nature. There is no suggestion here that the imagination is fit to do anything more than produce for us ideas that are ultimately diversions. They may no doubt be beautiful or charming or uplifting, but they are in the last analysis only recombinations of remembered experiences. They are not a form of knowledge of the universe.

This sort of view of the imagination has implications for the way in which art and creativity are understood and valued, and these implications will become clear presently.

Summary point: in the empiricist outlook, what the imagination does is simply to recombine memories in new ways. As Edmund Burke puts it: ' ... this power of the imagination is incapable of producing anything absolutely new; it can only vary the disposition of those ideas which it has received from the senses' (1958, p.17).

The uniformity of human nature

The point was made above, apropos of rationalism, that the truths discovered by the use of reason are universal. This belief assumes a particular importance when it is allied to a second, closely-related belief, namely that in all deep respects, human nature is the same across time and cultures, constant to a degree we would probably find hard to accept today. It was of course known that there were differences of manners, political institutions and aesthetic practices, not to mention religion; but it was held that these were either of a superficial kind, or were the result of unreason and so could in principle be removed by a dose of correct reasoning.

This belief in the uniformity of human nature can, in conjunction with assumptions of cultural superiority, be used to justify all manner of unpleasant colonializing practices. In the present context, it is appropriate to notice one of its more innocent consequences, in regard to the theory of aesthetic taste. Many theorists in the period before Romanticism believed that they knew what good or correct taste was, and believed they could prove how those who did not share it had had their taste perverted in various ways, some of them corrigible. Correct taste, as will be seen presently, is taste formed by acquaintance with the classics of the ancient world; what it is important to note here is the form of the argument regularly used to justify the conclusion that all normal human beings would accept this idea. Once again, Burke can furnish an example, from the 'Introduction on Taste' he added to the second edition of his *Enquiry*.

It was important for Burke to try to establish that aesthetic taste is by no means as subjective, not to say whimsical and unaccountable, as it is sometimes portrayed as being. He was proposing to write a systematic account of our experiences of the beautiful and the sublime, and should these experiences turn out to be unprincipled (i.e. irregular and capricious) then they would be undiscussable in general terms. You cannot write a systematic account of whimsy, and so unless Burke could prove to his own satisfaction that taste (our aesthetic preferences) works in accordance with discoverable principles, he could not begin his main enquiry. Fortunately, it seemed to him a fairly straightforward matter to establish the conclusion he wanted.

Taste is defined by Burke as 'that faculty, or those faculties of the mind which are affected with, or which form a judgement of the works of imagination and the elegant arts' (1958, p.13). In order to be thus affected or form such a judgement, three human faculties must be used: the senses, the imagination, and judgement. Burke claims that there is good reason to believe that each of these three elements of taste operates in a highly uniform manner. First, the senses: since the sense organs are the same in all human beings and operate in the same way, it must follow (Burke asserts) that all human beings perceive in the same way. What is sweet to me must be sweet to everyone else; what is bitter to me bitter to everyone else, and so on. Therefore, Burke concludes, the pleasures and pains of the senses must be the same for us all (excepting for cases of malfunction due to illness). Second, the imagination: as has been noted, Burke, like so many of his contemporaries, took the view that the imagination merely recombines elements of remembered experiences in new ways. Since the imagination can invent nothing, it follows (he thinks) that the imagination must be pleased or displeased with the images it recombines on the same principles as are the senses with their originals. Accordingly, he concludes that there must be as close an agreement with regard to the working of the imagination as there is with regard to the working of the senses. Third, judgement is involved in taste when works of art involve depictions of human character, action, motive, morality, circumstance, and so forth. The judgements we form of depicted humans are conducted on the same principles as our judgements of human beings in real life, i.e. the principles of reason. Since the principles of reason are universal, this aspect of taste can also be assumed to be highly uniform. Hence Burke believes he can justify the following conclusion:

> On the whole it appears to me, that what is called Taste, in its most general acceptation, is not a simple idea, but is partly made up of a perception of the primary pleasures of sense, of the secondary pleasures of the imagination, and of the conclusions of the reasoning faculty, concerning the various relations of these, and concerning the human passions, manners and actions. All this is requisite to form Taste, and the ground-work of all these is the same in the human mind; for as the senses are the great originals of all our ideas, and consequently of all our pleasures, if they are not uncertain and arbitrary, the whole ground-work of Taste is common to all, and therefore there is a sufficient foundation for a conclusive reasoning on these matters.

(1958, p.23)

It is not appropriate here to assess this argument, only to notice how readily Burke appeals to the idea of uniformity in several different dimensions of human nature. He feels able not only to assume, reasonably enough, physiological similarity in human beings, but also very great similarity in the workings of the imagination and in reasoning. In doing this he was merely using one of the key assumptions of the time, and he was far from alone: arguments of this kind, of varying degrees of sophistication, can be found in the pages of the many essays and treatises on taste which date from this period.

Summary point: it was believed at this time that human nature was extremely uniform in certain significant ways, including aesthetic taste.

The influence of the classics

Before turning (finally!) to the conception of art in the eighteenth century, it is necessary to say something about a very significant feature of the taste of the period, a matter (this time) less of logic than of history, the pervasive influence of the classics of the ancient world.

The cultural monuments left behind by the ancient world – Greece and Rome – have of course been a constant presence in European history, and there has never been a time in which their influence has been wholly absent. Indeed, it would not be possible to say what it is to be European at all without reference to a culture derived in so many profound ways, from metaphysics to politics, from these sources. Yet while this is true, it is also true that, especially in respect of aesthetic taste, there has been no period in European history in which the influence of ancient models has been more pervasive than was the case in the eighteenth century. There had been an efflorescence of translations from the classics during the period of the Renaissance, reinforced by later discoveries in archaeology (a process which continued in the eighteenth century), but not even these facts (I believe) can fully explain why classical models came to be regarded with quite such reverence in this period in particular. Well, even if there is no explanation which really accounts for it, the fact remains.

It requires an effort of historical imagination now to appreciate just how pervasive was the influence of classical culture at this time. Here are a few examples: in literature, writers would readily follow ancient genres – epic (derived from Homer and Virgil), lyric, satire, tragedy and comedy – indeed, with the exception of the novel, most of the literary genres which have been used in Europe were invented by the writers of the ancient world. The education of the time (restricted, of course, usually to fairly well-to-do males) was based firmly on the study of Latin and Greek. (Even in the late eighteenth century, when vernacular languages had become the regular vehicles for most forms of publication, a scholar could still write learned works in Latin and be sure of being understood throughout Europe. For example, the pioneering English Orientalist Sir William Jones (1746–94) published his studies of Persian poetry in Latin in 1774.) This education had ideally to be completed by a Grand Tour of Italy in order to view the remains of the Roman world at first hand, and the tourist (finances permitting) should have returned home with some *objets d'art* – casts of classical statuary, paintings of Roman remains, and so forth – as evidence of good taste and social status. Again, architects (notably the Scot Robert Adam) took ancient buildings as a major source of inspiration for their designs, and this inspiration could extend outside the house into the landscaped gardens, for which the *campagna* around Rome was a common source. The case with music is somewhat different, since no ancient music has survived, and the instruments of the time were in no real sense derived from ancient models. However, the myths, legends and history of the ancient world were the subjects of innumerable pieces of music (and accompanying dance) written in this period.

Not unexpectedly, this reverence for the classics made itself manifest in the area of aesthetic theory as well. It was widely accepted that good taste would manifest itself in a taste which was 'classical', i.e. either in a genuine liking for the Greek and Roman classics themselves, or for works in some way influenced or modelled on them. To take one example from hundreds, notice the assumptions Hume makes here in 'Of the standard of taste' when he describes how one's taste in literature may change as one grows older:

> A young man, whose passions are warm, will be more sensibly touched with amorous and tender images, than a man more advanced in years, who takes pleasure in wise, philosophical reflections, concerning the conduct of life, and moderation of the passions. At twenty, Ovid may be the favourite author, Horace at forty, and perhaps Tacitus at fifty.
>
> (1963, p.250)

Ovid is Publius Ovidius Naso (43 BCE –18 CE), a major Roman poet noted, among other things, for erotic verse; Horace is Quintus Horatius Flaccus (65–8 BCE), again another major Roman poet, noted for urbanity and satire; and Publius Cornelius Tacitus (*c*.55–117 CE) was one of the greatest Roman historians. Hume could just take it for granted that anyone likely to read his work would, as he does here, simply take as their measure and yardstick examples from the classics. These writers were part of the very fabric of cultivated life, and constituted fixed points of reference – it would be difficult to supply any modern analogue to this situation in the arts. Hume could assume with a certainty that was entirely justified that his readers would know precisely what he meant by these allusions.

This reverence for the classics had a number of consequences in the way in which art was thought about in this period, and in the next section we can begin to put together this idea with the others set out so far to articulate the view of art against which the Romantics in large part reacted. One consequence which is not difficult to foresee can be mentioned here. When faced with a body of work of such quality and authority as were possessed by the classics, artists and critics of later generations can react in a number of ways. In the eighteenth century, broadly speaking, the reaction was to regard these ancient works as *the* definitive models of what art should be like. Here is Sir Joshua Reynolds, president of the Royal Academy, addressing his fellow academicians in 1774 on the value of copying ancient works as part of the training of a painter:

> ... we must trace back the art [painting] to its fountainhead; to that source from whence they drew their principal excellencies, the monuments of pure antiquity. All the inventions and thoughts of the ancients, whether conveyed to us in statues, bas-relievos, intaglios, cameos, or coins, are to be sought after and carefully studied: the genius that hovers over these venerable reliques, may be called the father of modern art.
>
> From the remains of the works of the ancients, the modern arts were revived, and it is by their means that they must be restored a second time. However it may mortify our vanity, we must be forced to allow them our masters; and we may venture to prophesy, that when they shall cease to be studied, arts will no longer flourish, and we shall again relapse into barbarism.
>
> (1965, pp.84–5)

This extremely widespread reaction to the classics was summed up by the very important historian of ancient art Johann Joachim Winckelmann (1717–68): 'The only way for us to become great, and indeed – if this is possible – inimitable, is by imitating the ancients' (1985, p.33).

Summary point: in the eighteenth century, it was generally the case that classical culture was held in the highest esteem, and the great works of art from ancient times were taken to be models of what art should be.

The nature of art

Now at last we can deal directly with some of the central issues in aesthetics of our period. To repeat a point made in the introductory section of these units, views about the nature and value of art do not come out of the air, but are always related, in quite complex ways, to other phenomena in the culture of their day. Very few important concepts in European thought have changed so much and so often as that of art, and there is just no quick and simple way of understanding the history of this concept.

If you were to have asked any of the *cognoscenti* of Europe at this time to *define* art, you would have received in answer some version of this statement: that art is an imitation of nature. Works of art have in common that they are copies of some aspect of nature, including of course human nature. One of the main reasons why this would have seemed so obvious and so certain at the time was that it is itself a view which can be attributed to the most influential of Greek philosophers, and one of

the greatest thinkers in the entire European tradition, namely Aristotle
(384–322 BCE). The authority of Aristotle's views, and consequently his
influence on western thought, have been immense and incalculable, and
this applies in the area of aesthetics as much as to any of the many other
areas about which he wrote. Among his works is a short analysis of
Greek tragedy, which he regards as a species of poetry. This work, the
title of which is variously translated as either the *Poetics* or *The Art of
Poetry*, begins with a definition of poetry in general:

> Epic poetry and Tragedy, as also Comedy, Dithyrambic[1] poetry,
> and most flute-playing and lyre-playing, are all, viewed as a
> whole, modes of imitation.

(1940, p.3)

The Greek word for 'imitation' is *mimesis*, and you will regularly find this
theory or view of art referred to as the **mimetic theory**. (Additionally,
the adjective 'mimetic' can be used now in a different but related sense
as a synonym for 'representational' – as opposed to abstract – in the
description of works of art.) We need to spend a little time now seeing
just what this statement (that art is an imitation of nature) would have
been taken to mean at the time we are studying. We can begin by
looking at a typical and influential statement of the imitation theory by
Jean Le Rond d'Alembert (1717–83). It occurs in one of the most
influential – indeed defining – works of the Enlightenment, *The
Encyclopaedia* (*L'Encyclopédie*, 1751–72, with additions 1776–80), a
compendium of the most advanced knowledge of the day, based on the
principles of rationalism and empiricism as outlined above.

EXERCISE   Read the extract from d'Alembert's *Preliminary Discourse to the
Encyclopaedia* (*Discours préliminaire de l'Encyclopédie*, 1751) in
Anthology II (extract 2, pp.207–10), and answer the following question:

In what different ways, in d'Alembert's view, do painting, sculpture,
literature and music imitate nature?

DISCUSSION   Painting and sculpture imitate most closely the way things look to us in
ordinary experience. Architecture imitates the principle of symmetrical
arrangement so often to be seen in nature. Poetry (which can be
assumed to mean literature in general) represents to us the objects we
find in the world by means of the medium of language harmoniously
used, and appeals directly to the imagination. Music, which d'Alembert
speculates may have begun simply as a means of imitating sounds, has
become a sort of language by means of which we express our emotions

---

[1] A dithyramb was a type of choral poem which had begun as a hymn to Dionysus,
but gradually came to have a wider subject-matter. (Author's note.)

('passions' as he puts it). Any music that does not depict anything, he says, is just noise.

What d'Alembert says about music is worth remembering, as we will have cause to contrast it presently with the Romantic view of this art. It is clear that d'Alembert regards music as a relatively undeveloped art, from the point of view of the way in which its imitative potential has been exploited. D'Alembert wants music to be like language, a conceptual medium that can in a certain sense represent the world to us. Let us just bear this point in mind until we come to the Romantic view later.

In general, it should be clear that d'Alembert has to use the word 'imitate' in a number of senses to make plausible the assertion that all these arts can be called imitative: to say that the sort of shape-copying which was common in the representational sculpture of his day is relevantly like using the principle of symmetry in building design or representing the world via language is stretching the idea of imitation a great deal, though this did not trouble the imitation theorists of this period.

One important point to be clear about is that neither d'Alembert nor any other leading imitation theorist would have understood imitation to mean slavish or exact and exhaustive representation of the world, what we might call 'photographic realism'. Imitation as it was understood at this time was always subservient to the overriding principle of making something aesthetically agreeable, and it was held that in order to do this the imitation had to be selective. Broadly speaking, it was necessary to omit the ugly and deformed and copy nature at its best, *la belle nature* (literally: 'beautiful nature') as the theorists of the time put it. Just how much tidying up or improving on nature was desirable or permissible was the subject of debate, but there was agreement as to the general principle. Here is the Abbé Charles Batteux (1713–80), one of the most important imitation theorists:

> ... one must conclude that, if the arts are imitators of nature, the imitation must be one which is wise and enlightened, which does not copy in a servile way, but which, choosing objects and qualities, presents them with all the perfection of which they are capable: in a word, an imitation where one sees nature not as it is in itself, but as it might be, and as it might be conceived by the mind.
>
> What did Zeuxis[2] do when he wanted to paint a perfect beauty? Did he paint a particular beautiful woman, of whom his painting was a portrait? He brought together separate traits from several

---

[2] Zeuxis was one of the most celebrated of the painters of ancient Greece, working in the last part of the fifth century BCE. (Author's note.)

beauties; he formed in his mind an artificial (*factice*) idea, the result of bringing these traits together: and that idea was the prototype or model for his picture, which was true to life (*vraisemblable*) and poetic in its totality, and was only historically accurate in respect of its parts taken separately. This is the example given to all artists, here is the path they should follow, and it is the practice of all the great masters without exception.

(1989, pp.91–2; trans. R. Wilkinson)

This view was widely shared, and among important artists: exactly the same view is advocated by Reynolds as good practice to the members of the Royal Academy and it was followed by Reynolds himself in his own painting (see, for example, his *Discourses* 2 and 6 and his picture *Theory*, Plate 24.1 in the Illustrations Book). Surviving works of art from the ancient world were held to exemplify this practice, and this reinforced yet further the view that they made perfect models from which to copy.

It is with this important idea in mind that one has to understand the insistence on truth to life or verisimilitude as the chief aesthetic virtue among these writers. They would all agree that no art can succeed in which nature is not the model, in which nature is ignored fancifully; but what is meant by verisimilitude is imitation made with the aim of producing an overall effect of beauty. This is anything but 'warts and all' realism: the overriding imperative is to produce something beautiful, and if that requires discreet departures from exact copying of the model, so be it. Behind this belief that imitations should be of nature at its best, nature as it might be, *la belle nature,* is a moral consideration. As well as giving us the purely aesthetic pleasure we are supposed to gain in the presence of an idealized imitation, art was supposed to inspire and uplift us morally. Following a line of thought that can be traced back to Plato in the fifth century BCE, it was assumed that you were not likely to be uplifted or inspired by depictions of the ugly or disgusting aspects of life: hence the need to imitate nature at its best.

Summary point: the dominant eighteenth-century view regarded art as an imitation of nature, and the chief aesthetic virtue in this outlook, appropriately enough, is verisimilitude or truth to life. However, this is to be understood in the context of an overriding imperative to produce something beautiful. It was obligatory to improve on nature where just copying nature would not produce beauty. The imitation involved is always selective, and does not aim at what we now call realism in the arts.

Rules and the unity of the work of art

One of the features of eighteenth-century thought about the arts which seems most odd to people of our day (because we are heirs to certain

Romantic views we will come to below) is the readiness with which theorists and practitioners of the arts would formulate rules: rules for how to organize pictorial compositions; rules about what are the genres of art and about the impermissibility of varying or mixing them; rules about how many characters can speak at once in a drama; rules for the construction of plots, and so on, for all the arts and in some detail. As important as the rules themselves is the assumption which underlies them all, namely that aesthetic success will come to you if you observe them and will elude you if you flout them, and in particular that the extremely important aesthetic property of unity is likely to be destroyed if these rules are not followed. A work of art of any kind (it has been regularly held, and still is) must be a whole, must have an overall unity, and without this the work will not occasion a satisfying aesthetic experience.

There were a number of reasons for this preoccupation with rules, not least the reverence for the classics we have noted above, which had two particular consequences in this area. First, among the classic texts were works which themselves either were or could be construed as rulebooks, notably the *Poetics* of Aristotle, Horace's *Art of Poetry* and the work *On Architecture* by the Roman engineer Vitruvius (first century BCE). Granted the esteem in which all things classic were held, it is not surprising that any of the dicta in these works which could be construed as rules were accorded almost the status of holy writ. Second, the classics were a fixed corpus of work, held to have the power to please aesthetically through all time (an assumption grounded in the belief in the constancy of human nature), and in such a case, there is an irresistible tendency to study the practice of the ancient artists and if possible to extract rules from their example. Accordingly, even in areas where no ancient rulebooks could be found, critics of the day readily filled the gaps. Principles were found, held to be those on which the genuinely admired ancient works were constructed, and contemporary artists exhorted to follow them. This tendency can be seen at work throughout the eighteenth century, from (for example) the Augustan period in English literature at the start of it to the neoclassical period in painting later on.

While this was so, this fascination with rule-following in the production of works of art very soon gave rise to a problem within this view of art as a whole. The problem was that, quite obviously, rule-following did *not* always bring aesthetic success, nor did rule-breaking always destroy it: many of the works which followed the rules induced only jaw-breaking tedium, while some of those which broke them were evidently alive and gripping. The better theorists and practitioners noticed this very quickly, and tried to find some way of refining the rule theories to allow for this. This debate went on throughout the century. Here there is room to look at three examples, from the beginning, middle and end of the century respectively, the first from the poet Alexander Pope.

Pope had a due respect for the rules. In *An Essay on Criticism* (1711) he concludes his praise for the Roman poet Virgil, whose works he quite genuinely regarded as unsurpassable and composed in accordance with very strict rules, as follows:

> Learn hence for Ancient *Rules* a just Esteem;
> To copy *Nature* is to copy *Them*.

(ll.139–40, quoted in Butt, 1963, p.148; italics in original)

Pope could not disguise from himself, however, the uncomfortable truth that simply following Virgil's rules would not produce poems of the same quality.

EXERCISE   Read the following lines from *An Essay on Criticism*, and then give a brief prose summary of what Pope is saying here. (You can assume that by the phrase 'great wit' he means what others mean by the term 'genius'.)

> Some Beauties yet, no Precepts can declare,
> For there's a *Happiness* as well as *Care*,
> *Musick* resembles *Poetry*, in each
> Are *nameless Graces* which no Methods teach,
> And which a *Master-Hand* alone can reach.
> If, where the *Rules* not far enough extend,
> (Since Rules were made but to promote their End)
> Some Lucky LICENCE answers to the full
> Th' Intent propos'd, *that Licence is a Rule*.
>
> [...]
>
> Great Wits sometimes may *gloriously offend*,
> And *rise* to *Faults* true Criticks *dare not mend*;
> From *vulgar Bounds* with *brave Disorder* part,
> And *snatch* a *Grace* beyond the Reach of Art,
> Which, without passing thro' the *Judgment*, gains
> The *Heart*, and all its End *at once* attains.

(ll.141–9 and 152–7, pp.148–9; italics in original)

DISCUSSION   There are some effects in great works of art which just cannot be accounted for in terms of rule-following, and for which there seems to be no rule ('no methods teach'). All we can say about these is that it seems that only a 'great wit', a genius, can accomplish them.

What Pope has in mind are those special moments when some unpredictable element of a work of art, some aspect of it you cannot foresee because it has not resulted from the following of any discernible rule – some phrase in a poem or a piece of music, some movement in a dance, some line in a statue (and so on) – just takes your breath away and makes the inner walls come down; or, as we might now say more briefly, when something in the work *grabs us*, takes us over, and makes contemplation of the work a delight. This is what he means by the 'grace beyond the reach of art' which touches the heart directly.

Dr Johnson was exercised by the same issue, and makes another point concerning the rules advanced for successful writing. He suggests that there is a deeper principle by means of which we should evaluate all the so-called rules, and that is that justified or valuable rules are those which assist the artist to imitate or follow nature. Rules which are based only on local or ephemeral custom do not assist us at all in achieving this goal. As he puts it:

> It ought to be the first endeavour of a writer to distinguish nature from custom, or that which is established because it is right from that which is right only because it is established.

(Quoted in Greene, 1986, p.238)

Using this principle he dismisses as trivial the rule that there ought to be no more than three speaking characters on stage in a play at any one time – this is a rule which has only historical grounding in the original circumstances in which Greek tragedy evolved. By contrast, he advocates as more 'fixed and obligatory' (quoted in Greene, 1986, p.238) the rule that the action of a play must be single, since to have two equally weighted plots proceeding at once would destroy aesthetic unity. What Johnson does is to introduce a more basic notion (following nature), by whose use he can discriminate really useful and binding rules from pseudo-rules.

The question over the status of rules faced Sir Joshua Reynolds in a particularly acute form, since he had to decide, as president of the Royal Academy, to what extent he should *teach* his pupils to follow the rules of painting. His considered and reasonable response to the issue forms the substance of his eighth presidential *Discourse*, delivered in December 1778. He was abundantly aware that most of the so-called rules in the textbooks of his day had been ignored by the ablest painters at some time or other and, like Johnson, he concluded that there must be a way of separating true principles from mere local and temporary preference. The true principles of art, he argues, are those that assist the painter in achieving his/her primary goal, which is to engage our passions: the only justification for any rule is that it furthers the achievement of this goal. Not surprisingly, then, Reynolds does not advocate a slavish following of rules, but a much subtler and more reasonable position. The painter must be instructed in:

> the true meaning and cause of rules, and how they operate on those faculties to which they are addressed: by knowing their

general purpose and meaning, he will often find that he need not confine himself to the literal sense, it will be sufficient if he preserves the spirit, of the law.

(1965, pp.129–30)

This is as much as to say that the rules must be interpreted with artistic *judgement,* and that is in effect to reduce the status of the rules a good deal.

What should be noted, though, is that Reynolds (and he has this in common with Pope and Johnson) does not countenance the idea that rule-following is out of place in artistic creation. There are some valuable and useful rules, and these should be followed. The issue is only to find which the valuable rules are, and it is the observance of these rules that will lend the work of art its unity.

Summary point: in the eighteenth-century view of art, it was widely accepted that rule-following had a vital role to play in achieving artistic unity.

Creativity, genius and the status of the artist

If you put these ideas about the value of rule-following in the creation of works of art together with the empiricist view of how the imagination works, then a certain picture of creativity emerges as a matter of simple deductive logic.

EXERCISE   Looking back at these two sets of ideas, can you work out what follows from them about creativity?

DISCUSSION   To be creative can be little more than to have a capacity to recombine memories or elements of memories, in accordance with the rules which sum up the practice of the ancients, and this will result in the creation of aesthetically satisfying works.

You will probably feel (rightly, in my view) that this is just too pat, that there is more to imaginative creation than that. This account looks just too mechanical: if it were that easy, why are there not many more artists, and many more good works of art, than there are? Again, we have seen in the preceding section that just rule-following quickly came to seem an unsatisfactory way of trying to create works of art, since many works of art which observed the rules turned out downright dull. The people we want to single out as having artistic imagination are able to do more than apply formulae derived from ancient models, something odder, not predictable, harder to pin down. As the century wore on, it became more common to say that what these people had was a quality called genius, the capacity (as Pope so exactly puts it in the poem quoted in the previous section) to snatch a grace beyond the reach of art (i.e. beyond what can be produced by rule-following and model-copying). Genius appeared to begin where rules end, and this was an uncomfortable position for eighteenth-century theorists to be in. Very few were willing to give up the idea of rule-following completely, as we have seen, and attempts were made to make the theory more subtle. What also had to be done was to try to give an account of genius which did justice to its capacity to bend the rules, and yet which did not imply that the whole idea of rule-following was just a mistake and blind-alley.

One of the figures most exercised by this problem was Reynolds. While fully accepting the empiricist view of the mind and recombinative view of the workings of the imagination, he was (as we have seen) too sensitive a critic not to notice that, just as there was a problem about rule-following, there was a linked problem about the ability called 'genius', and in the sixth of his presidential *Discourses* (1774) to the Royal Academy, he set out to deal with this problem. He begins by stating his problem clearly:

> Genius is supposed to be a power of producing excellencies, which are out of the reach of the rules of art; a power which no precepts can teach, and which no industry can acquire.

(1965, p.74)

EXERCISE   In the following two paragraphs, Reynolds gives his answer to the problem of how to account for genius within his framework of beliefs. Read the paragraphs, and then write a short summary of his major claims.

> What we now call genius, begins, not where rules, abstractedly taken, end; but where known vulgar and trite rules have no longer any place. It must of necessity be, that even works of genius, like every other effect, as they must have their cause, must likewise have their rules; it cannot be by chance, that excellencies are produced with any constancy or any certainty, for this is not the nature of chance; but the rules by which men of extraordinary parts, and such as are called men of genius work, are either such as they discover by their own peculiar observations, or of such a nice texture as not easily to admit being expressed in words; especially as artists are not very frequently skilful in that mode of communicating ideas. Unsubstantial, however, as these rules may seem, and difficult as it may be to convey them in writing, they are still seen and felt in the mind of the artist; and he works from them with as much

certainty, as if they were embodied, as I may say, upon paper. It is true, these refined principles cannot be always made palpable, like the more gross rules of art; yet it does not follow, but that the mind may be put in such a train, that it shall perceive, by a kind of scientifick sense, that propriety, which words, particularly words of unpractised writers, such as we are, can but very feebly suggest.

Invention is one of the great marks of genius; but if we consult experience, we shall find, that it is by being conversant with the inventions of others, that we learn to invent; as by reading the thoughts of others we learn to think.

(1965, p.76)

DISCUSSION   It is not that the genius does not follow rules, rather that geniuses follow subtle rules of their own devising, and these subtle rules may well be extremely hard to express in words.

It would take us too far into distant philosophical territory to evaluate fully what Reynolds is claiming here. He is arguing that, because any event must have a cause, and because all causal chains can be articulated in law-like statements, then any masterstroke by a genius (which is an event) can be regarded as an instance of a law-governed occurrence, and then (crucially) that all statements of causal laws are relevantly like statements of artistic rules. Note that because he is not willing to give up entirely the idea of the value of rule-following, Reynolds has in effect to say that genius follows rules, only that the rules in question are of great subtlety.

Summary point: the empiricist account of the imagination, and the belief in the value of rule-following in artistic creation, entailed a fairly mechanical view of the creative process, from which in turn it followed that the phenomenon of genius was problematic in this view of art. Many had to admit that rule-following could not be the whole story; but it was not easy, within this framework of ideas, to give a convincing account of what it was acknowledged that genius could achieve.

All the ideas we have been considering help us to understand one of the features of eighteenth-century aesthetic thought which seems most surprising to modern readers when they first meet it, and this concerns what we can call the status of the artist. Because we are the heirs of Romanticism, we tend to think of artists as people who are in some ways different or apart from the rest of us. We generally assume they have some special imaginative talent or genius, tend to lead bohemian lives, perhaps, and can't really be expected to fit into the ordinary nine-to-five world, for reasons we will explore fully when we come to deal with Romanticism. None of these ideas were current in the eighteenth century. Prior to that period, the individuals we would call artists were regarded more like tradesmen than anything else: that is, someone who, like a carpenter, chef or metalworker, has through practice acquired a special skill, the ability to manipulate materials in a way that satisfies some human need. The special skill of the artist was to make beautiful things of some kind: poems, statues, pictures, pieces of music, and so on. If you needed an item of any of these kinds, you went to an artist and ordered one, just as you would go to a dressmaker for a new dress. Artists would have thought of themselves in this way: they thought of their business not as some sort of self-expression or the articulation of deep mysteries inaccessible to the untalented, but as the making of some sort of beautiful item.

This attitude is grounded in beliefs which go back to the ancient world. One of the most surprising truths in the history of western aesthetics, when you first meet it, is the fact that there is no word in ancient Greek or in Latin which means 'art' in the modern, post-Romantic sense to which we are used. The Greek term which is always translated as 'art' is *techne*, which means a skill or a knack, and is the root of our terms 'technique' and 'technology'. Just as a carpenter has the *techne* for forming items from wood, so (in Greek times) a painter simply had the *techne* for using paint, a sculptor the *techne* for using marble (or bronze, etc.), and so on. Add to this the Greek prejudice against those who worked with their hands rather than their brains, and the ground for the very long-lasting artisan-like status of many types of artist was laid. (The Latin word *ars*, from which our term 'art' is derived, means what *techne* meant in ancient Greek.) Artists were not separated out as a special type of individual in anything remotely like the modern way.

In the eighteenth century itself, artists (particularly painters) had to some degree shaken off this artificer/skilled craftsman status, and had come to be regarded more like what we would call practitioners of a liberal art; but this is not equivalent to the status which artists came to enjoy after the changes brought about by Romanticism. You need to be very careful, when studying the history of the European art world before the Romantic period, not to read into it, anachronistically, post-Romantic ideas about art and artists. It is worth recalling, for example, that Haydn, regarded by us as a major musical genius, was regarded by his employers as a servant, and had to show them that his fingernails were clean.

Summary point: in the eighteenth century, artists were not thought of in the modern, post-Romantic way. While they would have been, by and large, regarded as what we might call members of the professional classes, they were not conceived of as a group apart within the human race. (The Romantic conception of the artist will be described fully in what follows.)

Aesthetic experience

You have already read quite a lot about eighteenth-century views of aesthetic experience in the units on the Lake District tourists, about how distinctions were drawn between the states of mind brought about in us by objects considered beautiful, sublime and picturesque, and how these states were described within the framework of ideas furnished by a combination of rationalism and empiricism. Works of art could occasion these reactions in us as much as could nature of course, and so there is no need to repeat here the descriptions you have already read, which form part of the eighteenth-century view of art and the aesthetic dimension of life.

It is important, however, to notice a consequence of the conjunction of rationalism with the view of the imagination we have encountered above, and it is this. There is no suggestion in the eighteenth-century view of art that aesthetic experience, however intense, moving, uplifting or even shattering, is in the last analysis an experience which can furnish us with a truth we could not have discovered by the use of reason. One way of stating the principle of rationalism is that the only faculty which allows us access to truth is reason, which thus has the unchallenged status of the most important of the human faculties. The imagination may be able to wrap up these truths in aesthetically agreeable art-forms by judicious imitation, but this is a secondary and derivative role. Aesthetic experience, on this view, is in the last analysis simply a species of pleasure or diversion, a contemplative, refined and unusual pleasure no doubt, but pleasure nonetheless. That is why we seek it, not because it does something as serious as rational truth-gathering, or that reason cannot accomplish. Please just bear this in mind for the moment: why I have picked out this point will become clear soon enough.

Summary point: in the eighteenth-century view of art, aesthetic experience, however refined and intense, is in the final analysis a species of pleasure, a diversion.

The fixedness of the foregoing beliefs

One feature of the eighteenth-century view of the universe which seems most remote from us now is the stasis which is built into its view of the order of things. There was a certain confidence among the intellectual avant-garde that material and moral progress could be made through the application of rationalism in all areas of life; but there was no suspicion that rationalism itself could be seriously challenged. Newton had outlined a view of the universe as a stable, law-governed machine; it was assumed that the species of living beings were fixed, that human nature was, save for superficial accidents, uniform and unchanging at its deeper levels. In the area of aesthetics it was assumed that, since human nature was constant, the classics would continue to furnish satisfying aesthetic models, and that the genres of art for which we have classical models would continue to be the genres of art. Such progress as was envisaged – for example, in science and technology – would take place within this static, unchanging framework. The notion that reality might rather be like an organism, might be characterized by dynamic flux and change at the deepest level, might have something analogous to a will, is not present in this outlook, including its aesthetic dimension.

Summary

In the preceding section, you have been introduced to a number of ideas about art, and it is appropriate here to draw breath and sum up the main points made so far, to review the view of art that has emerged.

The eighteenth century believed in a universe which was law-governed (the laws being Newton's laws) and so orderly, resembling a great machine. It was assumed – and, as has been noted, there was no reason at the time to doubt it – that these laws and this order were fixed, and would remain the same for all time. Again, human nature was assumed to be, at deep levels, uniform across races and civilizations, and constant through time. Some races needed to be civilized (it was assumed) by contact with advanced, European ideas and institutions; but once the civilizing had been done, more European-like humans would emerge at the end of the process. The overriding impression was one of an orderly, fixed and fairly uniform cosmos.

These deep assumptions have their reflection in the view of art current at the time, though here the picture is complicated by the very powerful influence of the classics of the ancient world. From this source was derived the doctrine of mimesis, and the attendant critical standard of verisimilitude, neither of which was construed in a simple-minded way, but included the notion of selective imitation of the most beautiful aspects of nature in order to produce a morally uplifting effect. Again, it was assumed that the classics furnished models and standards of art appropriate for all times. Human nature being uniform at deep levels, it appeared to follow that what pleased in ancient times would also please us, since we differ from our ancestors only in superficial ways. It followed that the classic works of art of the ancient world could be regarded as patterns to adopt and models to copy. Further, since the canon of surviving works of art was pretty well fixed, it was possible to study this static body of work and draw from it rules which if followed appropriately would result in the creation of more fine works of art.

This view of art cohered well with the view of the imagination and of aesthetic experience that followed from the combined assumptions of rationalism and the empiricist method. All truth-gathering was held to be the work of reason reflecting on the data furnished by a disciplined use of the senses (i.e. following the empiricist method). In such a system, all that is left for the imagination to do is to rearrange memories and fragments of memories of first-hand experiences in ways which please our aesthetic fancy. These works of the imagination may be beautiful, picturesque or even in some cases sublime (though sublimity is more usually associated with works of nature), and they may move us, even deeply; but they are in the final analysis diversions, something *dulce*, designed to be pleasing, not a vehicle for any sort of truth which is either unavailable to us by any other means, or not restatable in purely rational terms, and by means of vehicles other than works of art.

With all this is mind, we can now move on to consider the view of art which succeeded this one in European history, the Romantic view of which we today are still the heirs. It has been necessary to dwell this long on the eighteenth-century view. It has its own intrinsic interest, of course; but additionally, without knowledge of it, the sheer magnitude of the change brought about by the Romantic movement – and the intellectual boldness needed to make it – are not evident. Again, to repeat, the Romantic view is the one which has shaped the modern view of art in European culture, and which we are likely just to take for granted until its relative newness, in historical terms, is pointed out.

3   The Romantic conception of art

Introduction

It is startling to reflect that by the time the first generation of Romantics had done their work (by around 1825 or so), virtually no artist or critic in Europe with any pretensions to be up to date would have accepted the view of art outlined in the foregoing sections of these units in anything like its entirety. They would have thought about art, and about the abilities of artists, in quite a different way. The changes in outlook were not just in detail but wholesale, and the sheer depth of the change can hardly be overstated. A view of art which had held sway for the best part of a century in Europe had been swept away, and in its place was a theory which is in many ways extremely modern and of which we are undoubtedly still the heirs.

This wholesale change did not come out of the air. The ideals and beliefs of the Enlightenment were challenged in a number of ways in various European countries throughout the latter half of the eighteenth century. One such manifestation was what is called the **cult of sensibility**. This phase in European culture has to do with the value placed on emotion, and its place in human life and in art, and was in part a readily understandable reaction to the severe rationalism of the earlier part of the century. It came to be felt that this pure rationalism was ultimately unsatisfying because it left something out. It came to be felt that it did not take proper account of the emotional needs of human beings, and it was therefore softened in various ways. Again, the aesthetic beliefs of the eighteenth century came to be challenged in various ways: instrumental music came to be more greatly valued than it was, for example, by d'Alembert. Equally, landscape painting without a historical subject rose in esteem and began to challenge the supreme status attached to history painting in the hierarchy of genres espoused by Reynolds. Another manifestation of the gradual departure from adherence to the ideals of the Enlightenment can be found in the *Sturm und Drang* ('storm and stress') movement in German literature in the 1770s. In various works from this movement one finds proto-Romantic elements: a Rousseauesque exaltation of freedom and nature; a high estimation set on folk art of various kinds; exaltation of genius, and so on. Yet while all this is true, and while Romanticism certainly had its precursors, going back decades in some cases, I would argue that nothing in this pre-Romantic phase of European culture quite approaches the depth of the shift in belief and value found in Romanticism proper.

Further, the change in aesthetic beliefs we are going to study in detail was related to changes in the wider world-view of the time, just as had been its eighteenth-century predecessor and as are indeed all theories of art of any real depth. Accordingly, as in the previous section, we need to begin in more general and abstract areas of thought, seemingly remote from art. These general areas of belief condition the aesthetic beliefs we are going to study, and set logical limits on them.

We are going to study the ideas at the heart of Romantic aesthetics principally via the writings of a small group of German thinkers active in the last decade of the eighteenth century and the early years of the nineteenth. These young men were not the only important figures alive at the time who can properly be called 'Romantics', and I will say something more about the complicated history of this phenomenon across Europe at the end of these units, remarks amplified at length in Audio 5, tracks 6–9: *The Romantic Circle*. However, these young Germans have the great virtue of being highly articulate and they state the new and radical Romantic doctrines with greater clarity, I would argue, than any of their contemporaries.

We will be focusing principally on the ideas of four men: August Wilhelm Schlegel (1767–1845; AWS from now on); his younger brother Friedrich Schlegel (1772–1829; FS from now on); the poet Novalis (1772–1801) and the essayist and critic Wilhelm Heinrich Wackenroder (1773–98). Biographical details about each of them can be found in the headnotes to the extracts from their writings printed in Anthology II (pp.210, 212–13, 219 and 220–1) and it would be appropriate to read these headnotes now.

One thing which will be clear even from these few details is that the members of this group of young men had a number of things in common. Most obvious is that they were all university educated. Between them, they had attended many of the leading intellectual

centres in Germany at the time, and many of their teachers were
important intellectuals in their own right. This is no group of rustics from
the backwoods: they are confident, articulate young men at home with
theory and abstraction, and this gives this particular phase in European
aesthetics a special character. These young men were used to discussing
the ideas which were at what we might now call the 'cutting edge' of the
intellectual life of their time: they were unafraid of theoretical
speculation and liked intellectual daring. When it came to taking on the
mighty edifice of the Enlightenment, they felt few qualms.

The nature of ultimate reality

The picture of the universe or what there is which lies behind the
aesthetics of the Enlightenment is, if dated in its details, in many ways
not unlike common sense: the universe is a great physical machine with
a definite and unchanging nature, out there, created by a god and
understandable by us in mathematical terms if we apply ourselves to
observing it carefully and reason correctly about what we observe in an
empiricist manner. This was close to being the single, 'official' view of
the time, to which all the leading lights would have signed up. When we
come to the ideas behind the Romantic aesthetic, by contrast, the picture
is different in two major ways: first, there was no single view of the
universe that had a comparable authority to the mechanistic view of the
Enlightenment. Second, the views that were advanced – even if, as I
contend, they have what one can call a common flavour – tend to be far
more remote from common sense, and strike most people as
counterintuitive when they first meet them. However, it is vital to say
something about them, since they lie behind the crucially important
Romantic doctrine of the nature and power of the imagination. All the
major tenets in the Romantic aesthetic presuppose these two basic
premises concerning the nature of reality and the ability of the
imagination to grasp it, and so it is necessary to have an understanding
of both.

First, let us consider the plurality of views. There were a number of
different views about the nature of reality current towards the end of the
eighteenth century and the turn of the nineteenth. Some were elaborated
by the major philosophers of the time: in Germany, these were Johann
Gottlieb Fichte (1762–1814) and Friedrich Wilhelm Joseph von Schelling
(1775–1854), both in succession professors of philosophy at Jena and
both known to the Romantics we will be concentrating on. Both these
philosophers – whose writings are of a difficulty which is the stuff of
legend – profess a version of a philosophy called, in a technical,
philosophical sense of the term, **idealism**. Idealism is the view that
ultimate reality is mental or spiritual in nature and none of it physical or
material (these are synonyms in these theories). The physicality of the
everyday world is therefore in some sense an illusion or appearance
only. This is not to be understood as meaning that all our daily

experience is dreamlike or deluding, but rather that, properly understood, what we call the material world is in fact a manifestation of a reality which is mental or spiritual in nature.

A major feature of what there is (the universe) is change, and so idealist philosophers have to give an account of how change comes about. Since reality is mental, and because what is mental has no separate components, this dynamism cannot be machine-like, the result of the operation of physical laws on interacting components. Insofar as it is like anything, it must be more like the action of an individual consciousness. Though the parallel cannot be pushed too far, the idea which emerges is that reality must have something like a *will*, and if an entity can be said to have a will it must also be possible to say of it that it *acts*. Thus Fichte, when he has to find a concept to describe the most fundamental property of the mental (i.e. the real) chooses to call this most basic of all properties of ultimate reality, not, for example, awareness, but rather the 'act' (German: *Tathandlung*; see Fichte, 1982, p.93). Again, Schelling developed the idea that history is the process by which reality gradually comes to full consciousness of itself in accordance with its own nature (see Schelling, 1988).

The details of these very complex and difficult philosophies need not detain us, but it is important to remember the great importance they gave to the idea of the will, an emphasis destined to have a long (and troublesome) history in Europe. In the Romantic period, the idea of the centrality of the will – taken somewhat out of its philosophical context it must be said – assumes great importance, an importance which extends even as far as the aesthetic ideas which are our concern here. It plays a notable role, for example, in the beliefs of Byron and is one of the defining properties of the type of hero he describes regularly, and which has come to be known as the Byronic figure, the heroic individual who defies a seemingly overwhelming and indifferent fate by sheer power of the will. His Childe Harold, whom you will meet later in this block, is one such individual, and Byron repeated the type several times: Conrad/ Lara (the corsair), Manfred, and the Giaour (for example) all being variations on this theme.

Again, it can be readily argued that this mental reality has to be a unity, i.e. there is only one such real mind, that the ultimately real is a single being. This has the consequence that all division of the universe into discrete or separate individuals has to be, in some sense, an illusion. Further, the one mind that is reality must also be infinite: the mental is by definition not spatial (it is not in any place at all) and without form, and what is existent but without form is infinite. It will be clear that reality thus conceived has most of the properties traditionally ascribed to divine beings, and this consequence has important consequences in aesthetics which we will notice below. Perhaps the most intelligible version of these ideas can be found in the theoretical work of the English Romantic poet Coleridge. Coleridge could read German and was greatly influenced by Schelling, and there is very little philosophical content in Coleridge's major theoretical work *Biographia Literaria* (1817) that cannot be found in earlier works by Schelling.

The conception of reality advanced by idealist philosophers, then, is both remote from common sense and from the Enlightenment view. This view coheres even if it does not logically coincide with other views that were gaining ground at around this time. One such is **pantheism**, the view that God is not transcendent (that is, logically independent of the creation) but immanent, that is, in some way present in all things in the world: not distinct from the creation. Since God is a mental or spiritual entity, this is not an easy view to state coherently if nature is conceived of as material; but it has nevertheless always had adherents, in our period notably Wordsworth, and one can see its influence in his poetry, notably *Tintern Abbey* and the ode *Intimations of Immortality from Recollections of Early Childhood* (see e.g. Bowra, 1950, ch.4). Again, the mystics of the world have always believed that direct communion with an ultimate, divine mental reality is possible, and indeed for the mystic such communion is the goal of life. In the mystic encounter, all sense of separate selfhood is lost and there is only a condition of oneness with the divine. William Blake was perhaps the best known mystic of our period, and his experiences markedly influence his works, both linguistic and visual. Again, there had been prominent in Germany throughout the eighteenth century an important version of Lutheran Protestantism called Pietism. (See Block 3, Unit 10, p.21.) For our purposes, the most important feature of Pietism was its intense inwardness: a belief in the power of individual meditation on the divine, a direct, individual approach to the ultimate spiritual reality of God.

I hope it is now clear why I said above that these views have at least a similar flavour. Common to them all is the assertion that there is an ultimate reality that is mental or spiritual or divine in nature. The universe of everyday life is either an illusion or it is at least not a machine, since the spiritual reality is omnipresent in it. For present purposes, the exact details of all these views do not matter.

Summary point: the early Romantics grew up in an age and ambience in which varieties of idealism, mysticism and pantheism were daily discussed. Reality was widely believed to be either spiritual in nature or such as to be intimately informed by spirit.

What we have to do now is investigate in some detail the far-reaching consequences of this way of looking at the world.

The power of the imagination

If you put together the basic assertion of idealism with the rationalism of the Enlightenment, a startling consequence emerges. Reason is the faculty which operates with concepts. The function of concepts is to mark differences in our experience which we find useful and which help us get about in the world: we make a basic difference between our own self and the rest of the world, and we then go on to divide the rest of the world into individuals of various kinds (animate and inanimate) with various properties, which act and interact in various ways. If you think about it, it becomes clear that concepts presuppose a reality in which there are divisions and differences: they have application only in such a reality. Accordingly, reason is of use only in a universe that consists of more than one thing. The difficulty arises when you add to this the fundamental assertion of idealist philosophies or the basic assertion made by mystics the world over: namely that reality is a oneness, a divisionless unity, and that all division of the universe into individuals is ultimately appearance only. If that is so, it follows directly that reason is in principle useless as a means of knowing such a reality, because no concepts apply to it. It is not possible to reason about such a reality. Reason is fine when limited to the world of everyday life, but can in no circumstances acquaint you with the one reality.

It follows further that, if you wish to become acquainted with reality, then studying the (ultimately unreal) day-to-day world by using the methods of empiricism is a useless way of proceeding. Reality is a mental or spiritual oneness: it is not *out there*, outside us, at all. The part of us most akin to it is our mind, and it follows that the way to reality is (so to speak) to journey *inwards*, into the depths of the mental realm. This at first sight startling (but logically inevitable) consequence is stated very clearly by Novalis.

EXERCISE Read the extract from Novalis's *Miscellaneous Observations* (Anthology II, extract 3, pp.210–11) and write a short paraphrase of it.

DISCUSSION The external world, the world of common sense, is unreal. The real world is spiritual, and is within us. In our normal everyday state of mind, this reality is hidden from us, but it is possible to penetrate the veils that disguise it from us.

A major question arises at once: as Novalis makes clear (and he is simply articulating a logical consequence of his basic world-view), reality is within us and is a oneness which is mental in nature, not material. If reason is in principle incapable of acquainting us with it, do we have any faculty that can do so? To this question the Romantics answered yes, and claimed that this faculty is the imagination. In order for this claim to be remotely plausible, they had to jettison completely the Enlightenment view of the power of the imagination as limited to that of making aesthetically pleasing recombinations of memories and bits of memories. From their new account of the imagination flowed an entirely different account of artistic creativity, of art, and of the role of the artist, and we need to spend some time getting a firm grip on their idea of what the imagination could do.

We can approach this by looking again at the nature of the reality with which the imagination has to acquaint us: recall that this reality is mental; that it is a unity (i.e. properly speaking, no concepts apply to it), and that it is without limit or infinite. Any faculty that can acquaint us with such a reality has to be extremely unusual in its mode of operation. In the following short passage from his *Philosophical Writings*, Novalis gives us a clue as to how, in such an outlook, the imagination must operate:

> The imagination is the marvellous sense that can *replace* all senses for us – and which already is so much directed by our will. If the external senses seem to be entirely governed by mechanical laws – then the imagination is obviously not bound to the present and to contact with external stimuli.

('On Goethe', paragraph 30, 1997, p.118)

Unlike the senses, the imagination is claimed by Novalis to be at the command of our *will*: while what we sense in the outside world is more or less out of our control, the imagination is ours to command. Moreover, Novalis appears to imply that while the senses are controlled by what he calls mechanical laws – the laws of science (such as Newton's laws of motion) which govern all the events in the external world – the imagination is not so controlled. He makes this explicit in another work, where he states that 'the imagination is ... an extramechanical power worthy to be called "magical"' ('General Draft', paragraph 43, 1997, p.135).

This is an extraordinary assertion. The everyday world, Novalis concedes, obeys the laws of science; but he is claiming that in addition the universe contains a realm that does not obey the causal laws which govern everything else there is. In the Enlightenment, it had been supposed that the imagination obeyed such psychological 'laws' as were claimed at the time to govern the mind as a whole, notably what was termed the law of association: if two events or items accompanied one another regularly in experience, then the occurrence of the memory of one would lead to the occurrence of the memory of the other. If you associate the smell of a particular food with a special restaurant, then recalling either will lead to your recalling the other, and much the same law governed the occurrence of the memories the imagination was held to rearrange. It is important to be clear how radically different is the view of the imagination Novalis is advancing here. He is claiming that no such causal laws apply to the working of the imagination as he understands it. As a matter of logic he has to say something like this: the laws of causality cannot apply to reality as he conceives it, since for causality to operate reality must consist of at least two things which can causally interact, and so if the imagination is to put us in touch with reality, it cannot do so by obeying causal laws. Small wonder Novalis thinks of it as *magical* – and he is choosing his words with care – for the magical is that which appears to defy conventional causal laws. Nevertheless, the magnitude of the claim has to sink in if we are to appreciate fully what the Romantics are going to claim as the role of art and the nature of the artist. For the Romantics, the imagination is no less than the faculty which has the power to penetrate all the veils of illusion which make up ordinary experience and lead us to direct acquaintance with the real.

Summary point: for the Romantics, the imagination supplants reason as the faculty by means of which we can be acquainted with reality, and the imagination, uniquely among the things of this world, does not obey conventional causal laws.

The nature of the artist-genius

In the Enlightenment, it was commonplace to refer to the person who accepted rationalism and used the empiricist method by means of the French term *philosophe*. As you learned in Unit 1 (p.10), this term does not mean quite what is meant in English by 'philosopher', which has a narrower and more technical focus. Rather, the *philosophe* was the person at the intellectual cutting edge of the time, the person who, free from superstition and not prepared to bow to authority however venerable, surveyed the evidence for whatever question was under debate dispassionately, trusting absolutely in the power of reason to reveal the truth about the universe, and making up their own mind in the light of the available evidence. All this changed dramatically with the coming of Romanticism. The imagination supplants reason as the faculty that gives us access to ultimate truth, and the figure who by common consent was specially endowed with imagination was the artist. Thus it came about that the artist and especially the artist with the greatest imaginative power – the genius – came to replace the *philosophe* as the final guardian of truth. The idea – which still lingers even now – that artists have some special power, that they are in some way set apart from ordinary mortals and cannot, perhaps, be expected to operate by the same rules, enters European consciousness at this time and on the basis of the ideas we have been discussing. As Novalis puts it: 'Only an artist can divine the meaning of life' (*Logological Fragments I*, paragraph 96, 1997, p.66). We need to look more closely at the Romantic conception of the artist and genius.

EXERCISE   Read the extract from Novalis's *Logological Fragments II* (Anthology II, extract 4, pp.211–12) and write brief answers to the following questions:

1   According to Novalis, what special ability does an artist have that a non-artist lacks?

2   Why is it wrong to suppose that painting is primarily an imitative or mimetic art?

3   How is the spiritual aspect of us related to the mechanical laws that govern matter?

Note: the Latin phrase *a priori* means 'prior to or independent of sense-experience'. For example, you know the truth of the statement 'All bachelors are unmarried males' independently of seeking out bachelors in the real world and verifying by observation that they are both male and unmarried. In order to know that this proposition is true, all you need to know is what the words in the sentence mean.

DISCUSSION   1   An artist experiences the world – both the outer world and the world of the inner life revealed by introspection – in a different way from the non-artist. Novalis claims that the artist experiences the world in a way that is 'quite active' and 'for the spirit'.

2   The essence of the art of the painter consists in 'the art of seeing with order and beauty', just as that of the musician consists in hearing with order and beauty. The painted image on the canvas, Novalis claims, is only the painter's 'secret sign', only the means used to communicate. The object of the painter is not to imitate nature, but to communicate something from within.

3   The spirit is independent of the mechanical order that governs the rest of nature.

This is not an easy passage to grasp, but the ideas in it are important and we need to dwell on what Novalis is claiming here: he is not gushing or indulging in hype, but choosing his words with care, and setting out convictions with which his companions would have agreed. A number of the ideas he puts forward relate very closely to the Romantic conception of art we will study in detail in the next section.

It may have struck you as curious that Novalis does not use the word 'imagination' here. He has chosen instead in this passage to use the term 'spirit' to mean the same thing, and this way of putting it would not have struck him as at all odd. Reality is ultimately spiritual, and the imagination – the faculty that penetrates to it – must itself also be spiritual or non-material. It is because it is spiritual in nature that Novalis can here remake the claim we have met before that the imagination does not work according to mechanical laws.

What, then, does it do? Notice that Novalis claims here that 'the beautiful, the subject of art, is *not* given to us nor can it be found ready in phenomena' (emphasis added). When an artist has created something beautiful, what has most emphatically not occurred, Novalis contends, is that he/she has copied or imitated some beautiful thing already existing in the natural world, even if tidied up and with imperfections removed. Art is *not* imitation. What occurs in the creation of beauty is that 'the spirit ... poeticizes the objects and the changes of the material'. Beauty is not something out there to be noticed and copied, a quality of things in the world: beauty is a manifestation of the activity of the imagination/ spirit. Artists experience the world with the benefit of a highly active imagination, and when they record these experiences in art they produce what we see as beauty: beauty is experience which has passed through the lens of the imagination. Novalis holds this to be obvious in the case of music, since music (he takes for granted) manifestly does not imitate anything in the outside world, certainly not in the same way that a painting might be said to imitate visible appearances: hence he states that '[t]he musician takes the essence of his art from *within himself* ...' (emphasis added). He goes on to insist, however (and logically he has to), that the same is true of painters. Painters might superficially be taken to be artists whose business is to imitate visible forms. Not so: the medium an artist uses in order to communicate to us his/her spiritualized experiences is accidental. In order to communicate at all in this world we need some medium of communication, some 'symbolic language', as Novalis puts it here. It can be words, musical sounds, paint on canvas, shaped marble (and so on for all the materials used by artists): it follows from the view of reality and the imagination we are considering that the medium is ultimately unimportant. What matters is the spiritual/ imaginative experience conveyed by it, and this message can be conveyed in a number of different media.

This is what lies behind Novalis's remarks here about artists hearing or seeing (etc.) *actively.* One of the most important aspects of the activity of the artistic imagination/spirit is that it informs and conditions the activity of the senses: the outside world as experienced via the senses is not just passively registered in the mind of an artist. Rather, it is moulded and transformed by it, made the vehicle for the artist's ideas and (as he insists) changed as the artist *wills.* The imagination is a truly formative, creative power. The artistic imagination, on this view, does not *imitate* the world, but in a special way *creates* its own, with a further goal in view that we will look at in the next section. When, in his poem *Dejection: an Ode* (1802), Coleridge laments the loss of what he calls 'My shaping spirit of Imagination' (l.86), this is precisely what he has in mind: the imagination (he believes) shapes or forms the world: it creates its own.

One more point about the artist as conceived of in this framework of ideas needs to be stressed. Reality is spiritual in nature, and so is the imagination which gives us access to it. This reality is infinite: in fact, it has, as we have seen, most of the properties usually attributed to God. Accordingly, it was regarded as divine by Romantics of the kind we are presently considering. It follows that the activity of the imagination is itself either divine or akin to it: God created the universe, and this creative power of the divine spirit is reflected and paralleled in the creative power of the imagination to shape and form whole new worlds. It also follows directly that the distinction between artist and priest collapses. To be an artist is to have a holy mission, to reveal the divine to those of us who are non-artists. An artistic genius is (literally) a sort of saviour. As FS puts it:

> The priest as such exists only in the invisible world. In what guise is it possible for him to appear among men? His only purpose on earth will be to transform the finite into the infinite; hence he must be and continue to be, no matter what the name of his profession, an artist.

('Ideas', paragraph 16, 1991, p.95)

More crisply, later in the same work, he says artists 'are Brahmins, a higher caste' (paragraph 146, 1991, p.108). Rarely has a greater claim been made for the mission and status of the artist, and it is echoed in both the works and the statements made by Romantic artists in the years that followed. One example will have to stand for many. The German painter Caspar David Friedrich (1774–1840), writing a statement of his artistic principles in response to an attack by conservative critics, describes the mission of the Romantic artist as follows:

> Is not the artistic spirit of our time, with an insensate, deplorable faith devoted to an imagined spiritual being without limits? Does it not follow, with childlike submission, every sacred commotion of its soul? Does it not give homage with blind abandon to every pious feeling as if such were in an absolute manner the purest and most limpid spring of art?

(Open letter to J.K.H. Schultz, 8 February 1809, quoted in Uhde-Bernays, 1960, p.142; trans. R. Wilkinson)

Friedrich is here summing up and pastiching, with considerable sarcasm and (non-Romantic) irony, views of the conservative critics he dislikes: he is in fact praising the religious inspiration of his artistic practice (and that of like-minded Romantics). He regards the grounding of art in religion as anything but 'insensate' and 'deplorable': for him faith *is*, as he says, the 'purest and most limpid spring of art'. In full-blown Romantic theory, art is a form of religion.

One can readily see the same spirit in Friedrich's paintings. For example, *Monk by the Sea* (see Plate 24.2 in the Illustrations Book), completed in the same year as the letter just quoted, exhibits precisely this religious feeling, attempting to convey to us Romantic intuitions of the infinite, and the same feeling informs much of this artist's work.

Summary point: the Romantics conceived of the artist-genius as the person endowed with a powerful imagination. The imagination is a spiritual and creative power that shapes realities

of its own. Since this power is akin to the creative power of God, the artist and the priest are one and the same.

The nature of art and aesthetic experience

It will be becoming clear by now that the eighteenth-century view that art is imitation, and that experience of it is, even if moving, in the final analysis a diversion from the serious activity of rational truth-gathering, will not fit with the Romantic ideas we have encountered so far. These new ideas demand a quite different conception of art and of the experience it affords us, more exalted and mysterious than their predecessors. As Novalis puts it, poetry (and the arts in general) serve the 'great purpose of all purposes – *the elevation of the human being above himself*' (*Logological Fragments I,* paragraph 36, 1997, p.56). We need to spend some time coming to grips with what this means.

EXERCISE   Read Wackenroder's short essay *Concerning Two Wonderful Languages and their Mysterious Power* (Anthology II, extract 5, pp.213–15), and write short answers to the following questions:

1   What are the 'two languages' of the title?

2   What do these languages allow us to comprehend?

3   What source of knowledge is to be preferred to the assertions of philosophers (paragraph 6)?

4   How is the effect of the two languages on us described in paragraph 8?

5   To which part of us does art direct our attention?

DISCUSSION   1   The languages of nature and of art.

2   Both languages allow us to perceive and comprehend heavenly things in their full force (paragraph 3). One can put this another way by saying that both nature and art, in Wackenroder's view, bring us into contact with an ultimate reality which is spiritual in nature.

3   Wackenroder claims that God has implanted in us what he calls 'dim intuitions' (paragraph 6), which are to be preferred to the reasonings of philosophers.

4   The effect of the two languages on us is remarkable, and is hard to describe. What appears to happen is that our faculties become in some sense far more deeply unified or integrated than is the case in ordinary experience. The senses and the intellect function in a unified and special way, as if they were some other, single mode of apprehension.

5   Art directs our attention to our inner self, to the spirit ('the invisible part', paragraph 9).

Let us concentrate on what Wackenroder has to say about the language of art rather than that of nature. He is announcing here a view of the nature and function of art typical of early Romanticism. Reality, as we have noticed many times, is spiritual in nature. In all philosophies which claim that there is such a reality, the ultimate goal of life for human beings is to come into as close a contact or accord with this reality as the philosophy in question claims to be possible: this is what Novalis means (in the fragment quoted at the opening of this section) by his phrase 'the purpose of all purposes'. We have a faculty that allows us access to the realm of spirit or the real, and this is not reason but the imagination. Of all human beings the artist-genius is the one most endowed with this faculty. The artist produces works of art, formed by the creative imagination, itself a function of the spirit and echoing its creative activity. Accordingly, the role of art in life, in the Romantic outlook we are discussing, is to bring us as close to the ultimate spiritual reality as possible. The purpose of art is not remotely to give us a diversion from the serious business of life, however refined the diversion may be; on the contrary, the purpose of art is identical to the most serious purpose a human being can have, namely to approach the divine reality. A shorthand way of saying this is that the function of art is to bring us closer to God, which in religious language is equivalent to saying that it brings us salvation. This is as bold a claim for the value of art as has ever been made. (Notice that this is the logical counterpart of the claim that there is no distinction to be made between artists and priests.)

This is the framework of belief that lies behind what Wackenroder is saying in this short essay. Art is a language which allows us to comprehend heavenly things (spiritual reality); it puts us in touch with the realm of spirit, both heavenly and in ourselves. (Remember: these are not different. The way to the spirit is to journey inwards, into the depths of consciousness.) We have ordinarily only a hazy, undeveloped awareness of these depths ('dim intuitions'): the experience of art unifies us by focusing attention on the real that is the spiritual.

Half-explicit in this essay is the view of the nature of aesthetic experience which logically has to accompany these other views. It is more explicit in the second of the three Wackenroder essays, *How and in what manner one actually must regard and use the Works of the Great Artists of Earth for the Well-Being of his Soul* (Anthology II, extract 6, pp.216–18).

EXERCISE   Read this extract and write short answers to the following questions:

1   To what does Wackenroder liken the art-gallery?

2   How does he describe aesthetic experience and to what does he liken it?

3   How do art and aesthetic experience relate to ordinary life?

4   In paragraphs 6 and 7, how does Wackenroder contrast the effect of works of art with that of works in which scientific disciplines are expounded?

DISCUSSION   1   To a temple, that is, a place of worship.

2   He describes it in terms of spiritual rapture, especially in paragraphs 3 and 4: saturation with ethereal light, illumination of the soul with higher revelation, freedom from the trivial activities of ordinary life, and so on. Aesthetic experience is likened to prayer, not conceived of as a self-regarding petition to God, but as a humble opening of the soul to God, so that God may enter the soul.

3   Aesthetic experience is wholly apart from the ordinary flow of life.

4   In scientific works, the meaning of the words is finite and can be exhausted. We can finally master what is meant, absorb it and put it to the practical use for which it was intended. (This would apply, incidentally, to more or less every treatise produced in the Enlightenment.) Not so with the best works of art: here there is no end or terminus to understanding them. There is always something new to be found in them.

Just as the distinction between artist and priest collapses in the Romantic outlook, so does the distinction between religious experience and aesthetic experience, and this is coherent with the view that art is a means to salvation. No doubt, generally speaking, it is not the case that aesthetic experiences are as intense or transformatory as the religious encounters described in the works of the great mystics, but these experiences are conceived of by Wackenroder as being of the same kind, as points on the same scale as it were, not as wholly disconnected types of experience, as would have been the case previously.

I have picked out point 4 above for a different reason. Here Wackenroder – typically of the Romantics – has put his finger on a property of some works of art, an aesthetic virtue, which gained hugely in importance as a result of the Romantic view of art. What he is talking about is what we now call depth or profundity. Only a small percentage of works of art qualify for this accolade, and they are usually at the summits of artistic production. What they have in common is that they cannot be summed up: they go on suggesting new ideas and new interpretations, and (a logically coherent accompaniment to this) the experience they provide does not become dull. We cannot get to the bottom of them: every time we dig there is a deeper layer to be found, a new significance, another convincing interpretation. You will no doubt have your own examples: I find there is something odd about even the idea that there could be a 'last word' about works such as *Don Quixote* or *The Tempest* or Beethoven's Piano Sonata op 111 or some of Rembrandt's self-portraits, and many (myself included) would put Goethe's *Faust* on such a list as well.

For the moment, note only this point: it is no accident, from a logical point of view, that this particular aesthetic virtue came to such prominence in the writings of Romantic theorists. For them, reality, the reality to which the imagination alone can penetrate, is ordinarily hidden deep behind veils of false belief and shallow, distracting everyday experience. We need help to get to it, the help furnished by artists via works of art. The better these works are, the more they stay with us: they get inside us and reverberate, as it were, in our memory and our own imagination, seemingly without end. When Victor Hugo (1802–85), the archetypal figure of French Romanticism, sets out to describe what separates second-rate artists from first-rate ones, this is what he says. Second-rate artists

> have neither exaggeration, nor shadows, nor darkness, nor monstrousness. What therefore do they lack?
>
> That.
>
> That, is the unknown.
>
> That, is the infinite.
>
> Investigate deeply then the meaning of these words, placed like masks on the mysterious qualities of genius. Beneath obscurity, subtlety and shadows, you find profundity; beneath exaggeration, imagination; beneath monstrousness, grandeur.
>
> (1973, p.95; trans. R. Wilkinson)

The rhapsodic nature of Hugo's prose does not disguise the typically Romantic view he advocates here: the Romantic work of art suggests the infinite, and because it is finite it can do it only by being inexhaustible.

The idea of these works having depth, especially concealed depth, suggests itself irresistibly as a metaphorical way of describing this remarkable aesthetic phenomenon.

Summary point: for the Romantics, art is a means to salvation, and salvation is the most serious goal any human being can have. The artist-genius forms a work which will stimulate the imagination of the spectator in such a way that the latter is brought into closer touch with reality. Aesthetic experience and

religious experience are of a kind, the former being anything but a diversion or rest from matters taken to be more serious. Aesthetic experience *is* the most important experience most people will ever have.

The unity of the work of art

I want now to move on to consider some of the major consequences of this view of the imagination, art and the artist. The first of these concerns the Romantic doctrine on how a work of art achieves the vital quality of being a unified whole. While the Romantics shared with their eighteenth-century predecessors (and indeed many artists from all periods) the view that unity is a condition for success in a work of art, they took a quite different view of what it means and how it is achieved. You will recall that in the eighteenth century it was believed that unity would be achieved by following the models to be found in the classics and epitomized in the rules either stated in classic works or deduced from classical practice. This is coherent with the view of the imagination as a recombiner of memories according to the rules of taste. Take the view that the imagination is a faculty which exhibits a power which is quasi-divine, and which does not imitate anything but *creates* its own worlds, and there ceases to be a reason to follow *any* pre-existing model, classic or otherwise. Again, the idea that the genres of art invented by the ancients are sacrosanct loses all its force. The imagination furnishes its own laws. Aesthetic unity comes not from conformity to any type of model or the following of rules, but from the internal consistency of the imaginative vision. This is how FS puts the point (he happens to be talking about the novel, but what he says applies to any kind of work of art):

> ... the dramatic context of the story does not make the novel a whole, a work, if the whole composition is not related to a higher unity than that of the letter which it often does and should disregard; but it becomes a work through the bond of ideas, through a spiritual central point.

> (Quoted in Wheeler, 1984, p.78)

It is consistent quality of imaginative vision that lends unity to a work of art, and no amount of rule-following can compensate for a failure in this vision.

This doctrine had far-reaching consequences in criticism, since it not only permitted but invited the appreciation of artists and works held in much lower esteem in the previous century. Notable among these was Shakespeare, for whom these Romantics had a profound admiration. What Shakespeare's plays do *not* do is follow the rules for the construction of drama universally supposed at this time to be advocated in the *Poetics* of Aristotle (and adhered to in neoclassical drama in the seventeenth and eighteenth centuries, especially in France): the unities of time, place and action. According to these rules, the action of a play must take place within 24 hours, must occur in only one location, and must concern one central plot, a story complete in itself. For the Romantics, Shakespeare's disregard for these supposed rules is of no importance. Applying his standard of imaginative consistency, FS arrives at this critical verdict:

> In the nobler and more original sense of the word correct – meaning a conscious main and subordinate development of the inmost and most minute aspects of a work in line with the spirit of the whole, the practical reflection of the artist – there probably is no modern poet more correct than Shakespeare.
>
> ('Athenaeum Fragments', paragraph 253, 1991, p.53)

This admiration was shared by AWS, who translated 17 of Shakespeare's plays into German, and the book in which they were published was extremely successful. Nor was this new admiration for Shakespeare confined to Germany but spread to France (though, for reasons we will return to, it took longer to take root there). It can be found, for example, in the two pamphlets written by Stendhal in 1823 and 1825, now always printed together as his book *Racine et Shakespeare*. Here Stendhal prefers Shakespeare to Racine, the paradigm exemplar of classicism in French drama. Shakespeare, Stendhal argues, free from the tyranny of following the so-called rules derived from Greek tragedy, is able more accurately to depict the movements of the human heart than can Racine. Again, the quotation from Victor Hugo about profundity (see p.48 above) is from his book, *William Shakespeare* (1864), a full-length eulogy of Shakespeare derived from Romantic principles. In the following year, his son Jean-François-Victor Hugo published a translation of the complete works of Shakespeare, for which his father wrote a preface.

Summary point: for the Romantics, the unity of a work of art is not guaranteed by the following of models of any kind. It is a consequence of the quality and consistency of the imagination which creates it. This manifests itself as internal consistency in the imaginative world of the work.

Wit and Romantic irony

The concepts of wit as the Romantics understood it and Romantic irony are both important in the Romantic conception of art. They are logically very closely linked to the belief in a spiritual reality accessible only via the imagination. It is not possible to pretend, however, that these concepts are easy to grasp at the first attempt, and we need to remind ourselves of some points already covered in order to see what they mean and why they were considered so important by the Romantics.

The context in which these ideas were developed, as we have seen, has at its basis the belief that behind the appearances of the everyday world is a reality which is a unity or oneness, which is spiritual in nature, infinite and divine and which is accessible not by reason but only by means of the imagination. Artists seek to convey to us the quality of their imaginative experience by means of works of art. In the context of these beliefs, the function of art is to stimulate *our* imaginations, so that we might come closer to union with the real. However, this entire enterprise – that of seeking to use art to bring us closer to the real – involves a major paradox, of which the Romantics were perfectly aware. Reality is infinite and spiritual, yet the artist must seek to convey it – and we to grasp it – by means of works which are finite and material. What is infinite and spiritual has no form, and cannot in principle be depicted, represented or otherwise meaningfully described. In a sense, the Romantic artist is seeking to do something known in advance and in principle to be impossible: somehow to suggest or convey the experience of the infinite and spiritual by finite and material means. In successful art, somehow, the finite has to suggest the infinite. The ability to make this suggestion by means of art the Romantics called 'wit', manifestly in a special, technical sense of the term. Here is a statement of this view by a less prominent member of the Romantic circle, Karl Solger (1780–1819):

> Many have explained wit as being the mere comparison of individual things in their interconnections; but this is in fact the very opposite of what wit really is. For them the finite remains simply finite; its connection to the infinite remains incomplete and the intuition of essence infinitely distant. True wit annihilates all that with a single blow, by discovering in every connection the essential intuition whereby things converge. Wit connects what is present and individual in things with this intuition, and in so far as presentness and individuality are for simple existence accidental and sporadic, it is only through this process of the wit that existence is unified.
>
> (Quoted in Wheeler, 1984, pp.141–2)

What Solger here calls 'the intuition of essence' is the vision of reality available only via the artistic imagination. What this vision reveals is that separateness in all its forms is an illusion; or, put another way, that all things are interconnected in ways unperceived in modes of experience where the imagination is not engaged. When the world is experienced imaginatively, the infinite is found to be present in the finite, and this revelation is made only by the property of the imagination the Romantics called wit. As FS puts it: 'Wit is the appearance, the outward lightning bolt of the imagination' ('Ideas', paragraph 26, 1991, p.96).

Summary point: in the writings of the German Romantics, 'wit' is the term used for the imaginative intuition of the infinite in the finite.

The paradox stated above – that Romantic art is an attempt to do something that cannot in principle be done – also lies behind the important doctrine of Romantic irony. Irony in its ordinary usage means, as Dr Johnson puts it in his *Dictionary*, 'a mode of speech in which the meaning is contrary to the words' (quoted in Bartholomew *et al.* 1992, p.xii). When language is used ironically, the user not only conveys the surface meaning of the words, but also indicates that they are to be taken as meaning something else as well, sometimes the reverse of the surface sense, sometimes a significance subversive of the surface sense (or part of it, or some belief presupposed by it) in another way. For example, when Gibbon castigates pagan historians for their inattention in not noting the darkening of the sun at noon at the time of the Crucifixion, what he is doing is indicating by the ironic use of words that he believes that no such darkening of the sun took place at all. Eighteenth-century texts are full of such ironies, which often allowed the writers to escape the wrath of the authorities.

Romantic irony is a more complex notion, and arises from the artist's awareness that any work of art will necessarily and in principle not be adequate fully to convey the experience of the infinite. The artist cannot allow the spectator (listener, etc.) of the work of art to fall into the trap of believing that the work is in any sense final or absolute or perfect, for it cannot in principle be any of these things. It is all too easy for us to be beguiled by the aesthetic charms of skilfully constructed artworks, and if we enter this state our own imaginations will not be stimulated in the way in which the Romantic artist seeks to stimulate them. The goal of Romantic art is to bring us not to a condition of mental stasis, but on the contrary to a state in which our imagination is constantly operative.

EXERCISE   Read FS's *Critical Fragments* (Anthology II, extract 7, pp.219–20), a statement of what Romantic irony is and what it does to us. FS here calls it 'Socratic irony', but he means exactly the same thing.

This passage, which is itself an example of Romantic irony, both exhibits and describes the condition of the true Romantic, both artist and spectator of art. Romantic irony is the attitude that both embodies in itself and arouses in us 'a feeling of indissoluble antagonism between the absolute and the relative, between the impossibility and the necessity of complete communication'. The absolute is the ultimate spiritual reality; the relative is the day-to-day world of individuals, including individual works of art. Complete communication with the real is the goal of all of us (necessary because it is our salvation), towards which the artist tries to assist us, while knowing full well – as do we – that complete success in this endeavour by means of finite works of art is impossible. It is essential that both artists and spectators continue to strive for this goal, in the full knowledge that it is impossible to achieve. Only by this continuous striving can we transcend ourselves, i.e. approach communion with the real.

How is this to be done in practical terms? FS gives us a clue in the phrase 'continuous self-parody': Romantic works of art composed in the light of this doctrine of Romantic irony are such that they in some way draw attention to their own limitations, to their own status as limited works of art, and this was an idea destined to have a long future in western aesthetics. Perhaps the most vivid examples in the early Romantic period are to be found in the plays of Johann Ludwig Tieck (1773–1853), where strikingly modern techniques are used to draw attention to the artificiality of the drama. Characters on stage will break off the action and begin to engage in critical debate about the play; then another actor, planted in the audience, will stand up and complain that such discussions are intolerable, and so on. Again, when you come to Goethe's *Faust*, you should consider the effect of the short Prelude on the stage (pp.31–3 of the *Faust* text). Here, Goethe deliberately draws attention to the fact that the audience is about to witness a play which is meant to divert: even if he is about to deal with some deep aspects of the human condition, Goethe does not allow us to forget that we are in the presence of an illusion whose shape is partly dictated by practical considerations of staging. (Quite a number of theatrical techniques made use of in the modern theatre are foreshadowed in these works.) Another technique is that of the use of the fragment form for the publication of these very ideas: you will have noticed in the extracts in Anthology II that many are from works which include the word 'Fragments' in their title, and much of the theoretical work which appeared in the key Romantic journal, *The Athenaeum*, appeared in this form. The choice of the aphoristic form is deliberate – these men could have written connected prose expositions of their ideas had they so chosen, but they preferred the fragment form of brief numbered paragraphs. It is less conventional (it allows different authors to appear in the same piece, as they regularly did, thus undermining ordinary notions of authorship), and requires the reader to do more of the work: the logical links between ideas can be omitted, the thought left incomplete for us to work out, thereby requiring *our* imaginative participation in reading and thinking.

The aim of all these techniques is, by drawing attention to the limited and artificial nature of the work, to prevent the audience from becoming mentally too comfortable, from becoming 'harmonious bores' as FS puts it here. If you are in a state of mental harmony, you are not striving, and if you are not striving, you are a bore. There can be no doubt that the Romantic ideal of unceasing search for communion with the real is a strenuous one, in both life and art. Romantic works of art are not designed to put you at your ease.

The justification for the term 'irony' is this: one aspect of irony in its ordinary usage is that it involves a certain degree of detachment. Romantic irony is the detachment of artists from their work, their awareness of its necessarily limited success. The truly Romantic spectator of art will have the same attitude.

Summary point: Romantic irony is the attitude which results from the conviction, shared by both artists and spectators, that the goal of Romantic art – the manifestation of the infinite in the finite – cannot be achieved, but must nevertheless be striven for ceaselessly. This attitude manifests itself in works of art which deliberately draw attention to their own limitations.

The Romantic and the classical

One thing that will be clear from the previous sections is that the Romantics with whom we are concerned were highly self-conscious: they were aware that they were doing something new. One way in which this self-awareness manifests itself is their meditation on the meaning of the term 'Romantic' or, put another way, their reflection on what it meant to be Romantic, and on what Romantic art is like. This in turn had consequences for their attitude to the classics, of which several of them, notably both Schlegel brothers, were considerable scholars. In this section we will investigate some of their best-known statements about what one can call the Romantic spirit, and how it relates to the classical.

EXERCISE   Read paragraphs 1–5 of extract 8 (Anthology II, pp.221–3), from the first chapter of AWS's *Course of Lectures on Dramatic Art and Literature* (1809–11), and write a brief answer to the following question:

What are the essential qualities of the figure AWS here calls 'the true critic'?

DISCUSSION   The 'true critic' has universality of mind. Such a person recognizes that the ability to create beauty is universal among humankind, and is able to perceive this beauty, no matter in what conventions or forms ('external accessories') it is embodied.

AWS is here articulating a principle that had widespread consequences in the arts. The imagination, the Romantics believed, is a faculty universal among human beings. Since experience imaginatively rendered – which is what gives a work what AWS calls here 'internal excellence' – is the most valuable of human commodities, it follows that any human creation which embodies it is to be valued. Thus all epochs of human history and all civilizations are of potential interest to the Romantics, and none has a claim to a unique status. Consequently, the Romantics took an interest in a very wide range of cultural artefacts and institutions. They were interested in the remote in time and the remote in place, in myths, folk legends and fairytales – it is no accident that the great fairytale collections of the Brothers Grimm were assembled in the first 20 years of the nineteenth century, since they were made directly under the influence of the Romantic ideas we are discussing. Any product of the imagination was valued by the Romantics, and they accordingly felt free to include legends, tales and so on, in their own works, and they did so in the belief that they were not just confections, diversions or mere examples of stages of the development of humanity more primitive than our own. For the Romantics they all embodied valuable imaginative truths, and this is a belief which has underlain revivals of interest in and collections of 'folk' culture ever since.

EXERCISE   Now read paragraphs 6–9 of AWS's text (pp.223–4) and write short answers to the questions which follow. (The reference, in paragraph 6, to new life being given to the study of ancient literature is AWS's way of referring to the Renaissance.)

1   How was the study of the classics of the ancient world perverted?

2   Why will mere imitation of ancient models not result in the production of successful works of art?

3   In paragraph 9, how does AWS define the term 'Romantic'?

DISCUSSION   1   The perversion consists in regarding the classics as furnishing models that are regarded not just as perfect *of their kind* but as *the only possible models* for successful artworks.

2   Successful art, AWS states, must come from within us: as he puts it: 'even what we borrow from others, to assume a true poetical shape, must, as it were, be born again within us' (paragraph 7). We must in some way put ourselves into the work of art, or it will be lifeless.

3   The Romantic is identified with the modern. He suggests that there is a modern or Romantic spirit which is quite distinct from the classical, deriving from a more recent phase in the history of civilization in which the remains of the civilization of the ancient world are blended with the culture of the northern (Teutonic) races.

These paragraphs contain some important Romantic ideas. The first point to note is that the Romantics were far from denying that the classics of the ancient world are indeed classics and deserving of the greatest respect: their admiration for these works was absolutely sincere. However, they add a qualification which was new: these classics may be perfect examples of their *kind*, but this kind is not the only one. History has not stood still, and a new spirit has evolved – the modern, Romantic spirit – equally deserving of respect and equally capable of engendering works of art of the highest quality.

Second, in his comments on the futility of copying ancient models, AWS relies on some ideas about art destined to have a long history, and which came to be commonplace in aesthetic theory. We have already met the idea that the unity of a work of art cannot be guaranteed by following any particular set of rules or patterns or models: the unity is derived from the consistency of the artist's vision. This is one aspect of the principle he here relies on explicitly, namely that in order to be successful, a work of art must 'be born ... within us'. Another way of putting this is that it is a necessary condition for aesthetic success that a work of art be a genuine expression of the artist's experience. You will often find in histories of aesthetics the idea that the Romantics believed that art is not imitation of nature but expression, usually of emotion, and indeed some Romantics (e.g. Wordsworth) do link aesthetic success with the expression of emotion, though not in any simple-minded way (see Wordsworth's *Observations Prefixed to the Second Edition of Lyrical Ballads*, 1801). However, as AWS's text here makes clear, the German Romantics at least took a rather more complex view. They certainly did not believe that just expressing yourself is likely to result in the creation of a work of art. Rather, what they are claiming is that unless artists really have something they wish to convey, unless there is some genuine and real imaginative experience behind it, the work of art will be lifeless. The classics of the ancient world are successful, in the view of the Romantics, precisely because they did this for the spirit of their own times, evolving art forms perfect for their purposes; but their times are not ours. History has moved on, and in modern times we have other concerns with which artists must occupy themselves: hence, any attempt to make art just by copying works from the past is bound to end in failure, for each age is different and requires its own forms of art. To be successful, modern art need not be like any previous model; rather, it must be true to the concerns that give it life. This is the idea that art can be authentic, which enters European consciousness at this point.

EXERCISE   Having claimed that there is a modern, Romantic spirit, distinct from that of the ancient world, AWS has to try to identify where the contrast lies, and this is what he goes on to do in the rest of this chapter. Read the remaining paragraphs (pp.224–9) and write a short answer to the following question:

How does AWS describe the key difference between the ancient and the modern?

DISCUSSION AWS locates the difference between the ancient and the modern in the area of religion, which he regards as 'the root of human existence' (paragraph 16). Greek religion, he claims, is a 'deification of the powers of nature and of the earthly life' (paragraph 14). Absent from Greek civilization is a vision of the life everlasting in the presence of a single spiritual reality or god, and the absence of real other-worldliness entails that we cannot find in their civilization 'any higher character ... than that of a refined and ennobled sensuality' (paragraph 15). This is to be contrasted with the Christian vision of God and immortality that informs the modern spirit.

What Christianity has given to the modern, Romantic outlook (AWS contends) is the belief that our real existence begins after death, in another world, spiritual, eternal and infinite. The soul cannot be content with this life, which is transitory and illusory (paragraph 24). The modern, Romantic soul is haunted by a sense of being exiled from its proper home, the realm of the spirit. It cannot escape 'indescribable intuitions of infinity' (paragraph 25), the intuitions which, as we have already seen, it is the ultimate business of art to embody and reinforce. However, again as we have already seen, these intuitions cannot be fully embodied in finite works: 'the modern can only do justice to its endeavours after what is infinite by approximation' (paragraph 26).

A certain conception of poetry in particular and art in general follows from these views, and it was set out most famously by FS, in a fragment which will be the last reading in this section.

EXERCISE Read *Athenaeum Fragment 116* (Anthology II, extract 9, pp.229–30) and write a short answer to the following question:

What does FS claim to be the 'real essence' (i.e. the most important property) of Romantic poetry?

DISCUSSION For FS, Romantic poetry is always in a state of becoming. It can never be said to be *finished*.

Behind the paradoxical rhetoric (which, as we have seen, is a typical Romantic technique for the stimulation of the imagination) is a rigorous deduction from beliefs we have already come across. Romantic poetry is an art form that embodies the modern outlook. The modern outlook is aware that each age constitutes its own chapter in the historical manifestation of the infinite spirit which is reality, and each age generates its own authentic art forms in which to bring those alive at the time to fuller awareness of the great imaginative-spiritual experiences which it is the business of art to convey. Accordingly, there can be in principle no fixed, final art form with which the Romantic outlook can be identified and in which it can be expressed or embodied. The Romantic outlook is always alive to its epoch, and every epoch is different. Change is constant, and so the art that reflects it must also change constantly (it is always in a state of 'becoming'). We rely on the imaginative genius or artist to respond appropriately to changes, for the artist is closest to the spirit, and so 'the will of the poet can tolerate no law above itself'. Any art which does not follow this ideal (for example, by relying on imitation of the art forms of the past) will be inauthentic and will fail. Hence all poetry should be Romantic, for Romantic poetry or art (FS contends) is just another name for art which responds authentically to its times.

Summary point: the Romantics believed that for art to be successful it had to be an authentic response to the experience of the artist and the age the artist lived in. They identified the Romantic with the modern, and the modern with the age in which human beings had been made aware of their other-worldly needs by the coming of Christianity. Since human experience is always changing, there can in principle be no fixed art forms with which Romanticism can be identified.

Communicating the incommunicable

In this final section, I want to consider two further important consequences of the Romantic doctrines we have looked at so far. These consequences concern, first, the use of symbols in art and, second, the special status accorded to music. We will consider **symbolism** first.

We have already come across a major paradox in the Romantic view of art, namely that in a sense it is an attempt to do what cannot be done, to convey by means of finite works of art what AWS exactly calls 'indescribable intuitions of infinity'. There is no way in which the experiences which mattered to the Romantics could be conveyed by anything like straightforward mimesis, and the Romantic theorists and artists were fully alive to this issue. They did not, however, content themselves with merely stating it. There is a typical way in which artists tend to respond when they are faced with this problem – that is, trying to communicate by artistic means experiences which these means are not ideally suited to communicate – and that is to use symbols of some kind.

Human conceptual structures have evolved to deal with those aspects of the world and of our own experience we have to deal with most often, and in these areas we have developed a rich array of distinctions. We have a huge vocabulary to describe the objects, life-forms and experiences which the vast majority of human beings have to deal with in the course of their daily lives. But what are we to do when the experiences to be communicated are rare and unusual, at the edges or outer limits of our awareness as it were, by no means experienced by all human beings even once in their lifetime, and indeed are in an area where conceptual distinctions do not readily apply? In such cases all that can be done is to try somehow to hint at the experience, to suggest it by some indirect means, and a common way of doing this, in the arts as in other areas of life, is to use symbols.

The symbols in which the Romantics were interested were not what philosophers call conventional symbols, such as red meaning 'danger' or 'stop' on various signs; or the referee's whistle signifying variously 'begin playing' or 'stop playing', as the context dictates. Conventional symbols can always be paraphrased and replaced by others – green might equally well mean danger, were the convention accepted. The symbols in which the Romantics were interested, and which were used in Romantic art-forms of various kinds, are quite different. They are words, images, shapes or sounds intended to stand for experiences not articulable in other ways. Such a symbol will be uniquely appropriate to the experience it is designed to convey and there will be no alternative or equivalent to it. If skilfully chosen, the symbol will suggest to us precisely the experience the artist is concerned with. As Solger put it in a letter to Tieck dated 3 August 1818:

> But where do we enjoy a perfect understanding of the eternal and guard it in ever-present contemplation? We feel a constant urge wherever possible to draw it into our presence by means of *individual* symbols.
>
> (Quoted in Wheeler, 1984, p.154)

The paradox at the heart of the Romantic aesthetic which we have already noticed in the context of the idea of Romantic irony appears in another form in the theory of symbolism. As Solger notes, symbols are *individual*, yet the experience they are ultimately designed to communicate is not of anything individual, but of a unified, spiritual reality. The ideal or perfect Romantic symbol would make the infinite (reality) manifest via the finite (the symbol). In practice, this ideal was impossible to achieve, but this did not make striving for it any the less urgent. Moreover, there is nothing in the theory which entails that there can be only *one* perfect symbol. Much as is the case in the logically very similar theory of Japanese *haiku* poetry, in the experience of the perfect artist the infinite is perceptible in everything finite, and the artist can with skill convey this experience to us by a variety of artistic means and subject-matters. Consequently, we can benefit from the experience of many different artists and works of art.

Let me try to make this abstract and difficult theory more concrete by taking an example from Block 7, Delacroix's 1830 painting *Liberty Leading the People* (Plate 32.28 in the Illustrations Book). This picture as a whole is a symbol, and is complex in that it includes other symbols. What precisely does Liberty here stand for? This image of a female is not just a personification of an idea, not just an artist's conventional device for the representation of something abstract and so not depictable. There is more to it than that. Delacroix is trying to convey something much deeper and less amenable to summary, an animating ideal of humankind, an ideal for which human beings are ready both to kill and to die, capable of shaping history, and in the light of which life should be lived, which institutions should both respect and foster. Again, Delacroix has enriched the symbolism by incorporating a pre-existing symbol. Liberty carries a flag, the tricolour, and this again – although not of course invented by the Romantics – is a symbol which is from the logical point of view of precisely the kind which the Romantics were concerned with. It is worth asking yourself whether you could devise a complete statement of what this (or indeed any other) national flag stands for: not just an area of the planet, not just the people who at any time inhabit it, not just a history and a culture. It stands for all these and more: but what is this more? Perhaps you might say it stands for what it means to be French: but what does that itself mean? Can that be summed up? The Romantics would say that the content of symbols such as these in principle *cannot* be summarized, and that is precisely why we have to use them. There are no complete literal prose translations (as it were) for Liberty and the tricolour, because the realities and experience for which they stand are inexhaustible and simply cannot be summed up. Moreover, if the symbol is successful, it will resonate in your memory for as long as you live, because it has triggered an experience that has no terminus. (You will see that this idea is very closely related to the conviction that reality is, as it were, of infinite depth, and with the belief that profundity is an important virtue in art.)

There is a very close link between the Romantic notion of a symbol and that of myth, in which the Romantics were also deeply interested. Myths were construed by the Romantics precisely as symbolic utterances of the kind we are considering. A myth is a story which somehow embodies a very deep and important aspect of human experience which cannot be articulated satisfactorily in any other way. They could not, however, be content simply to reuse the founding myths of European civilization, those of ancient Greece, for reasons we have already encountered. We are not Greeks, and while their myths are beautiful and articulated their profound concerns in unforgettable stories, times have changed, and the modern spirit must form its own myths. As has often been pointed out (see e.g. Berlin, 1999), what the Romantics did was to elevate certain more recent works of art or characters or stories to the status of myth. Thus it was, for example, that *Hamlet, Don Quixote* and the Faust legend achieved mythic proportions in the Romantic period and after, becoming the source of endless interpretations as profound articulations of significant aspects of the human condition. The legend of Don Juan/ Giovanni was another such theme given mythic status in this period. The fate of the final sextet in Mozart's *Don Giovanni*, which as Donald Burrows points out was dropped from performance for almost a century, is directly related to the Romantic symbolic interpretation of the Don Giovanni figure. Isaiah Berlin gives us the reason:

> Here is this vast, dominating, sinister symbolic figure, Don Giovanni, who stands for we know not what, but certainly for something inexpressible. He stands, perhaps, for art as against life, for some principle of inexhaustible evil against some kind of philistine good; he stands for power, for magic, for some sort of infernal forces of a superhuman kind. The opera ends with an enormous climax, in which one infernal force is swallowed by another, and the vast melodrama rises to a volcanic culmination, which was meant to cow the audience, and to show them amidst what an unstable and terrifying world they lived; and then suddenly this philistine little sextet follows, in which the characters simply sing peacefully about the fact that a rake has been punished, and good men will continue their ordinary, perfectly peaceful lives thereafter. This was regarded as inartistic, shallow, bathetic and disgusting, and therefore eliminated.
>
> (1999, p.123)

The sextet, the Romantics felt, was incompatible with their mythic, symbolic interpretation of the Giovanni figure, and reduced the whole piece to the status of a trite morality tale with a meaning which can be neatly summed up.

The mention of Mozart's opera leads us to the last two readings for these units. These readings concern music, for which the Romantics had a special regard, and we need to explore the reasons for this.

EXERCISE   Read paragraphs 1–7 of Wackenroder's short essay *The Marvels of the Musical Art* (Anthology II, extract 10, pp.230–2), and write a short answer to the following question:

How does Wackenroder here describe the effect of music on us?

Note: in paragraph 3, Wackenroder is *not* using the term 'wit' in the technical, Romantic sense described earlier. He is using it in a sense much more like its ordinary one: the 'desperate game of wit' he speaks of here is simply the state of ordinary people trying to best each other in some way, to outwit each other, a profoundly unquiet condition.

DISCUSSION   One can paraphrase Wackenroder's central thought in these paragraphs by saying that music transports us to the realm of spirit. It lifts us entirely out of the stream of daily life with its manifold disquiets: uncertainties, neuroses, violence, and all the other varieties of friction between egos. The experience music causes in us stands entirely apart from the ordinary experiences of life. Through it, 'we come close to divine blessedness' (paragraph 6).

EXERCISE   Wackenroder goes on, in the rest of this piece, to say more not only about the effect of music but also about its nature. Read the remaining paragraphs of the text (pp.232–4) and write a brief answer to the following question:

How does Wackenroder here characterize the nature of music?

DISCUSSION   Wackenroder describes music as a special kind of language, the nature of which is somehow to embody our emotions in (as he puts it) 'a superhuman way ... above our heads in incorporeal form' (paragraph 12). He repeats his claim that music causes in us the rare and very valuable condition of 'true serenity of soul' (paragraph 13).

Wackenroder has here indicated some of the features of music which (to this day) continue to fascinate and puzzle philosophers, and which have been much discussed. It does seem to be the case that in some way not yet understood music has a special relation with the emotions: we are very ready to apply to music terms drawn from the vocabulary of human emotions. We are quite at home describing pieces as sad or melancholy or triumphant or wistful, though it is not always the case that we feel when listening to them the mood we take them to embody: rather than feeling dejected when listening to a piece of music we would want to describe as dejected, we can feel moved or compassionate, and so on. Again, the emotions felt when we listen to music are odd in an important way, in that they are not (like emotions felt in ordinary life situations) causes of action. Rather (as thinkers in the Indian tradition who have meditated on this issue put it) we savour them in a detached fashion – this is what Wackenroder is indicating, I would guess, by his phrase 'above our heads'. I can feel the mounting terror in Schubert's Goethe setting, 'Erlkönig' (discussed by Robert Philip in Unit 28), but the terror is not mine as would be terror felt as the result of some real-life incident. It is experienced in a detached way, as if it were at a distance from the everyday self and its concerns. (This was also the case, you will remember, with the terror felt in the experience of the sublime.) It is this remarkable feature of the emotions as they occur in aesthetic experiences that allows us to feel serene while experiencing them, and explains why we are willing to undergo the experience of works of art which embody negative emotions which in real-life situations are at the limits of the bearable.

What Wackenroder has not done here is try to suggest any more technically how music can have the effects he describes. For such a suggestion we need to return to AWS, to a different book this time, his 1801 *Lectures on Belles-lettres and Art* (Anthology II, extract 11, pp.234–5).

EXERCISE   Read this extract now and write a brief answer to the following question:

In which feature of music does AWS find the key to its aesthetic power?

DISCUSSION   AWS locates the key to the power of music in harmony. He speculates that harmony, which he regards as a unity of diverse elements, may be a representation of what he calls 'the internal structure of life'. Harmony strives to capture the 'infinite in the indivisible instant'.

AWS is careful not to locate the special power of music in any musical elements that emphasize the passage of time (i.e. tempo and rhythm), since to do so would be to relate it too closely to our ordinary life, in which time moves inexorably onward. Reality – to which art should seek to lead us – is eternal or timeless, and the closest analogue to that he can find to this state in music is the simultaneous sounding of two or more notes. Consistently, he claims that harmony was developed contemporaneously with Christianity, that is, with the development of a religion in which there is a fully-developed conception of a timeless spiritual reality, 'when the psyche was looking inwards in its search for a higher life' as he puts it here. It is no surprise then to find him claiming that a church anthem can express 'striving for spiritual union [i.e. with God] in the dimension of the suprasensual'. The description of the aesthetic experience furnished by music which we found in Wackenroder is entirely consistent with this. Both writers (and FS and Novalis would agree) insist that serious aesthetic experience is transporting: it is isolated from ordinary experience as a result of its intensity, emotional purity and detachment, and by the way in which our awareness of the passage of time is modified by it. (In other words, we cease to be aware of the passage of time in such contemplative states. Normal time-consciousness returns only when the experience ends.) Music is especially fitted to bring about this condition also for a logical reason, namely music is an art that does not make use of concepts. Spiritual reality – divisionless, eternal, infinite – is in principle indescribable in terms of concepts devised to describe a reality of finite, temporal individuals. The closest we can come to a symbol for it in human life is an art which does not deal in concepts of individuals at all, namely music. The Romantics held that music is more like the reality art seeks to convey than any other art form. It is this logical and conceptual point which is the ultimate ground for the extraordinary powers ascribed to music in Romantic theory. (It is worth recalling the view of music we met earlier in the text by d'Alembert, where this art is said to be *undeveloped* in respect of imitative powers: the contrast in the status accorded to music could hardly be greater.)

Summary point: in their attempt to communicate experiences at the limits of the communicable, Romantic artists frequently used

the device of symbolism. They had a special regard for music, which they regarded as a non-conceptual art, in certain ways more analogous to the reality it seeks to convey than any other art form.

EXERCISE   Listen to Audio 5, tracks 6–9: *The Romantic Circle.* In this talk, Professor Nicholas Saul, Head of the Department of German at the University of Liverpool, describes in more detail some of the ideas and personalities of the people you have been studying in the sections on the Romantic view of art, and their relationship to Goethe, part of whose work *Faust* you are about to study.

---

4   Conclusion

In these units you have been introduced to a number of ideas, and before concluding this survey of ideas in aesthetics, it will be useful to sum them up, as in the table opposite.

The final point to be made in these units is to make this picture more untidy. A framework of contrasts like the one set out is easy on the memory, but has the drawback of making the history of these ideas, and their relation to artistic practice, look much neater than in fact it was. In the first place, it would be wrong to regard the Romantic ideas we have been discussing as a manifesto to which all the artists of the time, even in Germany, signed up at once and in its entirety, any more than it is true that all artists of the eighteenth century accepted the imitation view of art in every detail. It took time for these ideas to catch on, and even when they did, not all artists adopted them wholesale: life is never that simple. The relationship between the actual practice of artists at a given time to any theories about art with which they are contemporary is rarely straightforward. One important reason for this is that the theorists are not usually themselves artists, and consequently do not have first-hand experience of what is involved in making a successful work of art. In the case of the Germans whose texts we have read, Novalis is unusual in being both an important poet and a major contributor to the theoretical debate. The theorists of art can allow themselves a greater preoccupation with theoretical consistency and conceptual neatness than the demands of creative artistic work, it seems, usually permit. For an artist, the overriding imperative is to produce a work which does justice to the experience which has intrigued them and which they want to embody in a work of art, rather than to satisfy to the letter the demands of some theory. What one generally finds as a result is a situation such that artists will adopt whatever elements of theory help with the work in hand, or

Eighteenth-century view	*Romantic view*
The universe is a great machine, governed by mathematical laws. Material reality is not an illusion, but something out there, independent of us.	Reality is mental and a unity. All appearance of division and materiality is an illusion.
Reason is the human faculty that gives us access to reality and truth.	The imagination is the faculty that acquaints us with the real.
The activity of the imagination is the recombination of memories.	The imagination is a function of the spirit, which spiritualizes perception and can create its own worlds.
Human nature is uniform at deep levels in many areas, including that of taste.	There is a deep difference between the ancient and the modern or Romantic spirit.
The classics of the ancient world provide timeless models of artistic perfection which can be imitated with profit.	The classics are fine works, but are models for their own times only. Time does not stand still, and Romantic art changes with it.
Art is imitation of nature, though the imitation is selective and aims to produce works which are beautiful and uplifting.	Art is a manifestation or expression of imaginative, spiritualized experience.
Artistic unity can be achieved largely by following rules derived from the classics.	Artistic unity is the result of consistency of imaginative vision.
Creativity is understood as a tasteful recombination of the data of memory. Genius is a problematic concept.	Creativity is non-mechanical, exempt from causal laws, mirroring the activity of reality itself. The genius is the artist pre-eminently endowed with imagination.
The artist is a professional, a maker of beautiful things.	The artist is a quasi-saviour, who can lead us to communion with the real.
Aesthetic experience, however refined or intense, is ultimately a type of diversion.	Aesthetic experience is of a kind with mystical experience, an encounter with the ultimately real.

help them articulate their own experience of what creative work is like. Works of art, in general, are at best a partial fit with theories of art. This does not entail that theorizing about art is foolish: it has its own value in summarizing trends and making shifts in artistic preoccupations clearer; but it is a mistake to expect the art of a given period to exemplify neatly the theories that others have formulated about it. The best way to appreciate this in the present context is to look at examples of artists and works of art from the Romantic period included in this course, and see to what extent they reflect the point of view set out in the works of the German writers we have been considering.

A first point we can notice in this connection is that, although ideas of the kind we have been discussing were shared to some degree in other countries, it is not the case that they were accepted in every instance on the basis of a highly explicit theory such as was formulated by the young German Romantics. The closest parallel to their views in Britain (as has been mentioned) is to be found in the theoretical works of Coleridge, who had in effect taken them from German sources. Blake, by contrast, arrived at a similar view as a result of his natural, unforced and frequent mystical experiences, and Wordsworth as a result of his pantheistic intuitions in the face of nature. Byron, it should be stressed, did *not* accept the Romantic doctrine of the imagination, nor did he regard nature or the order of things as ultimately beneficent or a source of consolation. What makes Byron Romantic is his belief in the power of the will, and of the heroic quality it can lend to human beings.

Again, it is not the case that these ideas spread across Europe at an even rate. France, for example, where the eighteenth-century view of art had taken a profound hold, and preoccupied with the events of the Revolution and the Napoleonic Wars, took some time to adapt to these ideas, and when it did, did so in its own way. As one distinguished French critic has put it, when Romanticism crossed the Rhine it shed its metaphysics (Cabanis, 1964, p.47). Even in so complete a Romantic as Delacroix, whom you will study in Unit 32, there is a distinctively French emphasis in the artist's ideas, as Linda Walsh makes clear. While sharing a number of the ideas we have encountered, especially concerning the reality to be found within the soul itself, Delacroix retains a belief in the power and value of the intelligence or reason. It is worth pondering whether the grip of classicism was ever as loosened in France as it was in Germany or England.

EXERCISE Listen to Audio 5, tracks 10–11: *Romanticism in Practice.* In this talk, I develop this point about the complex relation of theory to artistic practice in the Romantic movement, and how Romanticism manifests itself differently in different countries.

Partly as a result of the grip of classicism in France, Mme de Staël, whom you have already met, felt the need to write a book, *On Germany* (*De l'Allemagne*, 1810), to explain developments in Germany to the French. In the present context, what is interesting is what she tacitly assumes that the French readers of her book will take to be the obvious point of view. Here she is explaining the German view of art:

The Germans do not consider, as one ordinarily does, the imitation of nature to be the principal goal of art; they consider ideal beauty to be the principle of all masterpieces, and in this respect their poetic theory is in perfect accord with their philosophy [i.e. idealism]. The effect one receives from the fine arts has not the least relation with the pleasure one receives from any imitation; man has in his soul innate feelings which real objects will never satisfy, and it is to these feelings that the imagination of painters and poets is able to give form and life. Music, the first among the arts, what does it imitate? However, of all the gifts of the Divinity it is the most magnificent, for it seems (so to speak) to be superfluous. The sun gives us light; we breathe the air of a tranquil heaven; all the beauties of nature serve mankind in some way; music alone has a noble inutility, and it is for that reason that it moves us so deeply.

The literary theory of the Germans differs from all others, in that it subjects writers neither to conventions nor to tyrannical restrictions. It is an entirely creative theory, it is a philosophy of the arts which seeks like Prometheus, far from constraining them, to steal fire from heaven in order to make a gift of it to poets.

(Staël, 1968, vol.II, pp.161–2; trans. R. Wilkinson)

What is interesting about this passage is what historians call the 'unwitting testimony'. Writing some 12 years after most of the Romantic ideas we have been investigating were first formulated, Mme de Staël could still assume that the imitation theory of art is the one her French readers would take for granted, together with all the apparatus of ancient models and rules that went with it – and she was right.

Romanticism did, however, in the end, become the dominant view of art in Europe, and we are to this day its heirs. Few now would accept the Romantic view in its entirety, with all its metaphysical trappings, but it remains true that a substantial number of the views put forward by the Romantics are still with us. The idea that an artistic genius is a figure apart in the human race, akin to the wild figure with flashing eyes and floating hair who has fed on the milk of paradise (at the conclusion of Coleridge's *Kubla Kahn*), is a Romantic invention: in the eighteenth century the artist was more like a tradesman whose business it was to produce beautiful things. The idea that art can be profound, that it can communicate something special to us that no other human invention can; the idea that artistic imagination is something rare and special and deserves to be nurtured; the idea that consistent imaginary worlds as objectified in art are valuable to inhabit: these ideas are all Romantic inventions, and have yet to leave European consciousness.

References

Alembert, Jean le Rond d' (1995) *Preliminary Discourse to the Encyclopaedia of Diderot*, trans. R.N. Schwab, Chicago, University of Chicago Press (first published 1751).

Aristotle (1940) *The Art of Poetry*, ed. and trans. W. Hamilton Fyfe, Oxford, Oxford University Press.

Bartholomew, M., Hall, D. and Lentin, A. (1992) *A206 Studies 1*, Milton Keynes, The Open University.

Batteux, C. (1989) *Les Beaux-arts réduits à un même principe*, ed. J-R Mantion, Paris, Aux Amateurs du Livre (first published 1746).

Berlin, I. (1999) *The Roots of Romanticism*, London, Chatto & Windus.

Bowra, C.M. (1950) *The Romantic Imagination*, Oxford, Oxford University Press.

Burke, E.A. (1958) *Philosophical Enquiry into the Origin of our Ideas of the Sublime and Beautiful*, ed. J.T. Boulton, Oxford, Blackwell (first published 1757).

Butt, J. (ed.) (1963) *The Poems of Alexander Pope*, London, Methuen.

Cabanis, J. (1964) 'Mme de Staël', in *Plaisirs et Lectures*, Paris, Gallimard.

Coleridge, S.T. (1965) *Biographia Literaria*, ed. G. Watson, London, Dent.

Fichte, J.G. (1982) *The Science of Knowledge*, trans. P. Heath and J. Lachs, Cambridge, Cambridge University Press (first published 1794).

Gordon, G., Lord Byron (1945) *Poetical Works*, Oxford, Oxford Standard Authors edition.

Greene, D. (ed.) (1986) *The Oxford Authors: Samuel Johnson*, Oxford, Oxford University Press.

Horace (1929) *Satires, Epistles and Ars Poetica*, trans. H.R. Fairclough, London, Heinemann (Loeb Classical Library).

Hugo, V. (1973) *William Shakespeare*, ed. B. Leuilliot, Paris, Flammarion (first published 1864).

Hume, D. (1963) 'Of the standard of taste', in *Essays: Moral, Political and Literary*, Oxford, Oxford University Press (first published 1757).

Hume, D. (1978) *A Treatise of Human Nature*, ed. L.A. Selby-Bigge and P.H. Nidditch, Oxford, Oxford University Press (first published 1739).

Novalis (1997) *Philosophical Writings*, ed. and trans. M.M. Stoljar, Albany, State University of New York Press.

Reynolds, Sir J. (1965) *Discourses on Art*, ed. S.O. Mitchell, Indianapolis, Bobbs-Merrill.

Schelling, F.W.J. (1988) *Ideas for a Philosophy of Nature*, trans. E.E. Harris and P. Heath, Cambridge, Cambridge University Press (first published 1797).

Schlegel, F. (1991) *Philosophical Fragments*, trans. P. Firchow, Minneapolis, University of Minnesota Press.

Staël, A.L.G. (1968) *De l'Allemagne*, 2 vols, ed. S. Balayé, Paris, Garnier-Flammarion (first published 1810).

Stendhal (1970) *Racine et Shakespeare*, ed. R. Fayolle, Paris, Garnier-Flammarion.

Uhde-Bernays, H. (ed.) (1960) *Künstlerbriefe über Kunst*, Frankfurt-am-Main, Fischer Bücherei.

Wackenroder, W.H. (1971) *Confessions and Fantasies*, trans. M. Hurst Schubert, Pennsylvania, Pennsylvania University Press.

Wheeler, K.M. (ed.) (1984) *German Aesthetic and Literary Criticism: The Romantic Ironists and Goethe*, Cambridge, Cambridge University Press.

Winckelmann, J.J. (1985) 'Thoughts on the imitation of the painting and sculpture of the Greeks', in *German Aesthetic and Literary Criticism: Winckelmann, Lessing, Hamann, Herder, Schiller and Goethe*, ed. and trans. H.B. Nisbet, Cambridge, Cambridge University Press (first published 1755).

Wordsworth, W. (1940–7) *Poetical Works*, ed. E. de Selincourt, 4 vols, Oxford, Clarendon Press.

Further reading

Angelo, P. d' and Duque, F. (1999) *La religión de la pintura*, Madrid, Akal.

Behler, E. (1993) *German Romantic Literary Theory*, Cambridge, Cambridge University Press.

LeHuray, P. and Day, J. (1988) *Music and Aesthetics in the Eighteenth and Early Nineteenth Centuries*, Cambridge, Cambridge University Press.

Martino, P. (1944) *L'Époque romantique en France 1815–1830*, Paris, Hatier.

Prawer, S. (ed.) (1970) *The Romantic Period in Germany*, New York, Schocken Books.

Schlegel, A.W. (1973) *Course of Lectures on Dramatic Art and Literature*, trans. J. Black, New York, AMS Press.

Stoljar, M.M. (1973) *Athenaeum: A Critical Commentary*, Bern and Frankfurt-am-Main, Herbert Lang.

Units 26–27
Goethe, *Faust Part One*

Prepared for the course team by Carmen Lavin, with David Johnson

Contents

Study components

Weeks of study	Supplementary material	Audio-visual	Anthologies and set books
2	AV Notes Illustrations Book	Audio 6 Audio 7	Goethe, *Faust Parts One and Two* Anthology II

Objectives

By the end of your work on Units 26–27 you should:

- understand the span of Goethe's life and work;
- understand the ways in which Goethe's play breaks with the traditional terms of the Faust myth;
- understand Goethe's own conception and literary ambitions for *Faust*;
- appreciate the impact of *Faust* on its first audiences, and the controversy it generated;
- have developed confidence in the skills of (a) close literary analysis and argument and (b) close listening to dramatic performance;
- have developed a questioning attitude to the relation of *Faust* to Enlightenment and Romantic thought.

1   Introduction

The Conclusion to Units 24–25 opened out the possibility that not all texts can be firmly defined in terms of the transition from Enlightenment to Romanticism. Over the next two weeks we shall be studying just such a text. While Goethe's *Faust Part One*, published in 1808, was written during this period, its thrust takes it out of the confines of any strict classification.

Goethe's œuvre was vast and encyclopaedic, and you may be asking why his *Faust*, in particular, should be such an important focus for this course. It was a work which gained recognition even during his lifetime as a masterpiece of European literature. It takes a story which had its origins in the transitions of one turbulent epoch, the Reformation, and it reworks that story in the raw energies and uncertainties of another turbulent epoch, Goethe's own. The drama transforms traditional understanding of the Faust myth and addresses the aspirations and the dangers in the human drive to achieve new possibilities, dramatizing the diversity of potentials in western culture. It provides us with lines of enduring and haunting beauty like those of Gretchen's spinning-song ('My peace is gone/My heart is sore'), which Schubert famously set to music (see Unit 28, pp.174–6), and expresses dramatic conflict between reality and aspiration in terms not conceived before. It also opens out any neat distinctions between Enlightenment and Romanticism, denying appropriation under either label.

We shall be studying *Faust Part One* in Robert David MacDonald's translation, your set text for these units,[3] with occasional reference to other translations, which you will find in Anthology II. The accompanying audios offer a sound performance of selected scenes, and the corresponding AV Notes should be used to help you to understand performance aspects of the play. Close examination of particular scenes in the play will provide a basis from which to stand back and look at the work as drama, the significance of Goethe's reworking of the fundamental premise in the Faust myth, the pact between Faust and Mephistopheles, the nature of the Gretchen story and the applications of terms like Enlightenment and Romanticism. The units conclude with a section on the conception and reception of *Faust*.

[3] Sections 1 to 17 of these units were written by Carmen Lavin; section 18 by David Johnson.

2   Johann Wolfgang Goethe: his life and work

While most English speakers have heard of Goethe, few have read his works. Bearing in mind the general recognition of Goethe's stature as a giant of world literature, this is curious. German speakers, for their part, are well acquainted with Shakespeare's plays, and indeed Weimar, where Goethe spent more than half of his life, has a prominent statue of Shakespeare in its park. There is one memorial to Goethe in England – underneath Prince Albert on the frieze at the base of the Albert Memorial in London's Hyde Park, a tribute from Victorian times when English interest in German culture and Goethe in particular was especially high.

Goethe (see Figure 26.1) was born in 1749 into a prominent family in Frankfurt am Main, one of the Free Cities of the Holy Roman Empire. Even as a law student at Leipzig he was writing poems and plays. He practised law in Frankfurt in the early 1770s, and then two works turned him into a literary celebrity – *Götz of Berlichingen* (1773) and *The Sorrows of Young Werther* (1774). In 1775 he accepted the invitation to take up ministerial responsibilities at the ducal court in Weimar, and he stayed based there for the rest of his life until he died in 1832.

Goethe lived through dramatic constitutional changes which altered the whole map of Germany in his lifetime (see the map of Germany in the 1780s in Figure 26.2). He lived through the social and ideological transformations following the demise of the Holy Roman Empire (which, as Voltaire quipped, was by no means Holy, nor Roman, nor an Empire, by the eighteenth century), upheavals following the French Revolution, and occupation in the wake of Napoleon's campaigns. The 'complete historical disjunction' in Continental Europe provided 'an experience of collective detachment from an irretrievable past such as England had not known since the Reformation of the sixteenth century and did not have to face again until the final dissolution of the [British] Empire in the twentieth' (Boyle and Guthrie, 2002, p.13). It is no wonder that German writers responded with a particularly keen sense of irony to differences between the ancient and the modern (as you learned in Units 24–25), between what was and what might be. Encountering change on this scale informs Goethe's articulation of the scope of human potential in *Faust*.

Luther had lived and preached in Weimar, Cranach had painted and Johann Sebastian Bach had made music there. Two of Bach's sons were baptized in the Lutheran church. The town was certainly marked by moments of outstanding endeavour, but it was in Goethe's lifetime that it gained a particular magnetic character as a centre of literary and intellectual creativity in Germany, even in Europe.

Figure 26.1   Karl Joseph Stieler, Goethe, *1828, oil on canvas, 78.2 x 64 cm, Bayerische Staatgemäldesammlungen, Munich. Photo: courtesy of Bayerische Staatgemäldesammlungen, Munich.*

Soon after Goethe's arrival in Weimar in 1775, the writer Johann Gottfried Herder (1744–1803) was invited to take charge of the Lutheran church there. Goethe had already met him in 1770 during his student days in Strasbourg. Herder's concern with nature and the natural had drawn him towards the influence of Shakespeare and the spontaneity and simplicity of the European folk-song heritage (he published two volumes of folk-songs in 1778), and he also awakened in Goethe an enthusiasm for medieval art and history which influenced Goethe's depiction of the sixteenth-century knight Götz of Berlichingen, landmark figure of the

Figure 26.2   Map of Germany in the 1780s, from Nicholas Boyle, Goethe: The Poet and the Age, *vol.1, Oxford, Oxford University Press, 1991. Reprinted by permission of Oxford University Press.*

The abolition of the Holy Roman Empire and Napoleon's reorganization of Germany were followed by the establishment of the German Confederation at the Congress of Vienna in 1815. Contemporary centres of intellectual and artistic activity included Leipzig, Berlin, Hamburg, Strasbourg, Heidelberg and Jena.

Sturm und Drang movement. Literally, *Sturm und Drang* translates as 'storm and stress'. Our current usage of 'stress' may be misleading here. The 'stress' in *Sturm und Drang* means to push forward, reach, even over-reach, in passionate rebellion against social and literary conventions (see Unit 1, p.44). Another important character at Weimar was Christoph Martin Wieland (1733–1813), a tutor at the court, renowned for his translation of Shakespeare's works and called by some a, if not the, German Rousseau. When the poet and dramatist Friedrich Schiller (1759–1805) came to Weimar in 1794, his relationship with Goethe proved to be a profoundly enriching experience for both of them.

In Units 7–8 and 24–25 you read about the phenomenal influence of Mme de Staël. When she wrote *On Germany* (1810, first published in English translation in 1813), all 1,500 copies sold in three days, and profoundly affected European attitudes to German culture. She describes the particular appeal of Weimar at this time, due in no small part to the enlightened interests of the ruling Duchess Anna Amalia, who in turn influenced her son August when at the age of 18 he took over the ducal rule, at the very same time that Goethe arrived in Weimar (see 'Madame de Staël on Weimar and the Germans', Anthology II, pp.237–8). Weimar, complete with an audience with Goethe, came on to the travelling agenda of the Englishman travelling in Europe, both alone and in the kind of tourist group which you have met in the units on the Lakes.

In 1802 Mme de Staël met Goethe and called him 'the representative of all German literature' (see 'Madame de Staël on Goethe', Anthology II, p.238). Thomas Carlyle began his 'First Notice of *Faust* in English', published anonymously in *The New Edinburgh Review* (January to April 1822) with the words: 'Goethe is likely to figure in after ages, as one of the most remarkable characters of his time' (quoted in Hamlin, 2001, p.560). Testimonies of Goethe's contemporaries throughout Europe record a sense of his colossal intellectual stature. Napoleon's first words, much quoted, when he met Goethe in October 1808, were '*Vous êtes un homme.*' (English renders this rather lamely as 'You are a man', but the original suggests a model for mankind.)

On the day after Napoleon's troops moved in and occupied Weimar in 1806, Goethe married Christiane Vulpius. His liaison with her developed soon after his return from his travels in Italy (1786–8), a time when he broke his relationship with the wife of the Duke's equerry Charlotte von Stein, for whom he had written exceptional lyrics through his early years in Weimar. There were many other loves in Goethe's life, but these were his longest relationships. He and Christiane Vulpius had a son in 1789. Their other children all died soon after birth. Not only Charlotte von Stein but both Christiane and their son died before Goethe himself, who lived, still writing, into a creative old age, completing his *Faust Part Two* shortly before his death in 1832. Reportedly his last words were a call for 'More light!'

Goethe's literary output is prodigious. His novels mark decisive turning-points in European literature. *The Sorrows of Young Werther*, written in 1774 in just four weeks, became a runaway bestseller, translated into English and other major European languages and setting a new trend in literature (a host of imitations followed), in behaviour – with a morbid sensibility taking hold – and even in fashion, with young men throughout Europe dressing in yellow 'Werther' stockings. *Wilhelm Meister's Apprenticeship* (1795–6) became the archetypal *Bildungsroman*,[4] establishing a literary prose form which influenced European writing throughout the nineteenth century. You will discover something of the reach of Goethe's poetry in Schubert's settings of some of his works in Unit 28. And his dramas explore issues of conflict and freedom in figures of the medieval knight, *Götz of Berlichingen* (1773), the historical champion of freedom in *Egmont* (1788), the Renaissance artist-hero in *Torquato Tasso* (1790) and the mythological *Iphigenia in Tauris* (1787).

So, what are the qualities which distinguish Goethe's writing? This is not a question that can be answered in just one line, but we can see something of the power of his writing when Faust articulates his fundamental conflict early in the play. On the one hand, he is filled with the urge to conquest, to soar in transcendence, while on the other, there is the urge to dig roots deep into the earth, to take on material experience. He is aware of some agonizing duality, opposite forces pulling him between raw sensuality and noble spirituality, something finite and something infinite, different aspirations and different states of reality:

> Two souls within me wrestle for possession
> and neither will surrender to his brother.
> One is of the senses, sensual,
> slaking his appetites like an animal:
> the other strives for purity of mind,
> to leave the world and all its works behind.
> (Scene 2, lines 137–42)

EXERCISE In the above passage Faust describes his inner conflicts and feelings in vivid terms. Read the passage again carefully and jot down what makes the lines vivid. Focus on the imagery and its compression, and the tense of the verbs.

DISCUSSION If you have not had much experience of looking at literature like this, you may well not necessarily think of the kinds of suggestions here and in subsequent discussions in these units. But don't be disheartened by

---

[4] Nineteenth-century novel tracing an individual's *personal* education and development, distinctive from the eighteenth-century *Erziehungsroman*, reflecting the forces of society in the development of the individual.

this. There are many different responses which may be useful, and if it would be more helpful, you could read through my comments before attempting the exercises and then set yourself the task of recognizing and understanding my comments. Alternatively, it might make more sense for you to work through the exercises on your own before seeing what I have made of them. The main thing is to find the approach that enables you to enjoy, understand and analyse the play.

The way in which Faust expresses himself is in terms of two 'souls' warring in his breast. The plural form accentuates his sense of a divided self. The first line, in just one line, expresses his anguish. (It is one of the many lines in the play which has been adopted in general cultural reference, rather in the same way as Hamlet's words 'To be or not to be'.) The intense imagery gives each competing 'soul' human attributes and charges the poetic tension of these lines with authority and passion. The words give physical force to emotional and metaphysical energies. This is more than simply a passing emotion. The present tense is unrelenting: this battle for unrealized potential is ongoing.

As we look more closely at *Faust*, keep the line about Faust's 'two souls' in your mind. (In Anthology II you will find alternative translations which you may like to look at to explore how every translation pushes the meaning out in different ways.) It is a statement which encompasses, in gigantic enlargement, the fundamental conflict of the drama.

Outside his literary productivity the diversity of Goethe's other contributions to virtually every field of knowledge is astonishing. His activities as a statesman encompassed his roles in a network of institutions as privy councillor, president of the war commission, director of roads and services and of mining projects, minister of education, librarian of the Duchess Anna Amalia Library (see Figure 26.3) and director of the Weimar Court Theatre. As a theatre director Goethe produced all Mozart's operas in Weimar, among them *Don Giovanni* (30 January 1792), and his designs for stagings of the operas still survive. He admired Mozart's genius unreservedly, as Johann Peter Eckermann (1792–1854), his assistant, editor and secretary noted on 14 February 1831. He had heard him as a seven-year-old in Frankfurt on 25 August 1763, and would have liked to have had a musical setting for *Faust* in the style of *Don Giovanni* (noted by Eckermann on 12 February 1829). Over 600 works, ranging from operas to plays and even dance theatre, were produced under his management.

Added to this, Goethe's scientific writings fill about 14 volumes, and his work in anatomy led him to the discovery of the *os intermaxillare*, the intermaxillary bone, in the human jaw. The breadth of his scholarship included optics (with particular research on the properties of colour and colour theory), geology, archaeology, sculpture, engineering, economics, morphology and mineralogy. He held a collection of 18,000 stones in the

Figure 26.3   Duchess Anna Amalia Library, Rococo Hall, Weimarer Klassik/ Goethe-Nationalmuseum, Weimar. Photo: Sigrid Geske/donated by Weimarer Klassik/Goethe-Nationalmuseum.

institute of mineralogy, and his art collection comprised 26,500 works. In the field of botany his extensive work on the structure of plants during his travels in Italy and his ideas about the *Urpflanze*, the archetype of all botanical species, testify to his thesis of unity and continuity, constancy and change, as balancing forces in all natural forms. Goethe's *Naturphilosophie*, philosophy of natural sciences, had an impact on the interconnections in all his literary output. His interests in new technologies of the age spanned the weapons of Napoleon's army, developments in communication, electro-magnetism, automation of spinning-wheels, Montgolfier's attempts at balloon flight and the construction of the Panama Canal.

Goethe's library held, among much else, volumes of Indian literature, oriental literature, literature in Latin, Greek and all the modern European languages, including the poetry of Cowper and Byron. He spoke seven foreign languages – Greek, Latin, Hebrew, English, French, Spanish and Italian. Goethe developed a concept of *Weltliteratur*, 'world literature', a poetic culture which might transcend ideological oppositions between oriental and occidental, secular and supernatural, without either having precedence over the other. He explored these in cycles of lyrics such as *West-Eastern Divan* 1819, modelled on the *Divan* of the Persian poet Hafiz (*c*.1325–*c*.1389), reflecting his interest in non-European culture. Commemoration in Weimar in the form of two sculpted seats, facing each other, one inscribed below with Hafiz's words and the other with Goethe's, recognizes the continuing value of his appreciation of other cultures. *Weltliteratur* was to be no international canon of great national works. Rather Goethe envisioned this paradigm as a cultural transfer to go beyond national and language boundaries in an expanding consciousness of the universality of human experience, stretching from antiquity to his own time and into the future. 'National literature is no longer of importance; it is time for world literature, and all must aid in bringing it about' (noted by Eckermann on 31 January, 1827, quoted in Gearey, 1986, p.224). You read about the Enlightenment belief in universal human nature in Units 24–25. What informed the breadth and scope of Goethe's thinking was above all a sense of life and literature and ideas as a continuing process, feeding into each other and interrogating each other in a progressive momentum.

3   Faust: myth, play and translation

The fascination of figures such as Don Juan and Faust in the late eighteenth century lies in the ways in which they exemplify huge individualistic drives. Not enshrined by either the Bible or the classical pantheon, they hold a flavour of something dangerous, even heretical. Myths surrounding both Don Juan and Faust derive from individuals who actually lived. Their biographies may be recorded in only sparse, unreliable terms, but the fact that their lives generated myths of great potency suggests that they exhibited impulses of a universal nature. So, where did the Faust legend start?

Historical roots: the legendary and historical Faust in the sixteenth century

Authentic details of the life of the historical Faust, Johann Georg Faust, are scanty. He is said to have lived in the small German town of Knittlingen between about 1480 and 1540, still a time with few distinctions between magic and medicine, which provided fertile territory for mystery and fantasy. Faust is said to have studied medicine, practised alchemy and provided horoscopes as he travelled around Germany, exploiting the credibility of his public and dabbling in necromancy and the occult. He gathered a reputation for impossible feats – producing a bunch of grapes in mid-winter, riding on a barrel of wine, working enchantments and wonders, and summoning up spirits, even of Helen of Troy. His ventures gave rise to tales about a pact in blood with the devil, and his reputation became overlaid with popular folk tales about knowledge illicitly gained through devious means leading to eternal punishment. Pamphlets in Faust's name outlined ruses to trick the devil, and Luther himself denounced him.

The first printed version of the Faust story dates back to the anonymous *Historia von D. Iohan Fausten*, published by Johann Spieß in 1587 in Frankfurt am Main. It conflates anecdotes of the real Johann Georg Faust of the early sixteenth century with the legend which took over from reality even during his lifetime. Here we have a fictionalized figure who conjures up armies of men, brings figures of ancient history back to life, and trades his soul to Mephistopheles for the promise of any wish for a period of 24 years, following which he is forfeit to eternal damnation. He goes to hell, and we must remember the enormous power which fear of hell held over medieval minds, so the moral appeal works as a moral warning. This becomes the Faust myth about the man who transgresses God's laws and is punished. Thanks to the invention of the printing press, it gained immediate popularity all over Europe, appearing in English translation in 1592 as *The Historie of the Damnable Life, and Deserved Death of Doctor Iohn Faustus*. The Spieß book is the original source of all subsequent treatments of the myth, continuing to hold potent appeal through the last five centuries and first treated dramatically by Christopher Marlowe (1564–93).

Faust in the eighteenth century

For English speakers the reference point is Marlowe's *Doctor Faustus* (based on Spieß, probably written between 1592 and 1593 and published between 1604 and 1616). It was not until 1818, over ten years after the publication of *Faust Part One*, that Goethe first came across Marlowe's play. He was familiar from his childhood with edited versions of it. These had been brought to Continental Europe by strolling players in the seventeenth century and were performed in a folk and fairground tradition by wandering puppeteers. The puppet-plays provided colourful entertainment for popular consumption: magical exploits fed interests in the attraction of the taboo and the fear of the devil. They presented Faust as larger than life, an agent in a spiritual argument with Mephistopheles which, by the late eighteenth century, was beginning to run counter to the rational emphasis of the Enlightenment.

In 1759 Gotthold Ephraim Lessing (1729–81) sketched out the first dramatization of Faust in which he is not damned. This Faust goes through all the traditional adventures, but his overriding concern for intellectual truth saves rather than condemns him. It is the first defence or rehabilitation of Faust. The myth of Faust underwent something of a relaunch during the Enlightenment, and the *Sturm und Drang* impetus in the 1770s spawned an array of dramatic treatments by minor German dramatists who converted it from a play about punishment, hell and eternal torment to turn Faust into a defiant cult figure setting himself against all social and moral conventions.

Genesis of Goethe's *Faust*

The first reference to Goethe's work on *Faust* dates from September 1775, but he had already been attracted to the idea in August 1771 when he returned from his studies in Strasbourg. Goethe retains the medieval setting: when we first meet Faust, it is in his Gothic study. This dark setting provides an unmistakable nod to the era of the original Faust story. Goethe, however, reworks the imperatives of the Faust legend out of a struggle between absolute forces of good and evil into a drama which expands these terms to grapple with the potential of the cultural heritage and aspirations of European man. Far from working with continuities in the tradition, Goethe is breaking the mould.

Goethe worked on his *Faust* over a period of 60 years (Figure 26.4 shows the garden house in which he wrote much of *Part One*), in fact during the whole span of the period covered by this course. It stands alone among Goethe's works: no other work occupied him like this one.

EXERCISE   Read MacDonald's account of the chronology of Goethe's work on *Faust* in the Introduction to his translation (pp.11–14 of your set book) and look at the Course Chronology. Take a few minutes to identify key events from these two 'bird's-eye' views of the context in which *Faust* was developed.

Figure 26.4 Ludwig Schütze, Goethe's Garden House in the Park on the Ilm in Weimar, 1827, colour engraving, 18 x 26.6 cm, Weimarer Klassik/Goethe-Nationalmuseum, Weimar. Photo: donated by Weimarer Klassik/Goethe-Nationalmuseum. KGr 1983/00526.

DISCUSSION   There are historical circumstances as well as cultural and personal ones which you might note.

1   *Contemporary events and beliefs*: the case leading to the execution for infanticide, not uncommon at the time, may well have been a seminal experience which affected Goethe as he was working on the play. We may forget in the second millennium the topicality for Goethe's contemporaries of infanticide by unmarried mothers and of execution. And we may also forget the widespread belief in witches, portrayed visually in Goya's *Asmodeus (Witches' Sabbath)*, shown in Video 2, band 1.

2   *The unpublished manuscript 'Urfaust'*[5]: for Goethe this was work-in-progress, a stage in his writing of the play, pre-dating the revisions and additions written in Italy in the late 1780s. Goethe destroyed these scenes, unaware that they had been transcribed by Luise von Göckhausen, a lady-in-waiting at the court. The manuscript was discovered by chance in 1885 in a descendant's papers. We shall not be studying *Urfaust* (or *Faust: Ein Fragment,* the fragment version published in 1790 under pressure from publishers). The text which we shall study is *Faust Part One*, with a short consideration of the end of *Faust Part Two* in section 13 and an examination of the conception and reception of *Faust* by David Johnson in section 18.

3   *The political turbulence of the time*: Goethe first started work on *Faust* before the American Declaration of Independence. The fragmentary version appeared just after the French Revolution, and *Faust Part One* was completed in 1806, the year of Napoleon's decisive battle over Prussia at Jena. Goethe's publisher Cotta travelled to Weimar to collect the manuscript, but the French occupation delayed publication until 1808. (Once published, performances of the play were suppressed during the Napoleonic occupation.) Goethe was writing during uncertain and volatile times of dramatic social and political change between the French Revolution, the Napoleonic Wars and political restoration.

Goethe's work on *Faust Part One* came in bursts over many years. Some early scenes were revised and even transposed. From 1794 on, contact with Schiller (see Figure 26.5) gave Goethe new impetus and revitalized his ideas. Schiller urged Goethe to work on with his *Faust* material, to turn it from a fragment – this 'torso of Hercules', as he called it in a letter to Goethe dated 29 November 1794 – into a play. Even at this incomplete stage, he thus invested the drama with monumental classical significance. Only in 1800, inspired by exchanges with Schiller (their ten-year-long correspondence, mutually productive, comprises over 1,000 letters), did

---

[5] *Ur* means 'original': the title was not conferred by Goethe, but by publishers of the 'pirated' manuscript when it came to light over 100 years later.

Goethe decide to divide the play into two parts. This concept of a division of the drama was a breakthrough, as was the writing of the pact between Faust and Mephistopheles in 1800. Work on *Faust Part Two*, constantly spurred on by Eckermann, occupied Goethe even before his completion of *Faust Part One* right to the end of his life. (We must remember that he was working at the same time on a huge output of other works, alongside his state duties.) According to Goethe's diary entries, final changes to the manuscript of *Faust Part Two* were made in January 1832. He made sure that it was locked away, so that it could not be published until after his death.

Figure 26.5   Ernst Rietschel, Goethe and Schiller memorial statue, erected outside the Nationaltheater, Weimar, 1857. Photo: Carmen Lavin.

Interest in the play was intense from the time of its first appearance. Coleridge and Shelley began translations, and Scott, Carlyle and a host of others followed suit. There have been countless incarnations in music and the pictorial arts as well as in literature (in diverse versions by Paul Valéry and Thomas Mann as well as Kathakali performances in India and Russian and Japanese recastings). In terms of critical works, there are innumerable literary investigations of *Faust*. Indeed, after Goethe's *Faust*, there *was* only one landmark Faust: Goethe's. Alexander Pushkin (1799–1837), who himself wrote a treatment of the Faust story in 1828, thought of Goethe's *Faust* as an *Iliad* of modern life.

Choice of MacDonald translation

There are hundreds of translations of Goethe's *Faust*. No work in German has been translated into English as many times. Some translations use archaic language while others sacrifice readability for rigorous accuracy. Often idioms are blurred. Some are stuffy. Others are trite. Overall there are extremely varying degrees of accessibility.

MacDonald's masterly translation has been used in acclaimed stage productions in major theatres in Scotland and in England. It doesn't necessarily translate line for line. It is not a complete translation. Some scenes (Dedication and Walpurgis Night's Dream[6] – the Golden Wedding of Oberon and Titania, scenes, incidentally, usually omitted from stage productions) and some speeches may be cut, but the persuasive strengths of this translation lie in its accessibility and dramatic bite, and in the way in which it captures the poetic spirit and theatrical power of the work. The vitality of the rhythms and the variety of style and idiom (lyrical, reflective, ironic, vernacular and farcical) impressively convey the registers and range of Goethe's language, the momentum of ideas and action. The nearness of MacDonald's renderings of Goethe's rhymes, rhythms and metres allows us close analysis of the language and imagery. While it certainly doesn't necessarily follow that what works in German also works in English, this translation gets very close to that equivalence. In particular, MacDonald's translation is particularly good at expressing wit and changes in mood, and it does so in a way which helps us to forget that we are reading in translation.

Selections from other translations are used in Anthology II alongside the German to allow comparison of the ways in which meanings can be teased out. The combinations of these versions invite you to respond imaginatively to the richnesses of Goethe's verse.

---

[6] Walpurgis Night: the eve of 1 May, when witches, according to German popular superstition, rode on broomsticks and billy-goats to revel with their master the devil, especially on the Brocken in the Harz mountains. So-called because 1 May is the day of St Walpurga, abbess of Heidenheim, who died *c*.778.

4 *Faust Part One*: overall shape of the play and accompanying audios

To give you a sense of the overall shape of the play, let me set out how groups of scenes relate and work together.

The context

Dedication (see Anthology II, pp.242–4)
Prelude on the stage
Prologue in Heaven

Opening sequences taking us into the 'reality' of the stage in front of us and into the heavenly sphere where the terms are set between God and Mephistopheles.

Faust's aspirations and his pact with Mephistopheles

1 Night – Faust's study
2 Outside the city gate
3 Faust's study

Introduction to Faust in his study and in his community, leading to the pact which he makes with Mephistopheles.

Transitions

4 Auerbach's cellar in Leipzig
5 The witch's kitchen

Transformation scenes, driven by Mephistopheles, setting Faust in another context and rejuvenating him.

First meetings between Faust and Gretchen

6 In the street
7 Evening – A small neat room
8 Taking a walk
9 Neighbour's house
10 Street
11 Garden
12 A summerhouse

Faust and Gretchen fall in love, with encounters engineered by Mephistopheles.

Developments in their relationship

13 Forest and cavern
14 Gretchen's room
15 In Martha's garden
16 At the well
17 On the ramparts
18 Night – the street in front of Gretchen's door
19 Cathedral
20 Walpurgis Night
21 Gloomy day – open country
22 Night – open country

While Faust explores the new exhilaration of his relationship with nature and the world, Gretchen becomes intensely aware of the **pathos** in her own life.

The relationship between Faust and Gretchen moves out of the control of either of them: Mephistopheles sees to this. He puts Faust into situations which unwittingly lead to the deaths of both Gretchen's mother and her brother Valentine – and to her conviction for infanticide following the death of their child. The death of Valentine precipitates Mephistopheles' escape with Faust into the macabre world of the Walpurgis Night.

Finale

23 Prison

Faust tries to rescue Gretchen, who is maddened with grief. She dies in the clarity of her recognition of the evil power of his companion Mephistopheles, while Faust is doomed by the pact he has made to continue the association.

Audios 6 and 7 provide a sound performance of selected scenes and the corresponding AV Notes explore issues of performance and performance history.

EXERCISE   Before beginning your study of the play itself, listen to Audio 6 (tracks 1–13) and Audio 7 (tracks 1–4) to capture a feel of the work. You may like to follow the text in your set book, taking into account that the audios do not give you every scene in the play (see the AV Notes). While you are listening, refer back to the outline above so that you can develop a feel for the overall dramatic shape of the play. As you listen, ask yourself two questions:

1   What do you think of Faust?

2   And what do you think of Mephistopheles? How credible a character do you find him?

Can you pick out incidents or quotations to support your views?

DISCUSSION   1   Faust's abilities are extraordinary. In the first Study scene his opening words register his vigorous mastery of every expertise of his time. His towering intellect establishes him as a great man. His achievements are legendary. In the text (2, 67–71) you will note that the townsfolk remember how he and his father – also presented as legendary – saved them from the plague. Faust's own recall, however, is different: he knows that his medical treatment led to as many deaths as it saved lives (2, 81–103). Right from the start there is no way in which he shares any exalted perception of his own self. The 'two souls' speech (2, 137–42) points to his raging predicament. He is intensely restless. Look, for instance, at lines such as:

> I wake each morning with a start of pain,
> knowing that by the time each day is done,
> I shall be forced to acknowledge, once again,
> not one desire has been fulfilled – not one.
> (3, 267–70)

The words given to Faust as he makes the pact with Mephistopheles could relate to the Romantic imperatives outlined in Units 24–25. There is, however, nothing of the medieval quest which characterizes particular forms of narrative Romantic poetry. It is not an escape. It is a search, a flight into the future. All the time he is struggling in the grip of a 'fundamental contradiction between the desire to know everything and the impossibility of knowing everything' (Muecke, 1970, p.76).

2   In the Prologue in Heaven, Mephistopheles enters heaven as the opposition party but not as Satan. As an agent of the devil, Mephistopheles would be a metaphysical entity, and this would

make him conceptually unreal as a 'human' stage character. He refers to his 'relative, the snake' (Prologue in Heaven, 92), but he himself is no personification of absolute evil. He changes shape, adopting different personae – from grovelling poodle (opening of scene 3) to travelling scholar (stage direction at 3, 90) to whatever suits his mercurial moment. He is a maverick master of improvisation.

In some respects, in his suave, man-of-the world pose, Mephistopheles is a very persuasive 'human' figure. He presents recognizable human traits – humour, capriciousness and bravado (Prologue in Heaven, 54–6 and 97–100). He has his tantrums (in the words used by him to recount the incident when the first jewels are 'impounded' by the priest, 8, 1–2). He can mimic (8, 22–8) and is never at a loss for a witty word. Representing perpetual cynicism (3, 106–7), he refuses to admit the essential integrity of Faust's love of Gretchen. Above all he enjoys generating friction and wants to destroy any spirit of affirmation. He flaunts his voyeurism, bursting into Faust's impassioned outburst (13, 36) and creeping in on the intimacy of Gretchen and Faust (15, 69).

You may find many other instances when he displays 'human' characteristics. Mme de Staël went so far as to call Mephistopheles the hero of the play (1813, p.182).

Keep in mind how you have begun to react to these two characters. Our examination of Goethe's poetic and dramatic resources in selected scenes will be punctuated with consideration of overall aspects of the play. As you pace yourself to divide your study between the next two weeks, you should aim in the first week to reach the end of section 10 of these units. In this and preceding sections we shall be looking at the following specific scenes:

- The Prologue in Heaven
- 1: Night – Faust's study
- 2: Outside the city gate
- 3: Faust's study

We shall also look at Christian iconography in *Faust* and at *Faust* as a drama, and we shall give particular consideration to the significance of Goethe's treatment of the pact between Faust and Mephistopheles.

Study in the second week will begin with an examination of the following scenes:

- 4 and 5: Auerbach's cellar in Leipzig and The witch's kitchen
- 7: Evening – A small neat room
- 13: Forest and cavern
- 15: In Martha's garden
- 23: Prison

We shall move on to make a brief sortie into *Faust Part Two* and review the particular significance of the Gretchen story and the dramatic effects of the play as a whole. Then we shall draw together ways in which we have explored the play in the context of the Enlightenment/Romantic axis of ideas and values. Section 18 on the conception and reception of *Faust* will conclude the units.

5   The Prologue in Heaven

Three sequences open – and postpone the start of – the play.

The Dedication (not in your set text but reproduced in Anthology II, pp.242–4) and the Prelude on the stage pass, and not until the Prologue in Heaven is there any reference to Faust. The sequences offer frameworks, both for each other and for the drama which follows. Each of them – Dedication, Prelude and Prologue – effectively becomes a play within the play, and then the play itself becomes another play framed within the play of these Prologues. The Prelude on the stage, giving us the theatrical establishment in interplay between poetic author, actor and pragmatic theatre manager, precedes the Prologue in Heaven. (Only a few lines of Goethe's original manuscript for *Faust Part One* remain. The rest he destroyed. Figure 26.6 reproduces lines from the Prelude on the stage.) Reality on earth, and not any old reality but the reality of the theatre – the reality, in other words, of what is conventionally taken to be the world of illusion – ironically sets up the heavenly world. It sets heaven up as a fictional construct. This makes the ordering of the opening sequences subversive right from the start.

EXERCISE

Now read the Prologue in Heaven (pp.34–6) and listen to it on Audio 6 (track 1), paying particular attention not only to the content but also to the effects of the verse. Note too the dramatic contrast, especially in the use of rhyme, rhythm and tone, when Mephistopheles speaks.

DISCUSSION

In the ceremonial of archangels extolling the glory of the created world, Raphael sings about the timeless harmony of stars and spheres, a vision of cosmic order, harmony and control:

> works, high and inconceivable,
> keep their first, glorious mystery.
> (7–8)

The slow, steady rhythms glide into each other. Regular form and nobility of language, evident in both original and translation, underline the order of the cyclical processes of the cosmos. The vocabulary is grandiose and measured. Gabriel describes the rhythms of day and night

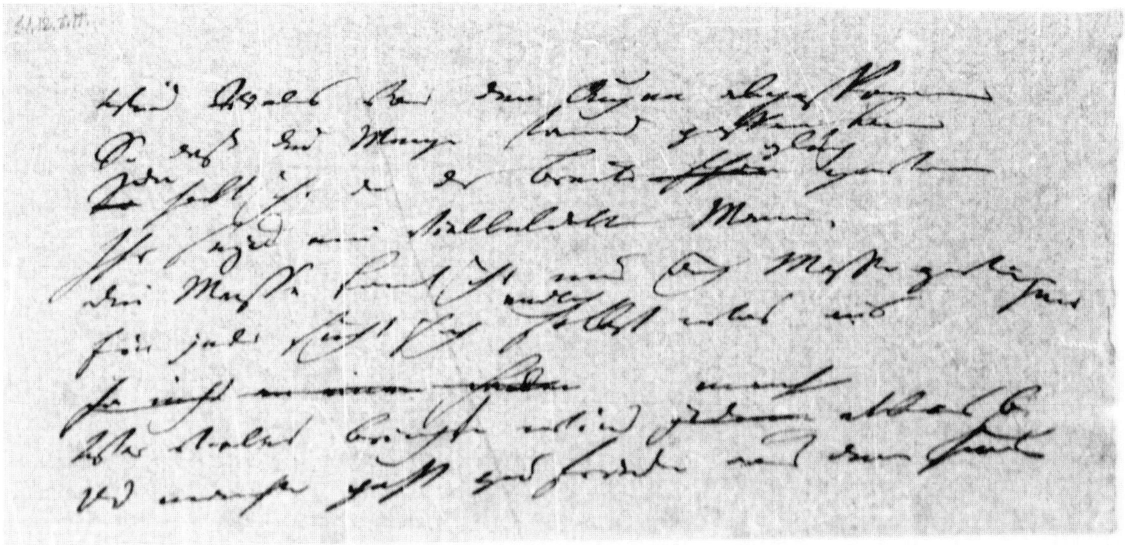

Figure 26.6   Goethe, Faust, *manuscript: eight lines from the Prelude on the stage, Weimarer Klassik/Goethe-Nationalmuseum, Weimar. Photo: donated by Weimarer Klassik/Goethe-Nationalmuseum.*

Direktor:
Wird vieles vor den Augen abgesponnen
So daß die Menge staunend gaffen kann,
Da habt ihr in der Breite gleich gewonnen,
Ihr seid ein vielgeliebter Mann.
Die Masse könnt ihr nur durch Masse zwingen,
Ein jeder sucht sich endlich selbst was aus.
Wer vieles bringt, wird manchem etwas bringen;
Und jeder geht zufrieden aus dem Haus.

Director:
Let many things unfold before their eyes,
Let the crowd stare and be amazed, for then
You'll win their hearts, and that's to win the prize;
You'll join the ranks of famous men.
Mass alone charms the masses; each man finds
Something to suit him, something to take home.
Give much, and you'll have given to many minds;
They'll all leave here contented to have come.
(David Luke, 91–8)

and in his turn Michael extols something of the sublime (in the Burkean sense examined in Units 16–17), a vision which inspires 'delight mingled with fear' (Beddow, 1986, p.29). He sings not so much of circular motion as of alternate and complementary spectacles of storms and calm, changing tides in 'a chain of mighty agency'. Regular metre creates the intonation of unchanging solemnity.

EXERCISE   Take a couple of minutes to note the effects of the first 16 lines of Mephistopheles' opening speech (pp.34–5). Read it aloud so that you can hear the effects. How would you describe the tone of the speech? How does it compare with the archangels' hymns? What is Mephistopheles saying? And how does he say it? (Look at his vocabulary.)

DISCUSSION   The cheeky and profane tone may take you by surprise. It is meant to. A disruptive presence has entered. Into the frieze of sonority of the archangels' almost disembodied hymn of praise, Mephistopheles enters like a court jester (God actually calls him a 'joker' later in the Prologue). He not only dismisses their perspective of creation: he wades into a personal invective against the humourlessness of heaven. His own particular concerns, he claims, lie not in planetary relations but in human beings, not included within the visions of the angels:

> the self-inflicted woes of men are all that interest me;
> the little god of the world, in the same situation,
> as odd as on the first day of Creation.
> (38–40)

The archangels have praised the cosmos: Mephistopheles talks about man. He punctures the eulogy with quite different expression, as he freely admits. The archangels have no interaction, no dialogue, either with each other or with God. Mephistopheles immediately makes clear that he is bypassing their impersonal strains and addressing God directly. The way in which he extends the length of the lines exaggerates the 'oddness' of the world rather than the 'first, glorious mystery' which the archangels have just repeated.

Mephistopheles taunts God for having given human beings the

> Schein des Himmelslichts;/er nennt's Vernunft –
> that glimpse of heavenly light,/ that he calls Reason.
> (42–3)

The use of the word *Schein* in German plays on two meanings – illusion, or glimpse, as well as radiance. This double meaning is important for the whole drama: it contains within itself both illusion and core, surface and substance, appearance and reality. Mephistopheles, seeing in Faust a prime example of the 'Schein des Himmelslichts' ('glimpse of heavenly light'), has nothing but scorn for both the meanings.

While God's speech is measured, both in its content and in its form, Mephistopheles' is flippant. They have not only contrasting styles but different agendas. Mephistopheles talks about seducing Faust's soul as if he is challenging God in the terms of good and evil which traditionally determine the Faust story, the theological absolutes of the sixteenth century. God, however, sees humanity from a different angle. He tolerates Mephistopheles because he sees him playing a definite part in the divine scheme, to spur humankind out of complacency.

MacDonald translates God's line in German 'Es irrt der Mensch, solang' er strebt' as:

> Men make mistakes, till they learn not to strive.
> (76)

This is a difficult line to encapsulate as succinctly in English as in German. A really close translation of Goethe's German would render this line as: 'Man [i.e. humankind] errs, makes mistakes, as long as he strives'.

In this rendering, however, the text is descriptive rather than prescriptive. It just says that errors necessarily occur as human beings strive. It does not say that they should not try to strive for fear of erring. The important point of this key line is the implicitly prescriptive one – that human beings *must* strive, even if in the process of striving they will inevitably make mistakes and lose their way. God is promoting ceaseless restlessness as a vital and productive, even essential, quality, rather than a flaw. Striving becomes the means to salvation for humanity rather than the route to damnation. This powerful premise, before the play itself begins, overthrows the driving theological principles of the conventional Faust legend. The Prologue may be set in heaven, but this is no orthodox theology.

The interchange between God and Mephistopheles leans on the opening two chapters of the Old Testament book of Job in which Satan challenges God to allow him to test Job's faith by bringing suffering upon suffering into his life. The religious parallel plays on the allegorical possibilities within the biblical account rather than reworking theological challenges. This is neither an Old Testament story of temptation nor a medieval morality tale about sin and damnation. It is more about the nature of human potential than about the nature of the Christian God. This is what coloured early reception of the play in England, leading to cries of 'pagan immoralism or amoralism' from Coleridge and Wordsworth (quoted in Hamburger, 1984, p.29), and bad taste and immorality from general readers. 'All German literature lay, as far as the nineteenth-century British public was concerned, under the twin suspicions of political Jacobinism and religious impiety. The one was assumed to lead to the other' (Boyle and Guthrie, 2002, p.14).

In the derisory way in which Mephistopheles refers to reason, the 'glimpse of heavenly light', it is already clear that the word *Schein* can hold differing meanings. Mephistopheles assumes that he has set up a wager with God for the soul of Faust. This is, however, no wager between equals: Mephistopheles is dependent on God's permission to act. While God is divine and represents the whole, Mephistopheles is no more than an underling.

This Prologue is the important initial premise for all that follows, a significant change from traditional settings of the *Faust* story in a council of devils rather than in heaven. This confrontation between God and Mephistopheles sets new terms on the traditional Faust legend even before the drama itself begins. As far as God is concerned, the issue is never in doubt. Mephistopheles' suggestion to corrupt Faust is effectively sanctioned by God, not because he wants Faust to be corrupted, but because he is confident that this will not happen.

God's presence on stage is as unusual for an early nineteenth-century play as it would be two centuries later – and carries a gravitas of another era, the time of the morality play of the middle ages. Let's think more closely about this. The archangels' song *fixes* the nature of creation: it is intoned as a timeless response to an unchanging pattern of the created world. Yet even the individual archangels express contesting views on the nature of the created universe. Raphael's vision of creation, with the sun and other planetary spheres circling around the earth in 'predetermined course', owes its origins to the geocentric ideas of Ptolemy (116–96 BCE). Gabriel, however, sets out the unchanging rotation of the earth in cycles of day and night in the heliocentric system of Copernicus (1473–1543). Between them they encapsulate the disputes of the time of the historical Faust.

God recognizes that everything – even Mephistopheles – has a purpose. This view of the universe has a oneness, and therefore it has meaning. This meaning involves constant *action* and consequently, by implication, change. Human inaction, *not* striving, is not an option. Action is a supreme obligation. Medieval consensus on matters eternal, *unquestioning acceptance of an eternal pattern*, is flying in the face of the dynamic urge to *probe, discover and challenge* contemporary knowledge about the earth.

EXERCISE   Look at the grasshopper imagery which Mephistopheles uses (45–50) and the gardener imagery of God (69–70). How does the contrast between their images reinforce their different views of humanity?

DISCUSSION   Both the images are drawn from nature. Mephistopheles reduces human activity to aimless 'leaping', 'flying' up in the air and then 'lying' on the ground. Human expression is no more than 'chirping', without purpose. The placing of these present participles at different rhythmic points in the lines, 'leaping' at the beginning of line 47, 'flying' towards the end, 'lying' near the beginning and 'chirping' in the middle of the next line, mimics an arbitrary grasshopper hop. Repetition of the participles with their echoing '-ing' sounds bounces the lines along without any destination other than 'the same old song'. There is no progress or achievement here. On the contrary –

> He pokes his nose in every sort of muck.
> (50)

Such is Mephistopheles' crude disdain of man, 'the little god of the world' (39), with his so-called gift of reason.

God's authoritative words give us the viewpoint of the gardener, a metaphor for himself. It is not restricted to ground-level insect life in the continuing present. On the contrary, his sights are set 'out of sight'. These three simple monosyllables, 'out of sight', are deferred to the end of the couplet: the couplet gives closure, but the words point to non-closure, an undetermined future. He recognizes potential in nature yet to grow. There is order in his world, and at the same time there is evolution: 'flowers and fruit', in other words the outcomes of human endeavours, are not 'lying in the grass' but 'lie ripening out of sight'. Play on the original Garden of Eden through reference to bountiful growth of 'flowers and fruit' enlarges the image out of strict confines of time in the present. The present participle 'ripening' has a purpose. While Mephistopheles concentrates on the visible, God looks at the invisible.

God and Mephistopheles are talking about different time-scales: Mephistopheles focuses on the fleeting present and God encapsulates the span and momentum of eternity. There is never any doubt that nature is an ultimate unity, always in flow and process.

6   Christian iconography in the play

Christian references map out a framework in the play. The Prologue, with the devil negotiating with God to try the limits of a human being, replays some of the Old Testament book of Job. Later (1, 238–47) there is the music of Christian ritual with the strains of the Easter hymn, and later still a Requiem (organ and choir in scene 19). Like Luther, the contemporary of the sixteenth-century Faust, Goethe's Faust works on a translation of the opening of the New Testament Gospel of St John. Gretchen questions him about Christian beliefs. And the last words of *Faust Part One* are (in relation to Gretchen) 'judgment' and 'atonement'. (Faust's death and ultimate 'salvation' come at the end of *Part Two*.)

There is, however, no dogmatic Christianity in *Faust*. Faust does not go to hell because he defies God. What Goethe presents is the problematic situation of western man of his time, still rooted in Christian tradition yet no longer with the consensus beliefs of the past.

Alongside the traces of Christianity in the play, there are magical rituals in the witch's kitchen and the Walpurgis Night revels. In itself the fact that Christianity and paganism set different scenes suggests some ironic interplay. In general terms Christianity and paganism address the common ground of the reader and the audience, the 'myths' which we hold in our heads about medieval images of hell and damnation, heaven and salvation, concepts which shaped centuries of European faith.

Notions of heaven and hell become relativized with the loss of a sense of absolute evil in Mephistopheles. As he proclaims when he introduces himself to Faust, he is no more than 'part of a part' (3, 118) of a spirit of denial. His name is a manufactured one dating from the time of the Faust legend in the sixteenth century. It draws on three Greek words which signify 'not loving the light'. Goethe invests concepts of heaven and hell with allegorical meaning to provide the imaginative framework for Faust's striving. The play presents God as an observer rather than a judge. He is present in the Prologue in Heaven, but after that he never reappears on the stage. Like us in the audience, he is viewing what then proceeds on the stage, witnessing it but not entering directly into the drama. Christian terms in the play do not *define* the play, any more than Romantic or Enlightenment elements define the work. The play defies any form of pigeonholing.

Scene 1: Night – Faust's study

The play begins with Faust the scholar in his dusty, cluttered study. In every way this comes as a contrast. After the dazzling light of heavenly realms the drama unfolds in night, in an enclosed and claustrophobic lonely darkness where a prison image prevails. The setting symbolizes confinement before any words are spoken.

EXERCISE   Read aloud the first ten lines of Faust's speech (p.39) and listen to them on Audio 6 (track 2).

1   Make notes on what Faust is saying. What attitude does he have to learning and knowledge?

2   Look closely at the vocabulary and form of the verse (in particular the tone, punctuation, rhythms and rhymes). Listen as you read aloud and consider their combined effect and significance.

DISCUSSION   1   Faust has exhausted all the fields of traditional learning – philosophy, law, medicine and theology – and he feels that he still knows nothing. He may have mastered institutionalized certitudes, but all that they amount to is perpetuation of petrifaction. Here is a man who wants to dispense with all the knowledge which forms the trappings of European cultural identity, not just from the time of the beginnings of the Faust story in the sixteenth century (see Figure 26.7), but also from the time of Goethe's contemporaries, the late eighteenth century, when Enlightenment confidence was being celebrated as a highpoint of civilization. Knowledge has immobilized Faust: he has come to a standstill. We are presented with erosion of beliefs rather than affirmation of the kind which has just been heralded in the Prologue in Heaven.

Figure 26.7   Rembrandt, Faust/The Alchemist, *c.1652, etching, 21 x 16 cm, Weimarer Klassik/Goethe-Nationalmuseum, Weimar. Photo: donated by Weimarer Klassik/Goethe Nationalmuseum. Schuchardt IS.177 Nr.0322.*

Goethe used a copy of this etching by Johann Heinrich Lips as the frontispiece for the first publication of Faust: Ein Fragment *(1790).*

2   This opening speech has the tone of a lament. Listen to the jumpy rhythms as you read the lines out loud, and look at the ways in which punctuation abruptly breaks up any sense of flow and order into an unsettling edginess. In the original German Goethe uses a sixteenth-century folk idiom for these opening lines called *Knittelvers*, a kind of doggerel. Even the structure of the verse he speaks confines Faust. Doggerel diminishes any suggestion of exalted status in these scholarly disciplines. It also has something of the language of the folk puppet theatre. Rhythmical and aural echoes of 'Philosophy' and 'Theology' run them into each other, trip them up over each other, and emphasize the futility with which they are now invested. This is reinforced by 'to my cost', encapsulating, almost in an aside, the disillusion of high expectations in Faust's study of theology. Coming after the Prologue in Heaven this phrase expresses the inadequacy of theological ideals to penetrate the fulfilment which Faust is seeking in common with other secular disciplines, which have all been 'grimly sweated through' and leave him a 'fool'.

Listen to the rest of the scene (track 2), noting that it omits the entrance of Wagner. Faust's ambition is

> to probe the secrets of the Universe;
> to learn its mysteries and recognise
> the force that binds all Nature's energies;
> (20–2)

and he turns first to the moon outside his study and imaginative release in nature. The way in which Goethe presents his passion for knowledge and revelation owes something to Paracelsus (1493–1541). Paracelsus was an alchemist and physician, a contemporary of the historical Faust: he conceived nature as a revelation of God, 'a spirit realm, a stepping stone to knowledge of something higher' (Brown, 1986, p.53). His aspirations to such knowledge as well as his revolutionary medical discoveries were considered controversial and heretical: they were seen as an urge into territory forbidden to humankind.

Faust turns for guidance to the writings of the astrologer Nostradamus (Michel de Notredame, 1503–66). Flicking the pages, he comes at random to the sign of the macrocosm (from the Greek *macros*, meaning 'great' and *cosmos*, meaning 'world'). This macrocosm (see Figure 26.8) is a sign which depicts a Renaissance view of the harmony of the universe in terms of concentric circles representing the planets around the earth. Outside the three rings of fire is the realm of God, displayed in the cloud. Nature, personified, acts as a conduit with a chain in one hand reaching down to the ape on the earth and a chain in the other reaching up to the divine cloud (Brown, 1986, p.55).

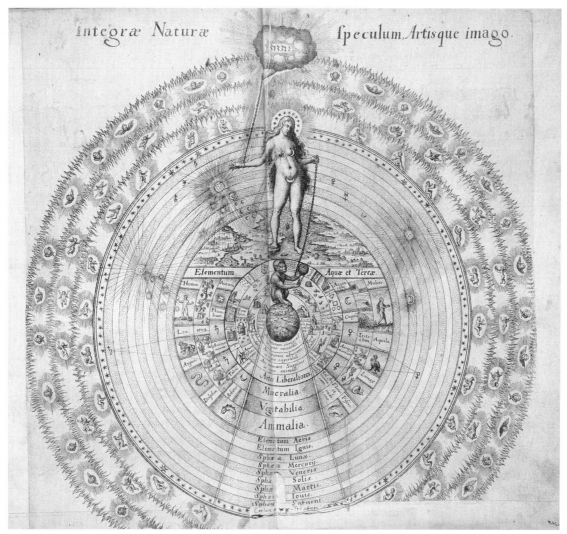

Figure 26.8   Robert Fludd, Macrocosm, *from* Utriusque cosmihistoria, *1617, Wellcome Library, London. Photo: courtesy of Wellcome Library, London.*

Fludd was a prominent follower of Paracelsus.

Finding the macrocosm sign in Nostradamus's book changes Faust's tone. 'Light dawns' as 'the red of dawn' inverts his dark mood and words such as 'open' and 'rise' signal a new rhetoric of excitement and expectation. But the elation capsizes when he realizes that this is no more than an abstraction, not the substance which he is after. It gives visual shape and pattern to a particular system of ideas. It is a *Schauspiel*, a play (*Schau* denoting seeing and *Spiel* a game). It amounts to a game or play for the eye:

> A great show, but no more than that – a show!
> (71)

We are reminded of the *Schein* of the Prologue in Heaven – the illumination as well as the illusion. Faust remains outside it, unengaged. There may be some meaning here beyond the rational knowledge which Faust has mastered in his learning, but there is no way in which he can connect with it. It is still a man-made sign, not the real thing.

Undeterred, Faust looks for something else: he turns more pages and finds the sign of the earth spirit. Once more he is overcome by his feelings, but this time it is not as an observer of symbols, standing outside, but as a participant taken over by forces which he can hardly formulate. The lines break up. Snatches of words – 'clouds', 'moon', 'vapours', 'beams', all visions of light, seize him:

> At each new pang I feel
> my senses reel
> (94–5)

When the earth spirit materializes, however, its energies go beyond anything he has conceived, and he cannot relate to its intensity and magnitude.

This spirit voices polarities of life and death ('cradle and grave') and unceasing movement. One present participle – 'weaving' – transposes into another – 'living', 'changing', 'blending, arranging' and one line surges into the next without a breath. This perpetual activity reminds us of the third archangel's hymn in the Prologue extolling tossing seas and of God's emphasis on the word 'strive'. The thrust of this poetic language expresses a spirit of dynamic creativity, sweeping over Faust but disenchanting him in the final statement:

> You're kin to the spirit that you comprehend:
> not me.
> (123–4)

The abrupt two monosyllables 'not me' – like Goethe's 'Nicht mir!'– leave a sudden silence as the spirit 'vanishes'.

Faust reads into the earth spirit only what he wants to find. Wagner's entrance comes as an ironic interruption. Wagner is Faust's assistant, a scholar in small format, so to speak, and his pedestrian utterances at this point, when Faust feels overwhelmed by the earth spirit, underline the difference between them. They confirm the reputation of which Faust is aware – remember how he realizes:

> True, I surpass the dull incompetents,
> (7)

in his first speech – just at a point when he is overwhelmed by the irrelevance of reputation. As a 'dull incompetent' Wagner entirely misreads Faust's situation. He relies pedantically on the very knowledge which plagues Faust, clichés derived from 'reciting plays', 'History', the words of 'great men'. He can do nothing but rehearse received opinion. Wagner diagnoses Faust's torments as no more than a search for intellectual reassurance which can be found in any of his books.

When Wagner leaves, Faust turns back to his memory of the earth spirit. Immersing himself in a kind of trance state his glance eventually settles on a phial of poison among his books and papers. The fascination for a suicidal death seems irresistible when at the last moment a new interruption comes, this time again from outside, in the sounds of the Easter chorus. The reference here is to Christ's resurrection; the hymn of praise touches his memories:

> the Easter hymn brings childhood flooding back to me.
> (243)

He has reconnected with himself and his resolve to commit suicide is broken:

> I have returned to earth.
> (247)

EXERCISE   1   How would you describe the main structural elements (such as the pace, the overall shape and the sequence of events) of this scene?

2   How is Faust presented?

DISCUSSION   1   The scene starts by night and ends at daybreak. This might symbolize opening of new purpose, but the shape and structure of the first scene move hither and thither as Faust keeps setting new courses, responding to one stimulus after another, shuttlecocking without apparent aim or resolution. This subverts the pattern and purpose enunciated by God in the Prologue in Heaven.

The scene can be divided into seven sections:

(i)   The first monologue (1–24)

(ii)   The address to the moon (25–45)

(iii) The invocation of the macrocosm (46–76)

(iv)   The summoning of the earth spirit (77–128)

(v)   The interruption of Wagner (129–172)

(vi)   The possibility of ultimate escape through suicide (173–237)

(vii) The sound of the Easter hymn (238–247).

The scene builds up in gradual intensification through signs and mysteries, invocations, interruptions and new directions. It is as if Faust is pushing at the edges and constantly being thrown back on himself again. Again and again his perceptions are dislodged as he finds that nothing is quite as it seems.

2   Faust is presented as a man of enormous erudition and at the same time with a colossal capacity for intense emotion, yet neither erudition nor emotion fulfils his desperate yearning for some understanding of 'the force that binds all Nature's energies' (22).

The acquisition of knowledge, which Faust decries in his initial outburst, is a burden because it is something *external* to him, external to his experience, external to his age (it is, after all, knowledge accrued through past ages), and external to his emotions. It is for this reason that it is 'a valueless inheritance' (40). Faust is looking for shortcuts to some internalized experience where the 'spirit's inward strife is stilled' (59).

Before we move on to look at more of the play, let's think about it in terms of its genre as poetic drama.

8   Some thoughts on *Faust* as a drama

Drama is a literary genre which presents conflict, dealing with events and moments which change people's lives. In this first scene Goethe presents an exposition of Faust alone, a man in acute agitation, in conflict between the limitations of his life on one hand and his unformed aspirations on the other.

Dramatic suspense depends on audience expectations and how they are met. On one level, this is a matter of the ways in which Goethe has changed the traditional terms of the Faust myth. On another level, dramatic tension is built up through the contrast between the knowledge to which we in the audience have access and the different knowledge available to the stage character(s). This is known as **dramatic irony**. The successive prologues delay Faust's entry, and from the Prologue in Heaven we in the audience know more than he does in his isolation on the stage. We know that Mephistopheles intends to challenge Faust. We have met them separately in the separate scenes. As you proceed, contrast the amount of information possessed by the audience with the knowledge that various individual characters have on the stage. Ask yourself as you read on what the effect of that contrast is.

The macrocosm, the earth spirit and the Easter hymn are dramatic devices which work as symbolic signs. The first enlists theatrical effects of the occult, the second embodies energies and processes of nature, while the third depends to a large degree on shared conventions which allow the audience to recognize the sound of the Easter hymn as representative of renewal framed in Christian belief. Each of these theatrical effects successively signals ways in which Faust's aspirations are thwarted. Keep watching out for particular dramatic elements as you continue your study of the play.

In terms of dramatic structure, the exercise at the end of the previous section allowed us to explore the *episodic* quality of the scene. Each episode could be seen as both complete in itself and incomplete. The theatrical potential of this loose form has bearings on the conceptual meaning of the drama, reinforcing the way Faust's drive is all the time *shifting*, moving in an onward search.

We have already begun to look at ways in which Goethe's language works in the play. As you study the play further, think about Goethe's use of imagery, symbolism and irony, and about the functions each may have. Listen out for different modes of language and words which are susceptible to differing interpretation.

9   Scene 2: Outside the city gate

EXERCISE   Read this scene (pp.46–50) and note the kinds of contrasts which provide the tension as the scene proceeds. Think particularly about contrasts in setting, concerns and dynamics of different groups and dialogues, and the different perceptions of Faust and Wagner.

DISCUSSION   While the previous scene in Faust's study took us through the night into the early morning, this scene begins in daylight and ends at dusk. We are flung out into the open into a whole new momentum of the outdoor world. Anonymous groups of characters – students, soldiers, citizens, girls – people a festival scenario. In dramatic terms, we move into a contrast from the private, enclosed life of the individual into the public life of the community. There is a spirit of *collective* arousal here and collective certainties, underlined with acclaim of Faust by one and all in the throng. Yet as the sun sets he is on his own with Wagner, and above all on his own with his uncertainties, enunciated in his words about the two souls which we looked at earlier. At the end of the scene, as daylight fades, Wagner and Faust see a dog. They see the same dog. But Faust sees things that Wagner doesn't, something beyond the prosaic character with which Wagner defines it. You may relate this to contrasts between certainties and uncertainties, between the definite and the indefinite, which mark the shift between Enlightenment and Romanticism (as outlined in Units 24–25).

10   Scene 3: Faust's study

Translation of the 'Word'

Read lines 1–40 of this scene (pp.51–2). Notice how inclusive Faust's language is. He talks of 'our savage urges', 'our hearts', 'our narrow cell', 'we can feel all is well.' Speaking in terms of 'we' and 'our', he has brought in with him from the previous scene, for all the personal anguish of the 'two souls speech', a common sense of humanity. Look back at the following lines:

> Here in the cheerful, noisy crowd, I can
> at last be what I always was – a man.
> (2, 54–5)

In scene 1 Faust is introduced to us as a reader, responding to a text. Now he turns to the opening chapter of St John's Gospel and sets about translating, or rather re-translating it. He chooses a text which expresses 'Life's primal source', and the word which he translates is 'Word': 'In the Beginning was the Word' (3, 31). The 'Word' translates *logos*, signifying the first principle of all things, God, in the opening words of St John's Gospel.

EXERCISE   How does Faust define the 'Word'? How many definitions does he suggest? What is the relationship between the definitions? You may wish to look at Barker Fairley's and David Luke's translations of this speech in Anthology II (pp.245–6).

DISCUSSION   Separating it from its context in the original text, Faust starts off with the authoritative doctrinal essence of the 'Word' and replaces it with 'Mind', still an abstract, cerebral concept. He moves on to a more fluid sense of energy, 'Force' (Barker Fairley gives 'energy'), and then he settles on 'Act' (David Luke translates this as 'Deed'). Faust is erasing one paradigm and substituting another, almost like a kind of wordplay. He is unfixing first principles, making the absolute relative, capable of transformation. He is looking at potential here, at the dynamic possibilities of the 'Word', in a meaning which is always approximate, never still, always becoming something else.

For Goethe an essential tension exists between a state of being and a state of becoming. Faust is challenging what happens to meaning when it stops just staying still. Rewriting the 'Word' becomes, in a way, an act of recreating it. In turn this affects the meaning of 'beginning'. 'In the beginning' becomes something which loses its finite definition of something past. It becomes always. It becomes a process, an 'act' always changing. The primal *logos*, creation itself, is action. Faust through this translation is demonstrating the concepts of beginning and ending to be no more than convenient human fictions.

We recall God's insistence in the Prologue on striving. Faust is not only striving to find meaning here, but the meaning on which he settles is 'striving' itself. He may not be able to articulate the inarticulable, but the main thing is that he keeps trying.

Mephistopheles' entry

Now read lines 41–256 (pp.52–8). Faust's efforts to translate the 'Word' run alongside his efforts to control the growling dog which has followed him into his study from the walk of the previous scene. He wants to control the bark of the dog just as he wants to control, in parallel, the 'Word'. Animal sounds juxtapose ironically with unresolved spiritual expression. We find that it is not just the meaning of the 'Word' which changes shape: the dog is changing shape too. Translations go along with transformations – 'some dreadful thing/takes shape' (51–2) – from dog to 'daemon', to apparition in smoke, to human being. This provides a dramatic entrance for Mephistopheles. As the dog, he has been distracting Faust from reaching a final truth in his translation of the 'Word'. Now he has resisted Faust's efforts to control him with his successive invocations of *Clavis Salomonis*, with the four elements of nature – Undine (water), Sylphide (air), Salamander (fire) and Gnome (earth) – and with the crucifix. He has been playing the kind of 'cat-and-mouse' game which we know he enjoys (Prologue, 81), for this travelling scholar is recognizable to the audience from the Prologue as Mephistopheles.

When Faust's attempts to exorcize the creature through the four elements of nature fail –

> None of the elemental four
> lurks in the beast
> (72–3)

– he recognizes some 'devil', and he tries to find a name for him among a host of labels:

> Prince of Darkness, Tempter, Lord of Flies,
> Old Gentleman, Adversary, Father of Lies.
> (102–3)

The variety of euphemisms subverts definition.

What Faust wants, though, is the equivalent of some 'translation': 'Who are you then?' (104). Mephistopheles gives him three versions of his identity, first as

> Part of the power which would
> work only Evil, but produces Good.
> (104–5)

He certainly is no more than 'a part'. We know that from the Prologue:
the view that Mephistopheles presents here fits in exactly with God's
view of him. A partial identity is, however, not what Faust is after.
Pressed by Faust, Mephistopheles' second introduction is as 'the spirit
that must constantly deny' (107). Defining himself in terms only of what
he is *not*, in negatives, is only to claim that he is destructive rather than
creative, negative rather than positive. He represents negativity. Faust
repeats his question and Mephistopheles proceeds with a third
explanation of himself:

> I am part of a part that, at the start, was All;
> part of the darkness that, though once complete,
> gave birth to light.
> (118–20)

Here he claims to be part of the chaos and darkness of the origin of the
world. Faust has just been trying to find some translation for the 'Word'
that there was 'in the beginning', and now, ironically, Mephistopheles
claims to represent that 'beginning'. The irony has a heretical flavour,
especially in the way that 'beginning' has become 'always'. This
depiction of the world, not surprisingly, is in total opposition to the
proclamations of the angels in the Prologue. Mephistopheles' view is that

> all things that live and grow
> deserve to have a final overthrow.
> (108–9)

(Whatever their deserts, God's gardener imagery in the Prologue has
assured us that 'all things that live and grow' will mature and progress
rather than be overthrown.) Mephistopheles proceeds to transpose good
and evil, light and darkness, insisting that light 'is doomed to fall' (121).
Once more, the Prologue provides the basic moral and spiritual structure
of the play, and Mephistopheles, for all his sinuous reasoning, is doomed
to disillusion.

It is Faust who first mentions the idea of a pact:

> a contract made with you
> would be adhered to?
> (177–8)

Mephistopheles hesitates. Faust's bantering tone is not conducive to him,
and he wants to buy a little time. He cannot leave: Faust effectively holds
him captive, because of the sign of the pentagram at the door. This
symbol is part of the ritual of the play, composed of a line which traces a
mystical five-pointed star shape signifying the five letters of the name of
Jesus (Möbus *et al.*, 1995, p.49). The fact that the line does not entirely
join up precludes Mephistopheles' immediate exit and allows him to

demonstrate his powers over this world, if only through the simple expedient of summoning a rat to his aid. The display is for the audience, though not for Faust, whom he has meanwhile conjured into sleep through the dream visions of the spirit song. In these short rhyming verses spinning visions of light and promise, Mephistopheles is working on Faust's senses to beguile him into associations which will make him receptive.

The pact

Read lines 279–456 (pp.58–64), as Mephistopheles returns to Faust, and then listen to the scene on Audio 6 (track 4). Note how Mephistopheles' comings and goings are riddled with devices of magic and superstition: until he establishes his pact with Faust he needs to move through rites of one kind or another to gain access. Faust comments sardonically that 'Hell has its rules and regulations too' (176), and these devices, doubtless, are some of them. We are in two worlds – the real world of Faust's study and the world of magic rites of Mephistopheles as one transformation succeeds another. His entrance now is in another garb.

EXERCISE   1   Trace the steps which lead to the pact between Mephistopheles and Faust.

2   What are the terms of the pact?

DISCUSSION   1   The steps are as follows:

(i)   Mephistopheles offers his services to Faust in this world:

> Here's my proposal:
> I place myself at your disposal,
> however it's expedient,
> I am your squire, your slave, your most obedient.
> (309–12)

(ii) Faust brings up the question of conditions.

(iii) Mephistopheles sets them out on the basis of something of a 'fair play', tit for tat, exercise, negotiating that he will do anything for Faust in this world provided Faust does anything for him in the next.

(iv) Mephistopheles' flippancy is countered by Faust's professed disregard for anything to do with 'over there': his concerns are only with this world. Remember his words in the opening scene: 'I have no fear of the Devil or Hell' (1, 12).

(v) Mephistopheles seizes the opportunity to offer to

> give you more
> than any man has ever had before.
> (333–4)

(vi) Faust tosses the offer aside. He and Mephistopheles once more have entirely different agendas. Mephistopheles is confident that he is leading the way and has the upper hand. Faust every time makes him take a step back, now claiming that his aspirations are of a kind which go beyond anything which Mephistopheles can offer him. Note the imagery which Faust uses:

> Where are
> the trees that put forth new green every day?
> (344–5)

This may remind you of God's imagery in the Prologue (69–70). And then he proceeds to set the terms:

> the day that I
> become a slave to pleasures that degrade me,
> that day's my last – I'll be content to die.
> (347–9)

(vii) Mephistopheles agrees the terms, which are confirmed in Faust's key words:

> If ever, as Time flows by us, I should say:
> 'This moment is so beautiful – let it stay!',
> that is the moment when you will have won.
> For me, the passing bell can sound,
> and from my service you'll be free:
> for me, the clock will cease its round,
> and Time exist no more for me.
> (351–7)

2   What it comes down to is this: if Mephistopheles can ever make Faust stop striving so that he ends up self-contented and inactive, then Mephistopheles can claim him.

Faust and Mephistopheles have been talking on different levels all along, Mephistopheles eager to secure what he no doubt perceives as a bargain, without understanding what Faust is asking for. Worldly gratification is all that Mephistopheles has in mind, while what matters for Faust is a more profound metaphysical totality, one which may include both pleasure and pain:

> I do not ask for joy:
> excitement, yes, the agony of elation
> (391–2)

Not only has he no fear of Mephistopheles, he has no expectation of him either:

> Poor devil, have you anything to give?
> (335)

He does not take Mephistopheles seriously: he takes him on in a spirit of defiance. Looking at different ways in which to translate the 'Word', Faust has been looking for alternatives, trying to move away from enclosed and finite definition to something more open-ended. This is just what his pact with Mephistopheles turns out to be.

The 'let it stay!' clause (352) is the only proviso to the deal, and Faust does not believe that he will ever want to say 'let it stay!' to the passing moment. With different terms from the traditional myth, Goethe's Faust has a different wish list from the desire for wealth and power of the traditional Faust. These are finite goals. Faust is not expecting such specific satisfactions.

Mephistopheles draws attention to the different modes of time operating for God and for humankind:

> The Universe was made for God alone.
> He suns himself in everlasting light,
> us He casts into darkness on our own,
> while you live in alternate day and night.
> (402–5)

God has eternity. Man's life is ruled by time. What Mephistopheles does not comprehend is that Faust wants to seize a moment which might encompass a sense of eternal fulfilment but never to rest within it: he wants always to be driven on to new stimulation. This reaches far beyond the terms of Romantic longing set out in Units 24–25.

Mephistopheles wants the pact signed, sealed and delivered. Faust finds the idea of a signed contract preposterous. This is not just another aspect of the material focus of Mephistopheles in contrast with the larger aspirations of Faust which neither can nor need to be defined in written form. It also emphasizes the lack of trust between the two.

The drama is set in motion. Mephistopheles, ostensibly Faust's servant (see line 312), massages the action. The pace accelerates, rushing on with new impetus. Dragged down at the beginning of the drama by the sheer weight of knowledge, Faust's pact with Mephistopheles sets him flying (look at the last words of the scene, p.64). The image of flight, as a fresh search, a liberation, sets a new course. The future, for Faust, becomes open and open-ended.

The significance of the pact in the play

Goethe inserted the pact between Faust and Mephistopheles while he was spurred on between 1787 and 1800 by Schiller's encouragement to develop his fragments into a complete play. The negotiation of the pact between Faust and Mephistopheles presents us with a reversal of the traditional bargain.

Traditionally Mephistopheles offered Faust the satisfaction of his every worldly desire on the understanding that on the stroke of 24 years Faust would pay in eternal damnation. (The conquest of knowledge was forbidden by the Catholic Church of the sixteenth century.) No fixed constraint or term binds Goethe's Faust. His whole life lies ahead, in fact more than his whole life, because in the witch's kitchen he is to be rejuvenated and given, literally, a new lease of life.

Nevertheless, the pact still depends on a specific understanding of time, and this is absolutely crucial. What Faust wants is to be able to use his energies *at every moment*, in every *Augenblick*, in essence a beginning without ending. He craves for a permanent condition in which all is forever potential. Each moment is to be a new start. It will both 'be' a moment and 'become' a new moment. One of Goethe's first poems written for the *Divan*, 'Selige Sehnsucht' ('Blessed Longing'), contains the injunction 'Stirb und werde!' (literally, 'Die and become!'). This enshrines the principle of *dying and becoming*, 'cradle and grave' in the earth spirit's words (1, 113), continuous organic renewal, which relates to Faust's reworking of meaning in the 'Word'. To stop striving is effectively to be damned.

It is not Mephistopheles who sets out the terms, but Faust himself. It is difficult to imagine a more positive statement of intent. Faust wants to grasp his own destiny. He does not want to leave it to the rewards or punishments of an outside compelling agency.

From now on Faust can never be free of Mephistopheles. Mephistopheles becomes a kind of alter ego. They both say no to the establishment. In this sense they are rivals. From now on they cannot do without each other.

11   Scenes 4 and 5: Auerbach's cellar in Leipzig and The witch's kitchen

EXERCISE   Read scenes 4 and 5 of the set text (pp.64–75) and then return to the unit.

In these two scenes, Mephistopheles appears as stage director. Faust is represented as the spectator in his own play. In Auerbach's cellar he watches from the sidelines. In the witch's kitchen he is both spectator and the central subject, captured among the crazy hissing and the crackling by the reflection of ideal womanhood as he looks into the glass –

> the beauty that seemed hardly possible
> (5, 145)

– rejuvenated, transformed into new potential. 'The ironic observer's awareness of himself as observer tends to enhance his feeling of freedom and induce a mood perhaps of serenity, or joyfulness, or even exultation' (Muecke, 1970, p.37). When we come to look at the significance of the Gretchen story in section 14, we shall consider again the dramatic significance of the mirror and the vision here.

12   The Gretchen tragedy

The Gretchen tragedy, as the latter part of the play is often called, is arguably the best-known part of the drama. On its own it has spawned a whole range of further treatments, especially in musical works. Gounod's *Faust* (1859) is one example: belying its title, it deals exclusively with the Gretchen story, and has been one of the works which has defined (or 'misdefined') *Faust* as the Gretchen drama.

The audience doesn't know anything about Gretchen, meeting her on stage for the first time at the moment when Faust sees her. Indeed, we are presented in a way with a new Faust, too, rejuvenated in the witch's kitchen. In a stage production the change would be visible. Differences between audience and stage character knowledge contribute to the dramatic tension of the play. The audience knows of Faust's relationship with Mephistopheles and the pact; Gretchen doesn't.

EXERCISE   Now read the rest of the play. Some of the remaining 18 scenes are very short (scene 22: Night – open country, the shortest, is only a matter of six lines long), and in the main they run in quite seamless progression into each other, even if considerable chronological time elapses off-stage (for instance, during Gretchen's pregnancy and imprisonment for infanticide). The intensity with which the drama moves is marked by passion and fervour, Shakespearean resonance (particularly of Juliet and Ophelia), and use of folk-song. When you have completed your reading, return to the unit.

Scene 7: Evening – a small neat room

The Prologue in Heaven gives us an introduction to Faust in the references of God and of Mephistopheles. The only introduction that we have to Gretchen is her decline of Faust's offer of his arm in the previous scene (6: In the street) and his reaction to her beauty and her modesty. Now we meet her on her own ground, so to speak, alone in her room in the evening.

EXERCISE   Listen to this scene on Audio 6 (track 6) and take a couple of minutes to consider the following questions:

1   How is the scene structured? How many separate sections can you find?

2   What are the poetic and theatrical effects of the song?

3   What happens to Gretchen in this scene?

DISCUSSION   1   The short scene divides into three parts. The song about the king is framed at the beginning by Gretchen's initial musings and at the end by her excitement over the jewels. Despite her protestations in the previous scene, she is attracted to Faust:

> I'd give a lot if I could know
> who that gentleman was just now.
> (1–2)

Thinking about him changes her feelings about the familiar surroundings of her room:

> I feel a sort of ... I don't know ... not right
> (7)

Even at the beginning of the scene, 'plaiting and putting her hair up', Gretchen feels defamiliarized. She is aware of something disquieting in these routines. By the end of the scene her everyday world has been overturned. There is no longer anything everyday about it.

2   The poetic effects of the song lie in its haunting symbolism. Here is a story from far away ('a Northern fastness') and long ago (suggested by 'it's told'), about enduring love, objectified and symbolized in the golden cup from which the king drinks before throwing it into the sea as he dies. Dying for him is not so much a matter of no longer breathing as no longer drinking from 'the sacred golden cup':

> never more drank he.
> (34)

Nothing more matters now. Two narratives are running alongside each other – what Gretchen is doing and what she is singing. The innocence of Gretchen undressing is juxtaposed with the eroticism of a legendary king clinging to his love even in his dying moment. In this song Gretchen is 'expressing her as yet barely conscious desire for the handsome stranger and the ingrained longing of every woman for a fidelity which will last beyond the grave' (Wilkinson and Willoughby, 1970, p.108). She is preparing for bed in conventional routines while she sings a song about a love which defies convention.

3   Gretchen has been singing about someone who is not actually there, and now the discovery of the jewels faces her with a parallel reality: her own world seems suddenly as unreal to her as that of the ballad king. The changed sense of herself and her surroundings, the ballad which evokes her unformed longings, and now her awareness of her own self in a transposed identity, expressed in turn through entirely different kinds of language – each gives intensity to a transforming moment for Gretchen. It is a moment where everything is charged with unknown potential.

In scene 14 (Gretchen's room) Gretchen goes on spinning at her wheel while she sings, and on stage the sight and sound of this mundane task invest the lyrical fervour of the lines with particular pathos, just as the passionate words of the song in this scene contrast with the routine of undressing at the end of the day.

Scene 13: Forest and cavern

Love transforms Faust's relationship with nature, opening sensations which transform his sense of himself.

EXERCISE   Listen to the scene on Audio 6 (track 11) and follow it carefully in the text (pp.88–91).

1   To whom is Faust addressing this opening monologue in lines 1–35?

2   What are the contrasts between the two parts of Faust's speech? Look at stress, alliteration and repetition.

DISCUSSION   1   Faust begins with the words 'Transcendent spirit'. Faust now feels privy to the vast processes of nature – 'All Nature and all Knowledge' (2) in access to 'Nature's deepest heart' (6). But the potential and the totality of the vision are not without their downside. The spirit allows him to soar, but it embraces negative as well as positive phenomena.

2   The monologue is divided: first Faust celebrates initiation into appreciation of all natural phenomena, in short, of all creation. The strong stresses reflect his new-found empowerment in recognition of

his 'kinship with all creatures' (10). There are rhetorical devices of contrasting alliteration ('province' and 'power' in line 3 against 'cold' and 'curious' in line 5) and onomatopoeia, also in the original German:

> a crash
> that echoes round the hills with hollow thunder.
> (14–15)

Repetition of 'now':

> Now the bright moon comes up before my eyes
> (19)

and

> now there float up before me [...]
> silvery forms of lost, forgotten worlds
> (20–2)

suggests two *simultaneous*, as well as different, experiences. The third 'now' as the second part of the monologue begins:

> But nothing perfect ever comes to Man.
> I see that now.
> (24–5)

stops at the caesura (breaking up the sentence mid-line), bringing a heavy pause into the line, as in the original German. Faust does not name him, but this is a reminder of his inextricable alliance with Mephistopheles. He laments the destructive energies which go along with this life-principle, ever-present in:

> this companion, whom already
> I can no longer do without
> (27–8)

The transposition between heights of elation and depths of degradation magnifies the conflict inherent in Faust's 'Two souls' speech which we looked at in section 2. He feels his needs being met, but this wish-fulfilment has a very high price.

The monologue marks a private moment for Faust alone – or so he thinks. The pact ensures that he can never be alone again. Mephistopheles is eavesdropping. The 'peace' to which he refers in his apprehension of the moon is over. Mephistopheles mimics Faust, taunting him in a parody of his euphoria:

> Of course – a supernatural delight!
> Lying there in the mountain dew all night,
> feeling yourself, 'at one' with earth and sky,
> swelling with immanent divinity
> (50–3)

The quotation marks around 'at one' ironically undermine any 'at one'-ness.

Mephistopheles proceeds to reduce Faust's claims to something much more prosaic, even coarse:

> your new-found powers of deeper penetration
> bring things – I hardly dare say how – to consummation.
> (60–1)

In the lewd insinuation of 'consummation' Mephistopheles is intent in turning love to lust, provoking Faust with his knowing account of Gretchen pining for him. When Faust, as he intends, reacts in rage, Mephistopheles' malevolence overrules Faust's exhilaration and converts it into a realization of the *destructive* nature of his love for Gretchen:

> Where is the happiness of being her lover
> when her own downfall's all I'll ever give her?
> (94–5)

Having felt at peace with nature at the beginning of the scene, he now refers to himself as

> outcast, homeless, wanderer, refugee,
> monster, restless, purposeless
> (96–7)

The cumulative way in which he brings out one word after another suggests that no word will do. Instead of joy in the creative elements of nature, he now uses imagery of violence and destruction:

> plunging like a cataract into the sea,
> hungering for the dark abyss.
> (98–9)

Faust cannot help himself: he cannot renounce his love for Gretchen, despite his knowledge that this can only precipitate some awful devastation.

This is exactly what Mephistopheles enjoys, as he flaunts his triumphant asides, bracketed in:

> (It starts to take.)
> (84)

> (There now, the fire burns up, he's on the boil.)
> (106)

The tremendous dynamics in their dispute orchestrate a huge contrast between Faust's monologue at the beginning of the scene and his frenzy of desire, convulsed at the end in despair. It is a tautly-built scene, starting with Faust's wonder and ending with Mephistopheles gloating over the way he has trumped him.

Scene 15: In Martha's garden

Gretchen does not know what Faust says in scene 13. He does not know what she sings in scene 14. Only the audience witnesses both and is aware of the unrelenting tension building up between them. The two scenes allow us to see first one and then the other alone, almost as if we are given simultaneous, rather than sequential, glimpses of each character alone. We can see how Goethe builds up dramatic effects through different kinds of contrasts, contrasts of mood and language within scenes and between them, contrasts of settings – inside and outside – and contrasts between characters, either between two, like Faust and Wagner, Faust and Mephistopheles, or between pairings like the ones between Gretchen's neighbour Martha and Mephistopheles.

Coming back into Martha's garden, Gretchen is ecstatic to be with Faust again. We meet them in mid-conversation just as Gretchen is asking Faust about his religious beliefs. As if rehearsing his catechism, she asks him:

> How much does your religion mean to you?
> (3)

When he broadens the question into a matter of the meaning of love, she persists:

> you don't even respect the sacraments [...]
> When were you last at Mass, or at confession?
> (10–13)

Insistently, now addressing Faust by his Christian name, she asks:

> Heinrich, please tell me, do you believe in God?
> (14)

Faust responds with rhetorical questions rather than with direct answers:

> Who can dare name God,
> and say 'He does exist'?
> Or what sane man resist
> the feeling, 'He does not'?
> (20–3)

These lines introduce a more fluid rhythm. The alternatives change Gretchen's terms. Faust is stretching the question out of its doctrinal essence. Do you remember how he worked over the meaning of 'Word' in scene 3? Once more he is addressing the problems of language, not in finding equivalent words for what has already been called the 'Word', but for something which cannot be encompassed in words at all. The most that anyone might do, Faust proceeds to say, is to rely on feeling, specifically the kind of feeling of the sublime which he has addressed in the forest monologue – a feeling of infinity within the finite. Faust's conviction of divinity in nature owes much to the influence of the philosopher and theologian Spinoza (1632–77), whose belief that God could be sensed pantheistically in everything, both visible and invisible, insisting that finite phenomena allow some apprehension of the divine, was condemned during his lifetime as heretical and subversive. Goethe shared his regard for Spinoza with, among other contemporaries, Coleridge. Among the phenomena to which Faust refers – 'stars' (28), 'all Creation' (29) – his focus falls on Gretchen with the words 'your generous heart' (33). It is enough to feel:

> Feeling is all.
> (38)

There is no moral imperative here.

Gretchen is disturbed by Faust's answer, but she wants so much to be convinced that she is prepared to align his answer with the orthodox view:

> So the good Father tells us, although he
> puts it a little differently.
> (40–1)

The ironic contrast between Faust's huge, passionate statements and Gretchen's simple, unquestioning doctrinal beliefs is full of intense pathos. The irony is compounded by Gretchen's reference to 'the good Father'. Presumably this is the same priest who snaffled her jewels, to Mephistopheles' fury (8, 24–31). The shift to rhyme and steady rhythms again after the free-flowing energies of Faust's words emphasizes her firm faith. Immediately after this interchange she turns her thoughts, not insignificantly, to

> that man who goes around with you
> (42)

– and here is someone whom *she* cannot name. She not only cannot name him but her whole moral sense feels threatened by his malevolent presence.

> When that man comes through the door,
> even my love for you becomes unsure.
> (50–1)

This is of course just what Mephistopheles, the spirit of negativity, is aiming to do. Whatever good impulses Faust has or engenders in others, Mephistopheles always undermines them. Gretchen feels tainted to such an extent by him that

> when he's here I cannot pray
> (52)

and what disturbs her is that Faust is exposing himself to moral contamination by his association with him:

> you feel it too, you know it's so.
> (54)

This is the line which tells us why she has been questioning Faust about his religious beliefs. It is an opportunity for Faust to take a stand; the pact, however, denies him the opportunity. He knows that he is playing with words when he says to Gretchen:

> Sweetheart, there is no earthly need to fear him.
> (45)

and is only going through the motions when he brushes her very real fears aside with:

> It's just an antipathy.
> (55)

Gretchen's instinctive loathing of Mephistopheles, on the one hand, and her absolute trust in Faust, on the other, reflect her essential purity. Nevertheless, although it is Faust who provides the sleeping draught so that her mother is not awakened when he visits her that night, it is she who invites him to her room. So she is not entirely the victim.

EXERCISE   Looking at the text (pp.92–4), listen to the scene on Audio 6 (track 13). What is the dramatic significance of Mephistopheles' entrance just as Gretchen departs?

DISCUSSION   It is a matter of 'talk of the devil', literally. He has been eavesdropping again. As in previous scenes (2 and 13), his entrance reminds Faust that he can never be rid of Mephistopheles. Mephistopheles' reference to him as a 'transcendental lecher' (72) debases Faust's exalted credo. Faust is just as passionate in his revulsion of Mephistopheles now as he was passionate in his love for Gretchen earlier.

Think about this in relation to dramatic irony. Dramatic irony can arise just as much out of different knowledge which the characters of the drama have – like Mephistopheles' awareness of Faust's every move – as out of different knowledge which the audience has from that of characters on the stage, which we have discussed previously. This irony affecting the relationship between Faust and Mephistopheles means that Faust, after the pact, can never be alone any more. Mephistopheles becomes an alter ego. He impersonates Faust's own critical faculties.

Escalation of the drama and consequences of the pact

Some of the dramatic effects of the play lie in what we *don't* see and hear, what happens off-stage. In the gossip of the next scene (16: At the well) we hear of Barbara, unmarried and pregnant, and socially ostracized. Gretchen's identification with Barbara's plight and the way in which she implores the Virgin Mary in the repetitions ('woe' and 'tears' and 'misery') of her prayer in scene 17 alert us implicitly to her own condition: nothing is directly stated. It is Valentine who publicly shames her as a 'whore' in scene 18 during which he is killed, albeit inadvertently, by Faust. By the time that Gretchen cries out for air in scene 19 (see Figure 26.9), the jeer of Mephistopheles about her 'mother's soul' tells us that Gretchen's mother is dead. We never see Gretchen's mother on stage, but she is a constant reference-point in Gretchen's life.

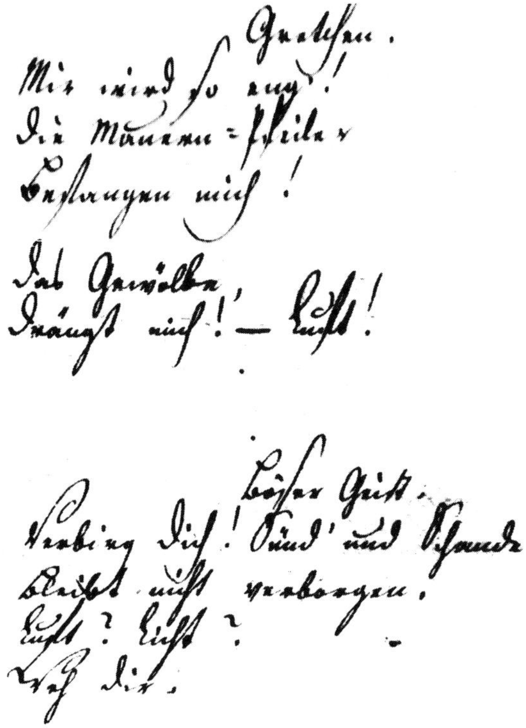

Figure 26.9 Goethe, Faust, *manuscript: ten lines from the Cathedral scene, Weimarer Klassik/Goethe-Nationalmuseum, Weimar. Photo: donated by Weimarer Klassik/Goethe-Nationalmuseum.*

Gretchen:
Mir wird so eng!
Die Mauerpfeiler
Befangen mich!
Das Gewölbe
Drängt mich! – Luft!

Böser Geist:
Verbirg dich!
Sünd und Schande
Bleibt nicht verborgen.
Luft? Licht?
Weh dir!

Gretchen:
I cannot breathe.
The minster walls
close in on me.
The vaulted roof
is choking me –
give me some air!

Mephistopheles:
Trying to hide?
Sin and shame
cannot be hidden.
Calling for air and light!
Creature of shame!
(MacDonald, 19, 25–36)

In the pact, Faust has committed himself to keep on actively striving. When he falls in love with Gretchen, Mephistopheles does his best to turn Faust's love for her into no more than lust. He tries to drag Faust away and confuse him in the din of manic Walpurgis Night energies (scene 20) of a profane and alien world, but here a vision of Gretchen appears in Faust's sight. Limits of time and space, in realistic terms, are eclipsed. She stands with the ring of execution around her neck, combining her past and her future. Mephistopheles attempts to persuade Faust that

> It's an illusion, lifeless – there is nothing there.
> (181)

In the only scene in prose in the play, scene 21, Faust implores Mephistopheles to help him to rescue her. He is beside himself, desperate to free himself from Mephistopheles, who delights in devaluing Gretchen:

> She's not the first.
> (8)

But there is nothing Faust can do: he is dependent on Mephistopheles.

Scene 23: Prison

In Martha's garden we break into the exchange between Gretchen and Faust. In scene 23 we break in again, but this time Gretchen is alone, singing, no longer in the open light of a garden but in the dark, confined space of the prison. Dramatic transformation is at the essence of the play, but the violent transformation in this song is no progressive process. It is about being murdered by a mother (Gretchen's reference to her child), a mother who is a whore (an echo of Valentine's accusation), devoured by a father. Her mind wanders into the fairytale about the mother cooking the flesh of the killed child and the father eating it and turning into a bird, to be immortalized by the Brothers Grimm in the collection they were to publish in 1812. The idiom of folk-song gives Gretchen the vocabulary through which to express her feelings. In these wild, disconnected snatches this Gretchen seems almost unrecognizable, a stranger.

To Gretchen, Faust is unrecognizable: she mistakes him for the executioner:

> I have never
> set eyes on you in my life before.
> (23–4)

He cannot find what to say:

> Oh, no!
> (16)

> Oh, God, how can I stand this any more?
> (25)

Faust may have toiled over the way to express the 'Word', but now it is Gretchen who has all the words, delirious and tormented as they are. She speaks about 'My friend' (Faust, of course):

> he's not here today.
> (20)

She talks of 'my child' and everyone is 'they':

> they took it from me
> (29)
> they said that I had murdered it
> (30)
> They're singing songs about me
> (31)

EXERCISE Some of the dramatic effects of pathos arise out of echoes from earlier parts of the play. Can you think of any as you read lines 1–38 (pp.109–10)? In what ways do these echoes contrast with earlier resonances?

DISCUSSION *Magical symbols*: for Faust the magic of the potion of rejuvenation in scene 5 has meant life and freedom. The magic in Gretchen's song is macabre: it becomes a nightmare full of gruesome death.

Flowers as symbols: 'They threw away/my flowers' (21–2). In scene 11, Gretchen picks the petals off the daisy – 'just a game' (64), coded play where each petal alternates certainty with uncertainty of Faust's love:

> He loves me – he loves me not – he loves me – not –
> he loves me – not – he loves me – not – he loves me!
> (66–7)

Now such innocence is subsumed in public shame.

Songs: 'They're singing songs about me' (32). The echo is two-fold. First, the line (from scene 23) recalls scene 16 where Gretchen learned the common gossip about Barbara. It is at this moment in the play that she realizes that, sharing Barbara's fate, she has moved from social integration to alienation. Second, she hears voices not so much speaking as singing, as if she is now becoming public property. Gretchen feels that her fate has become the subject of popular ballads. She feels tormented by public accusation. Singing has been the medium through which we have had access to Gretchen's intimate longings. To hear her talking about others singing is now to penetrate into her intimate fears.

Religion: as Faust falls down on his knees in front of her, Gretchen mistakes his gesture as one of prayer – a gesture craved in reassurance in her question to him about his faith in scene 15.

When Gretchen does recognize Faust's voice, all that matters to her in her trance-state, urgently, is his kiss, while for him all that matters, urgently, is her escape. She refuses to escape when he urges her:

> FAUST:
> To freedom. Out into the world.
> GRETCHEN:
> Into the world? No, not for all the world.
> Into my grave, yes.
> To meet my death, yes.
> I'll go to everlasting sleep,
> or I'll not move another step.
> (93–8)

Breaking the five regular beats of the rhyming pentameters, Gretchen is confronting her life head on. No escape is possible for her. She accepts her judgement. She is as clear-sighted as she is confused, seeing her past, present and future simultaneously. While she re-enacts the murders of her mother and her child, she enacts the moment-by-moment sensations of her execution day ahead in front of the gathering crowds in the square:

> The death-bell tolls, the rod is snapped:
> now they seize me, my wrists are strapped,
> to the scaffold they drag me, violently.
> (142–4)

She feels the feelings not just of herself but of all the spectators:

> On his own neck, each man can feel
> the breath and twitch of falling steel.
> Crack! and the world fades, silently.
> (145–7)

Meanwhile, she gives very practical instructions to Faust about the graves:

> Give the best place to my mother.
> Next to her put my brother.
> then me a shade – but not too far – to the side.
> And put the baby here – on my right breast:
> there will be no one else to share my rest.
> (81–5)

She may be crazed, but at the same time she sees clearly.

Dawn brings new urgency to Faust's pleas to Gretchen, underlined by the entry of Mephistopheles. Gretchen has shuddered in fear at Mephistopheles' proximity before: it disturbed her to such an extent that she could no longer pray (15, 52). Now she *can* pray, and does, asserting –

> I am on holy ground, in sanctuary.
> (151)

The floor beneath her which had earlier in the scene been

> the pit of Hell
> where the devils dwell
> (36–7)

is converted into sacred territory: Gretchen has passed through a process of acceptance and repentance:

> Judgment of God, in Thee I place my trust.
> (153)

By submitting to judgement on earth, she is placing hope for atonement in heaven. This final scene with all its pathos has a momentum in which Gretchen acquires a new strength in the balance of her relationship with Faust, whose words are few and desperate. Her last words and thoughts are for him:

> Heinrich, I shudder now to look at you.
> (158)

She fears for Faust as long as he cannot dispense with Mephistopheles. The clarity of her gaze reveals her moral autonomy in this last moment.

EXERCISE Listen to the scene on Audio 7 (track 4) and note how the openness at the end of the play is enhanced through the breakdown of verse and rhyme. When you have finished listening, return to the unit.

Caught between Gretchen and Mephistopheles, Faust is silent. Mephistopheles' verdict condemns Gretchen, but immediately an off-stage voice (that of God from the heaven of the Prologue, perhaps?) counters and caps with a verdict of redemption, as Mephistopheles takes Faust away, leaving the voice calling after him. The contradiction of the verdicts juxtaposes two German words – *gerichtet* ('judged' in the sense of 'condemned') and *gerettet* ('rescued' or 'saved') – which have rhythmical and aural echo ('ger-tet') in their beginnings and endings. The visual and aural repetitions in these two weighty words of condemnation and salvation introduce ambiguity and uncertainty into the absolute terms.

13   *Faust Part Two*: resolution?

Faust Part Two is not required reading for this course, but a glance at some overall aspects of its structure, content and ending at this point offers a context to your understanding of *Part One*. Unlike *Part One*, *Part Two* is a five-act play, following the structure of classical drama. *Part One* is concerned with the personal and emotional expansion of Faust's life. By the time that *Faust Part Two* ends, Faust has been swept back to the fall of Troy and forward to the capture of Missolonghi – a span of 3,000 years of European civilization from the classical times of ancient Greece to the contemporary political fight for freedom in modern Greece. Feudal decadence is exposed in the court of Charlemagne, and ancient mythology is reworked in Faust's marriage to Helen of Troy and the birth of their son Euphorion (based on Byron, for whom Goethe had unreserved regard).

By the end Faust is an old man, still pushing against boundaries, this time in great irrigation schemes to reclaim territory for the land he rules. Mephistopheles is still intent on wilfully undermining any noble venture. While Faust, now blinded by Mephistopheles' assistant Care, believes that he is hearing the sound of shovels working on the construction of dykes and canals, he is actually hearing his grave being dug, as Mephistopheles has instructed.

EXERCISE   Read Faust's last speech (lines 47–74, pp.210–11 of your set text) and the alternative translations by David Luke and Barker Fairley in Anthology II (pp.247–9). Then return to the unit.

EXERCISE   Look back at the terms of the pact between Faust and Mephistopheles in *Part One*:

> If ever, as Time flows by us, I should say:
> 'This moment is so beautiful – let it stay!'
> that is the moment when you will have won.
> For me, the passing bell can sound,
> and from my service you'll be free:
> for me, the clock will cease its round,
> and Time exist no more for me.
> (3, 351–7)

Can you identify how the words of Faust's final, grandiose vision of a future 'paradise' for 'millions', to 'crown' his 'life's work', relate to the terms of this pact?

DISCUSSION   Affirmation of the urge to action underlying his terms in the pact with Mephistopheles in *Part One* is projected as a guiding principle to inform the lives of future generations. In *Part Two* (act 5, scene 4), Faust expands his focus from his own potential to the social ideal:

> standing upon free soil, a people also free.
> (68)

At this moment, which he ironically supposes to be the ultimate realization of all he could strive for, he says:

> Then to the fleeting moment I could say:
> 'You are so beautiful – can you not stay?'
> (69–70)

Mephistopheles is exultant, convinced that he has won the pact:

> Time wins. The clock stands still.
> (81)

He speaks too soon. Faust's *conditional* statement – 'I could say' – does not confirm that he does say. As David Luke puts it, he 'might say', or, in Barker Fairley's version, 'could almost say'. On the fine line of this distinction, Faust proceeds towards the final intercession of Gretchen, now a penitent in heaven, to the salvation which God in the Prologue in Heaven had anticipated.

Faust dies in the midst of his visions. They are not yet realized for him. Only if they were realized could he address the 'fleeting moment' unconditionally. And only then would Mephistopheles win the pact.

This is no orthodox 'salvation'. Look at the climax in the last words of the play in the Chorus Mysticus in your set text (p.223) and the alternative translations in Anthology II (p.249):

> All that shall pass away
> is but reflection.
> (233–4)

Barker Fairley translates 'reflection' as 'symbolical only', and David Luke as 'a parable'. Reflection, parable, symbol – these words seem like an equivalent to Faust's search for different words to express 'Word' in scene 3. The transitory, the ephemeral, life on earth, is, cannot be more than, some approximation, some image. The final couplet signals the decisive importance of Gretchen, Goethe's 'das ewig Weibliche' (later to appear in Mahler's Eighth Symphony), variously given as 'Woman in all of us' (MacDonald), 'Eternal Womanhood' (David Luke) and 'the eternal in woman' (Barker Fairley).

Ultimately, Faust is redeemed by love and depends for his 'salvation' on the value of his relationship with Gretchen. 'Salvation', so much a part of the traditional Faust story, is a religious concept. In the end, though,

Faust's final justification celebrates his worth as a total human being, a *Mensch*, more than spiritual fulfilment in terms traditionally understood. God in the Prologue sanctioned his 'striving', and this unceasing striving determines his ultimate 'salvation'. He has pushed his potential further and further, reaching beyond himself in an ultimate quest for the good of humanity. His continuing striving is sanctioned in a continuing process. Nothing is finally resolved. There is no full stop to eternal striving.

14   Contribution of the Gretchen story to the play as a whole

In the Gretchen tragedy Goethe has Mephistopheles coming up with something irresistible. Here is the antithesis to Faust's intensely intellectual, non-physical life, a way to tangle him up and lure him into hedonistic worldliness. He's foiled, of course, but not before this innocent Gretchen is led to commit murder time after time.

Let's take a moment to look at what happens to Gretchen. In her 'small neat room' as the title to scene 7 announces, the simple vocabulary reveals an uncomplicated, un-self-conscious character. Yet right from the start all is not quite so innocent. She is bedazzled with the jewellery. Here is a sizeable casket. She hangs the jewels around her neck. And from then on she sees herself in a different light. It is as if she is looking at herself in a metaphorical mirror, seeing a reflection of herself which transforms her (and some stage productions use the mirror prop effectively to underline this). Opening the casket of jewels awakens her sexual desire.

Gretchen is presented as both innocent and not quite so innocent. Off she goes, behind her mother's back, to her neighbour Martha, hardly a woman of impeccable morals. And she is not averse to administering a sleeping draught for her mother while she leaves the door open for Faust.

Goethe has Gretchen using folk-song, a poetic form which characterizes her in natural spontaneity. Goethe did not incorporate actual folk-songs into the play: what he has done is to write lines which are like those of a folk-song. When she is agitated she instinctively draws on communal folk resources, like the narrative of the king of Thule, for reassurance. When she sings as she spins (scene 14), the repeated refrain and repeated rhythm of both voice and spinning-wheel similarly anchor her in her state of distress.

The structure of the Gretchen scenes has a fluidity which provides a fresh sense of immediacy, changing the pace after the more contained nature of each of the preceding scenes of the play. We come into a scene mid-stream, so to speak, into conversations which have begun before the scene begins (scenes 11 and 15, for instance). The scenes are characterized by allusiveness. Information is withheld from the audience, or only imparted indirectly (like Faust's seduction of Gretchen, Gretchen's pregnancy, her mother's death, and her murder of her child). This element of suggestion rather than presentation affects audience perception of Gretchen. There is more to her than we know or see.

Gretchen appears more often than not alone on stage – whether going to bed, spinning, praying, isolated in the cathedral from the intonations of the requiem mass, or, until Faust's arrival, in her prison cell. Let's think more about this. This is a character conceptually confined by community mores. Goethe presents her in comparison or contrast with the institutional securities on which she relies. She refers to her mother, the priest ('the good Father' – 15, 40), local gossip (scene 16), and the judgement of the community ('They're singing songs about me' – 23, 32). They are references to *absent* social voices. Yet in prison, beginning the scene crazed, the lines show how she finds her own voice by the end and is able to pray, despite Mephistopheles' proximity. Earthly authorities have become irrelevant. It is her own choice to refuse to be rescued by Faust. She does not blame him. She loves him to the end.

So this Gretchen not only comes to terms with herself and thus achieves a kind of freedom at the end of *Faust Part One*, but also becomes the intercessor for Faust at the end of *Part Two*. Her power lies in the love which she has awakened in Faust and which becomes ultimately the conduit to his redemption at the end of *Part Two*.

Gretchen has been variously seen as a witch (Schöne, 1993, pp.177–9), a saint (Wittkowski, 1997, p.291), and as the character who steals the show (Mason, 1967, p.207), and the balance between interpretation of her as a sacrifice and as an autonomous being has swung back and forth ever since the play was published. The integration of the Gretchen story is central in dramatic terms in the play. The concern over the extent to which she is a victim and the extent to which she develops her own autonomy is one of the reasons why 'it will always be open season on *Faust*' (MacDonald, 2002, p.15).

15   The scale of the drama in *Faust Part One*

Let's stand back and give some thought now to the monumental scope of the play. We have geographical locations – specific ones such as Auerbach's cellar in Leipzig and less specific ones such as Faust's study, the street or the prison. We have seasonal locations – Easter, for instance. These are the stuff of the everyday recognizable world. On another level, we have the illusion of the theatre: the Prelude on the stage actually puts the theatre on the stage. On yet another level the Prologue in Heaven takes us away from the here and now of this world altogether. And we have a further level in the Walpurgis Night, rampant with witches and warlocks out on their annual rampage. The scale of the drama is immense: it dips in and out of biblical time, medieval time, Goethe's own time, magical time, as well as mythological time. Time is telescoped and foreshortened: we start on the eve of Easter, race through the Walpurgis Night, and come (off the page and unnarrated) to Gretchen's mother's death and Gretchen's pregnancy, childbirth and infanticide (both cited retrospectively in the last scene in the prison cell), so that by implication there are gaps of great stretches of time. Goethe is not restricting himself to any confines of time or space or even genre in the mix between fantasy, realism and myth.

Alongside the expanse of the play in terms of place and time comes the lack of conventional Acts to divide the play. This has given rise to treatment of the work as two dramas – a *Gelehrtentragödie* ('tragedy of the intellectual') and a *Gretchentragödie* ('Gretchen tragedy'), each with a separate momentum. When *Faust Part One* was staged in 1829 for Goethe's eightieth birthday, it was divided into five, six, and (in Weimar) eight acts.

The colossal reach of the play is played out in large-scale scenes which express the communal voice (scene 2, for example) and intimate scenes given to a single voice, like Gretchen's in scenes 7, 14 and 17 and Faust's monologues, like the one which opens scene 1, and the one in scene 3 (261–78). The songs and the dances of the different groups in the Easter walk (scene 2) become a kind of pageant. The presentation of heaven on stage refers back to the medieval conception of the three-deck world – heaven, earth and hell – which was a convention of the morality play. The influence of Shakespeare, hailed as seminal for the *Sturm und Drang* movement because of the power of his expression of nature and the natural, underlines Faust's existential despair and Gretchen's fragile mental state (*Hamlet*), as well as the depiction of the witches (*Macbeth*). And there is all the magic of fairytales in the ride on magic horses, the witch's potion, and the casket of jewels. Part of the impact of the play lies in the combination of genres, in the ironies and alternatives with which they overlay one another.

One example lies in the different opening sequences which we considered in section 5. The Prelude on the stage challenges the illusion with which we suspend belief as we watch a play in the theatre. It places the stage squarely on the stage. Then comes the Prologue in Heaven, complete with God and his archangels, and we switch into conventions which are far from realistic, reminders of the medieval morality play. If we then look at the ordering of these scenes, the placing of heaven within the framework of the preceding Prelude on the stage sets it, arguably, within temporal bounds, eliminating the space between timeless heaven and temporal earth. This ironically displaces the supernatural claims of Heaven.

Within these genres the huge spectrum of Goethe's language takes in *Knittelvers* (scene 1), rhymed verse, free verse and prose (scene 21) in an astonishingly supple use of rhythms. There is abstract philosophical vocabulary (for instance in Faust's first monologue in scene 1) and informal familiarity (even in Mephistopheles' quips to God in the Prologue), while lyrical tenderness between Faust and Gretchen contrasts with rather more earthy ironies between Martha and Mephistopheles in scene 11 and wanton exchanges in the Walpurgis Night. In Gretchen's songs Goethe evokes energies of folk-songs and ballads, and he places her against other idioms in the liturgy of the Cathedral scene.

EXERCISE   We have one play on the stage. The play is dipping into events and narratives which are going on continually, even when our attention is not being directed towards them. Imagine that you are in the audience. Can you think of any examples where we are aware of some action either on- or off-stage which isn't fully revealed? What are the effects of this device?

DISCUSSION   Here are some examples.

- The Easter chorus, off-stage (1), becomes a reminder of the Christian promise of resurrection. The *Dies Irae* from the requiem mass (19) is a reminder of God's wrath. We do not see the singers. Inclusion of these particular aspects of the liturgy become metonyms, symbols in musical terms of salvation and damnation, the stark outcomes to the traditional Faust tale.

- Cameo dramas give a voice to one group after another (2). Three citizens discuss politics and economics, press reports and war. Girls eager to attract the boys enlist the advice of a fortune-teller. In the soldiers' chorus all is talk of conquering the girls. The effect is one of simultaneity, of different representative groups in concerns which typify the ongoing social life of the community.

- A narrative which is not directly revealed is the one about Gretchen's mother. She is a large presence in Gretchen's life but one without a part on stage. Gretchen wishes her there with her at home in scene 7 for reassurance. In scene 8, Mephistopheles is furious that her handover of the jewels to the priest has upstaged him –

    She has a nose for sin.
    (11)

  Widowed, with her son in the army, and with only Gretchen left at home, she is so exacting (11, 30) that Gretchen realizes that she would stand between herself and Faust ('My mother – no', 12, 4).

Only in the whisper in Gretchen's ear in the Cathedral (19, 2) do we learn that she has died from the sleeping-draught (presumably provided by Mephistopheles) handed to Gretchen by Faust (15). Her 'play' runs in parallel to the gathering tensions of Gretchen's life. Her absence on stage encourages us to imagine her rather than see or hear her directly. Because she doesn't appear, her presence becomes hearsay and the influence of hearsay, an agenda of strict morality which exerts a constant pull on Gretchen.

You may have thought of many more instances. There is the story of Martha's husband, Herr Schwertlein, for instance, in scene 9, or the seething orgies of the Walpurgis Night in scene 20. The density of these examples is such that while we are watching or reading the play, other 'plays' amplify the breadth of the drama by bringing in a realization that there is always more going on than we ever see on stage. They all have distinct closures in their own separate ways: they contrast with the open-endedness of the drama as a whole.

The multiple frames of *Faust* do away with the monolithic didacticism of the traditional Faust legend. Goethe may share the enthusiasm of the age for education, but education for him is not a didactic, imposed programme: it is more a matter of discovering the potential within the self, and discovering that the potential is never completed. The emphasis is on inner response, not on external prescription. Going hand in hand with this is the move away from Enlightenment reliance on reason alone to recognition of the value of the sensual and the imagination. For Faust the learning derived from books alone can only ever be the beginning.

16   Enlightenment/Romanticism and *Faust*

Classical order, balance and control which we associate with the Enlightenment on the one hand, and unrestrained creativity and fertility which we associate with Romanticism on the other, are tendencies in all art at all times. During the period in which Goethe wrote *Faust* they gained particular, acute emphasis in tension with one another, as Units 24–25 have shown. Concern with the human condition, with what it means to be a human being, is central throughout the period from the Enlightenment to Romanticism. While Enlightenment literature explores the way in which the individual relates to society, Romanticism focuses on the way in which the individual relates to him or herself. Enlightenment, a particular expression of classicism, is underscored by social consensus. Romanticism celebrates the inner drives of the individual, sometimes in a transitional, intuitive state. Individualism, counter to the Enlightenment ideal of integration, drives Faust – just as it does the Byronic figures which follow in the nineteenth century. Youth, elevated by Romanticism to the condition of the sublime, is given to Faust following his pact with Mephistopheles. But classical elements run alongside Romantic elements in the drama. And *Faust* is a text which resists neat categorization on the Enlightenment/Romanticism axis because it cannot be *contained* by cultural periodization. Just because *Faust* falls into the Romantic period is not enough to define it as a Romantic text.

In *Faust Part One* the figure of Mephistopheles introduces himself to Faust as

> part of the darkness that, though once complete,
> gave birth to light, which fights now to defeat
> its mother, darkness, but is doomed to fall,
> because it's fettered to material forms.
> (3, 119–22)

In this 'tendency to mythologizing personification' (Brown, 1986, p.77), Goethe has Mephistopheles casting himself in terms which we associate with a classical context. He sets Faust in one, too, when he chides him for 'playing at self-pity':

> it's like a vulture, feeding on your mind.
> (3, 302)

The image comes straight from the myth of Prometheus.

Long before the classical context of the second part, the drama has classical bearings. Goethe himself shared in the recent excitement of the discovery of the statue of Zeus of Otricoli (*c.*4 BCE) when he saw it in Rome. He was affected to such an extent that he used it in his rendering of the earth spirit in scene 1 (see Figure 26.10).

Classical and Romantic impulses are not necessarily mutually exclusive. Neither are they exhaustive in their description of any particular text. Goethe's *Faust* may lend itself to identification of Romantic elements. Faust exemplifies the Romantic urge to pursue intensity, rather than accumulation, of experience. The 'two souls' speech expresses Romantic despair, aspiration without resolution. Another aspect of Romanticism, the fascination for madness in the paintings of Goya (see Video 2, band 1), is here in Gretchen's wandering mind and in the dark side of life with which the play opens. Goethe, however, distances himself from the more excessive forms of Romanticism, satirizing the Gothic in the witch's kitchen, and always wary about lack of balance. His comment 'Klassik ist das Gesunde, romantisch das Kranke' – 'Classicism is health, Romanticism is disease' (quoted in Schöne, 1993, p.239) – voices his caution about pathological extremes inherent in Romanticism.

Figure 26.10   Johann Wolfgang von Goethe, Night, Appearance of the Earth Spirit, *1810–12, pencil drawing, 22 x 17.1 cm, Weimarer Klassik/Goethe-Nationalmuseum, Weimar. Photo: donated by Weimarer Klassik/Goethe-Nationalmuseum. 1367 Corpus IV, Nr.224.*

In scene 1 Faust is tormented by doubts:

> All my laborious studies only show
> that Nothing is the most we ever know.
> (10–11)

Everything he learns is not enough: that is the point which he is making. The play is about knowing everything and knowing nothing, about a perpetually questioning mode of being. Emphasis on the possibility of change elevates change to prime status.

Identification of specifically classical or specifically Romantic words and references does not, however, confer any more than partial definition to the play. The play is a key work in Goethe's oeuvre. And Goethe's own particular position in relation to the shifts of aesthetics is important to understand. Romanticism doesn't succeed Enlightenment directly in German literature in any straightforward, sequential process. The cultural shifts between Enlightenment and Romanticism are neither homogeneous nor equivalent in all the arts in every country in Europe at the end of the eighteenth and beginning of the nineteenth centuries. The *Sturm und Drang* passions of the 1770s broke decisively with Enlightenment ideas in Germany, and the *Sturm und Drang* decade in its turn was superseded by the dominance of what is known as the period of Weimar classicism. Goethe was a leader of both these movements, while concurrently (as you learned in Units 24–25) the brothers Schlegel and others were initiating the Romantic programme in Jena and in Heidelberg. In other words, exponents of Romanticism and classicism were producing work simultaneously and in close proximity (Jena and Weimar are only a few miles apart), all aware of each other. While the Schlegel brothers were consciously promoting a Romantic manifesto, Goethe, with 'his sovereign detachment from the ideologies with which his age teemed' (Boyle and Guthrie, 2002, p.14), remained independent of any deliberate programme of ideas. He didn't subscribe to the mechanisms of eighteenth-century Enlightenment any more than to the programmes of idealism which characterized German Romanticism.

In German bibliographical classifications the period between 1770 and 1830 is also known as the 'Age of Goethe'. Goethe, and his *Faust* in particular, resist historicist labelling. Faust stands for an archetype which exemplifies both Romantic aspiration and the challenges of Enlightenment knowledge, without relying on either. Labels become invidious. No easy formula will do. The Prologue and the ending to *Part Two* assure us that life is not irrational, that order is possible. God and nature, extolled by those archangels, are immutable in harmony, but in a harmony driven by an active principle. The play embraces above all a new *dynamic* approach to life and knowledge. The process of becoming is what matters. The increasing emphasis on evolutionary explanation which you met in your studies of Mungo Park finds another expression in *Faust* in the discovery of more and more potential through striving towards self-realization.

Faust's predicament resists conclusive interpretation. The play carries the conviction that the greatness of humanity lies in its struggle rather than in its achievement, where knowledge may offer all its explanations, but what needs to be faced is still mysterious and open, always evolving. Goethe's point is that continual striving is the very point of human existence.

17   In summary

Study of Goethe's *Faust Part One* has pointed you to consider:

- the stature of Goethe in world literature;
- the relation of Goethe's *Faust* to its mythological and historical context;
- the scope of Goethe's play with its extended genesis, its radical reworking of premises and conceptions of the human condition;
- the scale of the literary and dramatic qualities of the drama;
- the significance of the play as a work both of its age and beyond its age.

We turn now to consider the conception and reception of Goethe's *Faust*.

18   The conception and reception of Goethe's *Faust*

Introduction

Two questions frame this final section of our discussion of Goethe's *Faust*. First, how did Goethe himself conceive of *Faust?* In other words, what were his ambitions and concerns for the play? This involves examining Goethe's thoughts on literature in general and on *Faust* in particular, as expressed in his literary criticism, letters and conversations. Second, how was *Faust* received by Goethe's contemporaries? Like many acclaimed works of literature, *Faust* attracted passionate and widely divergent responses. From a safe distance two centuries hence, it is easy to forget these often ill-tempered critical disagreements, but they deserve our attention as they attest to the excitement Goethe's play generated. Further, Goethe's own thoughts on the conception of the play, and the controversial early reception history of *Faust*, illuminate the relationship between *Faust* and the intellectual currents of the day, notably those of the Enlightenment, Romanticism and German cultural nationalism.

Goethe's *Faust* mutated during the 60 years he wrestled with the play. The conception and reception of *Faust* should therefore be gauged in relation to the four main periods he worked on it. My principal focus is on the conception and reception of our set text, *Faust Part One*, but as there is much of interest in Goethe's writings relating to the other three versions, and in their respective reception histories, I discuss them all in chronological sequence below.

Urfaust (*c.*1776)

Conception

The *Urfaust* or 'original *Faust*' was planned when Goethe was in his early twenties and living first in Leipzig, then in Strasbourg and Frankfurt. Goethe sporadically wrote up sections of the play between 1772 and 1775, and read extracts to his immediate circle of friends. These readings were the play's only exposure. Luise von Göckhausen transcribed this version in 1776, but her transcription was only discovered much later, and published for the first time in 1887. Goethe's conception of literature at this early stage of his career was influenced both by the proto-Romantic *Sturm und Drang* movement, which elevated the individual artist-genius to the status of supreme authority, and the ideas of Johann Gottfried Herder, who had arrived in Strasbourg shortly before Goethe. Herder was angered by the political fragmentation of the German-speaking peoples of Europe into many small kingdoms and states, and in response undertook a programme for promoting the German language and German culture. The historian David Blackbourn emphasizes Herder's originality, and his powerful influence not only on Goethe's generation but also on subsequent writers:

> He and other eighteenth-century writers discovered (or invented) the German 'Volk' and the genius of local culture some time before the Grimm brothers and the Romantic poets.

(Blackbourn, 1997, p.37)

Herder's influence on Goethe is evident in two short essays of the 1770s. In 'On German architecture' (1772), Goethe first considers contemporary Italian architecture, and asks, 'Did not the genius of the ancients rise from the grave and fetter your own, Italian?' (quoted in Gearey, 1986, p.4), and then admits that his own architectural tastes had been 'fettered' by the 'genius of the ancients'. Goethe never doubted that classical architecture was a supreme achievement and appropriate for the ancient Greeks and Romans, but he objected to its uncritical elevation in his own eighteenth-century German world. He concedes that in judging Gothic architecture by classical standards he had applied the wrong criteria and inevitably found it wanting:

> Under the heading 'Gothic' ... I listed all the synonymous
> misconceptions that I had ever encountered, such as indefinite,
> disorganized, unnatural, patched-together, tacked-on, overladen.
>
> (Quoted in Gearey, 1986, p.5)

In Strasbourg, however, Goethe experienced a dramatic conversion, as
the Gothic splendour of Strasbourg Cathedral (see Figure 26.11)
destroyed his former prejudices. His enthusiasm was based in part on an
appreciation of the cathedral's formal qualities – '[as] in the works of
eternal nature, down to the smallest fibre, all is form, all serves the
whole' (quoted in Gearey, 1986, p.6) – and in part on the fact that it
exemplified a distinctively German architecture. He addresses Erwin von
Steinbach (1244–1318), the master-mason of the cathedral, in exultant
terms:

> And should I not grow angry, divine Erwin, when a German
> scholar, on the word of envious neighbours, fails to see his
> advantage and belittles your work with the misunderstood term
> Gothic, when he ought to thank God for being able to proclaim:
> This is German architecture! Our architecture! The Italians cannot
> boast one of their own, much less the French.
>
> (Quoted in Gearey, 1986, p.8)

Goethe then addresses his German-speaking readers, and instructs them
to embrace the cathedral as part of their heritage:

> Approach it and experience the profoundest feeling of truth and
> beauty of proportion, sprung from the strong, rough-hewn
> German soul.
>
> (Quoted in Gearey, 1986, p.9)

Goethe's essay 'Shakespeare: a tribute' (1771) emphasizes similar
concerns, notably a resistance to the uncritical elevation of classical
criteria, and a keen appreciation of *modern* men of 'genius', in the fields
of architecture (von Steinbach) and literature (Shakespeare) alike. In
much the same way as he accuses contemporary Italian architects of
being fettered by 'the genius of the ancients', Goethe turns on French
playwrights and accuses them of a similar slavish obeisance to classical
Greece:

> Little Frenchman, why are you wearing Greek armor? It is much
> too big and heavy for you.
>
> (Quoted in Gearey, 1986, p.164)

By contrast, Shakespeare refused to be cowed by the rules of the
ancients, and produced a drama true to nature. Goethe repeatedly
describes the impact of Shakespeare's drama upon him as literally a
happy shock of 'enlightenment'. He writes:

Figure 26.11   John Carter, West Front of Strasbourg Cathedral, *Victoria and Albert Museum, London. Photo: Bridgeman Art Library.*

> When I had finished reading the first [Shakespeare] drama, I stood there like a man blind from birth whom a magic wand has all at once given light ...

Further:

> Now when [I read Shakespeare], I saw what harm the keepers of the rules had done me in their dungeon ...

and:

> [Our] corrupted taste, however, so beclouds our vision that we almost require a new Creation to escape the Darkness.
>
> (Quoted in Gearey, 1986, pp.163–5)

He concludes his tribute with a rallying cry to German poets, and a final insult to the guardians of classical standards of taste:

> To work, gentlemen! Take your trumpets and drive forth those noble souls from the Elysium of so-called good taste, where, drowsy in monotonous twilight, they live, yet do not live.
>
> (Quoted in Gearey, 1986, p.165)

In these passages, Goethe presents the renunciation of the classical and the embrace of the modern in the form of Shakespeare as a movement from darkness to light.

These two essays suggest that Goethe's creative ambitions in writing *Urfaust* were influenced by at least two important considerations. First, Goethe followed Herder's project by trying to produce a literary equivalent of Strasbourg Cathedral, a work of distinctively *German* character that refused to bow down to the restrictive aesthetic criteria of classical Greece. Second, he assumed, or, more accurately, was assigned by his peers, the role of universal 'man of genius', a successor to Shakespeare, who would by his work be both true to nature and serve what he understood to be the cause of Enlightenment.

Reception

As Goethe's *Urfaust* was never completed or published, and its only audience was Goethe's immediate circle, there is no reception history to discuss. However, it is worth mentioning Goethe's affectionate memories of his first sympathetic audience, who 'willingly listened when I read my finished or unfinished works aloud [and] encouraged me' (quoted in Hamlin, 2001, pp.514–15). Also, subsequent generations have praised its poetic and dramatic power, with the twentieth-century playwright Bertolt Brecht an especially keen fan of the *Urfaust*. For most critics, however, the incompleteness of the *Urfaust* has been a substantial obstacle to enjoying it, and speculation as to why Goethe failed to finish the work has proliferated. The recent Goethe biographer Nicholas Boyle, for example, has argued that in the 1770s Goethe could dramatize but not resolve the opposition between Faust, 'the "revolutionary autonomous genius" of the *Sturm und Drang* tradition, and Gretchen, the representative of an organic German national "social and religious network" of the kind admired by Herder' (Boyle, 1992, p.225).

Faust: A Fragment (1790)

Conception

In 1788, at the age of 40, Goethe started work on *Faust: A Fragment* while he was in Rome, then completed it a year later in Weimar, and published it in his *Collected Works* of 1790. Notwithstanding his fresh enthusiasm for *Faust*, Goethe once again foundered after making swift initial progress, and submitted his work-in-progress for publication as a fragment. In his *Italian Journey*, Goethe emphasizes his strong sense of continuity from his efforts on *Faust* in the 1770s to the *Fragment* 15 years later.

Reception

Word had spread in literary circles about the power of Goethe's *Urfaust*, and much anticipation therefore accompanied the publication of the *Fragment* in 1790. Initial reactions, however, were mixed. The long wait for its appearance had raised expectations since the 1770s, but the inconclusive nature of the *Fragment* meant for many that those expectations were simply not met. Goethe's associates in the literary world were more generous, with Schiller likening the *Fragment* to 'the torso of Hercules' and Henrik Steffens (1773–1845), the leading Norwegian Romantic, declaring euphorically that 'this work captivated me in a way hitherto unknown' (quoted in Hamlin, 2001, p.551). With an equal measure of hyperbole but more critical insight, Schelling also applauded the *Fragment*, and identified two qualities in the work that have fascinated critics ever since. First, Schelling reads the *Fragment* as a creative reflection on the limits of the Enlightenment: '[the *Fragment*'s] initial direction is to satisfy ecstatically the insatiable desire beyond the aims and limits of reason' (quoted in Hamlin, 2001, p.555). Schelling even suggests that what the character Faust teaches is that 'an initiation into the basic principles of devilry [is] the appropriate basis for an enlightened perspective on the world' (quoted in Hamlin, 2001, p.556). Second, in acclaiming the originality of Goethe's *Faust*, Schelling emphasizes its distinctively German character:

> The kind of fate [it demonstrates] is unique and would deserve to be called a new discovery, were it not to an extent already present in the German temper and thus represented in its essential form in the mythological person of Faust.

> (Quoted in Hamlin, 2001, p.556)

Finally, present-day critics who have had access to both the *Urfaust* and the *Fragment* have noted that the latter displays a more self-conscious formal structure, a change that was prompted by Goethe's gradual distancing of himself from the anti-classicism of Herder and his circle.

Faust Part One (1808)

Conception

In 1797, at the age of 48, Goethe returned to *Faust* at the repeated prompting of Schiller, writing the Dedication and the Walpurgis Night's Dream in that year, the Prison scene and Prelude on the stage in 1798, and the Prologue in Heaven in 1799. In 1800–1, Goethe continued working on scenes for the first half of *Faust Part One*, and also began writing scenes for *Part Two*. He then halted all work on the play until 1806, when he prepared the final manuscript of *Part One* for publication in the 1808 edition of his *Collected Works*.

Goethe's writings of this period convey a sense of the complex mix of often-contradictory ideas that animated German intellectual life. In his 1795 essay 'Response to a literary rabble-rouser', Goethe continues to attack the deference which contemporary German critics accord to the classicist aesthetic standards of both ancient Greece and Rome and contemporary France. Goethe explains this deference in relation to the weaknesses of German national culture, and sees its cure in the contemporary impulse to Enlightenment. Insisting that critics should look at 'the individual circumstances which formed our German writers ... to find criteria by which to judge them' (quoted in Gearey, 1986, p.190), he identifies the absence of a unified German national culture as a major obstacle:

> Which [respected German writer] would not admit with some regret that in the beginning of his career he often pined for an opportunity to place the unique gifts of his individual genius at the service of a common national culture which unfortunately did not exist? To be sure, the education of the higher classes through foreign customs and literature was quite beneficial, but it also prevented the Germans from developing sooner as Germans.

(Quoted in Gearey, 1986, p.191)

According to Goethe, writers of an earlier generation (like himself) had struggled to resist 'foreign customs and literature' and had tried to develop an indigenous literary tradition. The cultural landscape for the young German writer of the 1790s as a result is more accommodating:

> [The] young man who enters in now enjoys a much larger and better defined circle than the writer of earlier times, who only after groping his way in the faint light of dawn was able to

> expand the circle, and that only as it were by chance. The would-be critic who wants to help us find the way with his feeble torch arrives too late – daybreak is here, and we will not close the shutters again.

(Quoted in Gearey, 1986, p.192)

As in his essays of the 1770s, here too Goethe uses a metaphorical transition from darkness to light to characterize the shift from the cultural forms of classicism to the forms he characterizes as 'enlightened', 'modern' and 'national'.

A rather different combination of ideas is to be found two years later in the pages of Goethe's correspondence with Schiller, as the two poets discuss their work, and in particular Goethe's progress on *Faust*. In a letter dated 23 June 1797, Schiller observed sympathetically that 'the demands on *Faust* are both philosophical and poetical, and you may turn in whichever direction you please, the nature of the subject will force you to treat it philosophically, and the imagination will have to accommodate itself to a rational idea' (quoted in Hamlin, 2001, p.518). Goethe accepted the force of Schiller's comments, and on 27 June replied:

> Your remarks about *Faust* ... coincide very well with my own projects and plans, only that I shall make this barbarous composition accommodate itself more to my wishes, and I propose rather to touch upon than to fulfil the highest demands. In this manner, reason and common sense will probably beat each other about like two boxers, and afterwards sit down amicably together.

(Quoted in Hamlin, 2001, p.519)

Two key shifts are embedded in this exchange. The first is Schiller's reference to 'imagination', still at this stage to be subordinated to 'reason', but one of the central preoccupations of Romanticism, and a term of reference of increasing importance in Goethe's own work. The second is captured in Goethe's somewhat scornful reference to his earlier version of *Faust* as a 'barbarous composition' that needs to 'accommodate itself more to my wishes'. In the second half of the 1790s, Goethe expressed a renewed sympathy with classicist aesthetic values, and recoiled from his unqualified enthusiasm of the 1770s for – as he now saw it – a limited German culture. Indeed, by the 1790s, Goethe and Schiller had become the two best-known representatives of Weimar classicism. However, rather than simply dispense with his earlier concerns, Goethe sought in *Faust Part One* to integrate or synthesize the opposed elements: philosophy and poetry; the classical and the Romantic; Enlightenment reason and Romantic imagination; and reason (derived from high culture) and common sense (derived from popular culture).

Reception

It is important to register the immense status Goethe enjoyed at this stage of his career, to the extent that responses to the work of 'Goethe the poet' were coloured by the judgements (mostly generous) of 'Goethe the man'. The satirical description of meeting Goethe by the poet Heinrich Heine (1797–1856) captures nicely the adulation of Goethe by his contemporaries:

> I am convinced that he was a god ... Some claim to have detected a trace of cold arrogance about his mouth; but this is also a feature proper to the eternal deities, indeed to the father of the gods, great Jupiter, with whom I have already compared Goethe. Truly, when I visited him in Weimar and stood before him, I glanced involuntarily to one side, half expecting to see beside him the eagle with the thunderbolts in its beak. I was on the point of addressing him in Greek; but as I found that he understood German, I addressed him in that language.
>
> (Quoted in Williams, 1998, p.280)

Goethe's god-like stature did not protect his *Faust Part One* from critical attack, although in German-speaking Europe at least, the balance of the early criticism was favourable. Of those hostile to *Faust*, the most prominent critic was the Church, with furious objections to the play's irreverent content from Catholic and Protestant authorities alike. Other critical voices included the Enlightenment thinker Friedrich Nicolai (1733–1811), who objected to the irrational excesses of the play; the younger generation of German radicals including Ludwig Borne (1786–1837), who identified Goethe and his play with the reactionary political establishment; and Wolfgang Menzel (1798–1873), who was particularly appalled that the character of Faust went unpunished for destroying Gretchen. More enduring than these negative judgements, however, have been the fulsome accolades for *Faust Part One* by many of Goethe's more influential contemporaries. Schelling, Georg Wilhelm Friedrich Hegel, Mme de Staël and Christoph Martin Wieland were but a few of the eminent figures who declared the play a work of genius.

The reception of *Faust Part One* beyond German-speaking Europe was also controversial, and we turn now to consider how it was received in England. Drama in England at the time was in a particularly moribund state, so new plays from Europe were eagerly anticipated.

EXERCISE   Read the following early reviews in English of *Faust Part One*, the first by William Taylor (1765–1836) in the *Monthly Review* of 1810, and the second by Thomas Carlyle (1795–1881) in the *Edinburgh Review* of 1822. Identify what each of the critics likes and dislikes about the work.

1   William Taylor:

> [*Faust* is] an uncouth though fanciful mixture of farce and
> tragedy, of profaneness and morality, of vulgarity and beauty, of
> obscenity and feeling ... Who can refrain from grief on receiving
> such trash from the Goethe who in his *Iphigenie in Tauris*
> approached nearest of all the moderns to becoming a rival of
> Sophocles? ... [The Walpurgis Night scene] of enchantment is
> described with a force of imagination and a truth of psychology
> which aspire to vie with Shakespeare ... On the whole the
> absurdities of the piece are so numerous, the obscenities are so
> frequent, the profaneness is so gross, and the beauties are so
> adapted to German relish, that we cannot conscientiously
> recommend its importation and still less the translation of it to
> our English students of German literature.

> (Quoted in Hauhart, 1966, pp.25–6)

2   Thomas Carlyle:

> [*Faust* is] undoubtedly one of the most singular [works] that have
> ever appeared in Europe. We scarcely know under what class to
> arrange it, or how to mark out its rank in the scale of literary
> dignity. As a mere drama, its faults are many; and its beauties,
> though of a high order, are not of the highest. There is not plot
> sufficient to create dramatic interest; and though many scenes are
> of great power, and many situations of high tragical effect, they
> hang too loosely together to constitute a perfect work of this
> class. Perhaps the most striking peculiarity of the whole
> performance is the wonderful versatility of talent which it
> implies. To group together the wicked scornful malignity of
> Mephistopheles with the pastoral innocence of Margaret, the
> chaotic gaiety of the Brocken, and the impetuous enthusiasm of
> Faust, was a task few could have meditated, and none but
> Goethe could have accomplished. It presupposes a union of
> poetical and philosophical powers, such as have rarely met
> together in the history of the mind.

> (Quoted in Hamlin, 2001, p.562)

DISCUSSION   1   What Taylor likes about *Faust* can be covered rather swiftly! His only
words of praise are for the Walpurgis Night scene, which he
commends for its Shakespearean-style imagination. The list of what
he dislikes about the work is substantially longer: it fails to match the
classical standards set by Sophocles and approached by Goethe
himself in *Iphigenia in Tauris*; it combines dramatic elements best
kept separate – farce and tragedy, beauty and vulgarity, profanity and
morality, and obscenity and feeling; it abounds with absurdities and
obscenities; and its positive qualities are peculiarly, indeed uniquely,
German. Taylor's response to *Faust* was an extreme one, but it was

not entirely untypical. Even writers sympathetic to Goethe (such as Coleridge) were hesitant in acclaiming *Faust*, as they complained of its incoherence, its incompleteness, and the lack of a dramatically satisfactory tragic catastrophe. Indeed, Coleridge much preferred Schiller's plays *The Robbers* and *Wallenstein*, and translated the latter into English in 1800, with disastrous financial consequences for himself and his publisher (see Ashton, 1980, p.5).

2   Carlyle is also critical of certain aspects of *Faust*. He argues that the plot lacks dramatic interest, and that the structure of the whole work is too loose. However, Carlyle embraces the very qualities in *Faust* that Taylor dislikes. He is impressed with the fact that *Faust* exceeds existing generic categories, and confounds critical efforts to allocate it a specific class of literary work. Further, the mix of dramatic elements that so annoy Taylor appear as great strengths to Carlyle, as he warmly applauds Goethe's ability to combine such different elements and qualities. He is particularly impressed with Goethe's combination of the philosophical and the poetical in one creative work. Carlyle's view of *Faust* was the one that gradually gained wide acceptance in the nineteenth century, both in Germany and in other parts of Europe, although Carlyle's own enthusiasm for *Faust Part One* moderated in his later years, and he declared a strong preference for *Faust Part Two*: '*Faust* is intrinsically but a small poem ... Of the two I find considerably more meaning in the Second Part' (quoted in Hauhart, 1966, pp.61–2). As in German-speaking Europe, in England too, praise for Goethe's *Faust Part One* from figures such as Lord Byron, Percy Bysshe Shelley and Sir Walter Scott gradually prevailed, although the dissemination of the play in England was hampered by the absence of an accurate translation.

Faust Part Two (1832)

Conception

In 1816, Goethe had worked out a plan for *Part Two*, but he only started reworking the early drafts of it from March 1825 to June 1826 when he was 76 years old. Goethe completed and published the *Helena* fragment from *Part Two* in the 1827 edition of his *Collected Works*. From the spring of 1826 to the summer of 1827, Goethe completed five further scenes of *Part Two*, and then from the latter half of 1829 to July 1831, he wrote the remaining scenes. On 29 August 1829, there was the first ever performance of *Faust Part One* in Weimar to celebrate Goethe's eightieth birthday. The final version of *Part Two* appeared shortly after his death in 1832 in his *Posthumous Works*. Goethe attempted in *Faust Part Two* both to resolve the creative challenges set up in *Part One*, and also to give dramatic expression to certain new concerns, as the criticism of his final years reveals.

EXERCISE   The four extracts below are taken from Goethe's writings of the 1820s. Read them and then answer the following questions:

1   What are Goethe's views on literature in the 1820s?

2   How do they differ from his views on literature in the 1770s?

Extract 1: 'Conversations with Eckermann' (July 1827):

> 'I wonder', said Goethe, laughing, 'what the German critics will say [of *Faust Part Two*]? Will they have freedom and boldness to get over this? Understanding will be attempted in the manner of the French; they will not consider that the imagination has its own laws, to which the understanding cannot and should not penetrate. If imagination did not originate things that must ever be problems to the understanding, there would be but little for the imagination to do.'
>
> (Quoted in Hamlin, 2001, p.536)

Extract 2: 'Conversations with Eckermann' (September 1827):

> 'It is high time that the vehement opposition of Classicists and Romantics be resolved. The essential thing is that we develop our minds; from what point we do so would be insignificant, were it not for the danger of being misled by false models. We are grateful to richer and purer insights into Greek and Roman literature for liberating us from monastic barbarism during the fifteenth and sixteenth centuries. From such a lofty vantage point can we not learn to appreciate everything in its true physical and aesthetic worth, both what is ancient and what is modern?'
>
> (Quoted in Hamlin, 2001, p.537)

Extract 3: 'On World Literature' (1827):

> National literature is no longer of importance; it is the time for world literature, and all must aid in bringing it about. Everywhere we read and hear about the progress of the human race, of good prospects for the future regarding relations among nations and human beings. Whatever the situation may be in this respect ... I wish nonetheless to point out to my friends that I am convinced that a world literature is beginning to develop, in which an honourable role is reserved for us Germans.
>
> (Quoted in Gearey, 1986, pp.224–5)

Extract 4: 'On Carlyle's *German Romance*' (1828):

> It is evident that the best poets and writers of all nations have for some time been concentrating their efforts on universal human concerns. In every specific literary mode, whether its content is historical, mythological, mystical or fictional, we increasingly see a writer's national and individual characteristics illuminated from within by these universal concerns.

(Quoted in Gearey, 1986, p.207)

DISCUSSION

1   There are three central elements to Goethe's views on literature in the 1820s. The first is that he proclaims the priority of the creative imagination over critical understanding. Goethe thus repeats one of the fundamental assumptions of Romanticism; indeed his declaration in extract 1 that the 'imagination has its own laws' might well be read as an accurate epigram for Romantic ideology. Second, as regards the major cultural debates of the decade – between classicism and Romanticism, or the ancients and the moderns – Goethe refuses to take sides, and argues that an independent effort to 'develop our minds' (extract 2) should take precedence over giving exclusive allegiance to either position. Third, Goethe promotes the emergence of a world literature that transcends the limits imposed by national literatures. Convinced that poets of all nations are concerned with matters of universal relevance, Goethe experiences the critical demands made by the custodians of national literary traditions as restrictive and parochial.

2   There are both continuities and changes in Goethe's views on literature from the 1770s to the late 1820s. The most obvious continuity is Goethe's sustained faith from 1770 to 1827–8 in the power of the imagination. However, it is worth noting that whereas in the 1770s Goethe's writings are couched in the terms of 'Enlightenment' and 'reason', with 'imagination' less prominent, in the 1820s the term 'imagination' itself enjoys centre-stage. The two main differences in Goethe's views on literature from the 1770s to the 1820s derive from his changed attitude towards German culture. In the 1770s, under the influence of Herder, Goethe expressed uncompromising hostility towards the dominant forms of classicism and dedicated his efforts to building a German national literature. By the 1820s, this attitude has shifted in two important respects. First, rather than trying to elevate modern German culture at the expense of the classical, Goethe promotes the equal appreciation of 'what is ancient and what is modern'. Second, the aspiration of the 1770s to nurture a German national literature is replaced by the ambition to contribute to the emergence of a world literature. It is true that for Goethe Germans are given 'an honourable role' in this enterprise, but the shift from 'nation' to 'world' as the organizing principle for literary production is still a major shift.

Reception

Initial responses to *Faust Part Two* were a mixture of hostility and bafflement, with even loyal supporters of Goethe and of the earlier versions of *Faust* expressing reservations. As with *Faust Part One*, Christian and Enlightenment critics also complained about Goethe's irreligious and irrational excesses in *Part Two*. Two examples of the latter kind of criticism capture the spirit of these negative responses. F.T. Vischer (1807–87), a great enthusiast of *Part One*, wrote a satire of *Faust* in which Faust spends time in purgatory where his penance is to explain Goethe's *Part Two* (Williams, 1987, p.50). Another fan of *Part One*, the English critic Abraham Hayward (1803–84), complained:

> We are wholly at a loss to conceive how the pleasure of draining bogs, or even of contending eternally for existence with the sea, could be of so exalted a nature ... indeed Faust had only to be born a Dutchman to enjoy this last pleasure from the first.

> (Quoted in Hauhart, 1966, p.44)

By the end of the 1830s, however, more generous reviews of *Part Two* began to appear in German, with warm praise for the poetic language and the extravagant set pieces. Although there were still critics who remained unconvinced by the work, by the 1870s both *Part One* and *Part Two* had been absorbed into the official canon of German literature, with severely edited versions set for compulsory study in the German education system. Arguments about Goethe's *Faust Part Two* continue, but there is a growing consensus that Goethe's elaborate imaginings here have a particular resonance for the present. Marshall Berman is one such critic, who concludes his sympathetic discussion as follows:

> [*Faust*] is also a challenge – to our own world even more than to Goethe's own – to imagine and create new modes of modernity, in which man will not exist for the sake of development, but development for the sake of man. Faust's unfinished construction site is the vibrant but shaky ground on which we must all stake out and build up our lives.

> (1988, p.86)

For Berman, Goethe's fascination with the rapid modernization of Germany after 1806 is expressed in the action of *Faust Part Two*, and because of Goethe's great poetic skill, *Part Two* precisely anticipates the subsequent global expansion of industrial capitalism. The contrast between Hayward's nineteenth-century scorn for Faust's building projects and Berman's twentieth-century sympathy for what they represent could not be more marked.

Conclusion

In a conversation with Eckermann on 13 February 1831, Goethe expresses hope for the fate of his *Faust*:

> [T]he only matter of importance is, that the single masses should be clear and significant, while the whole always remains incommensurable – and even on that account, like an unsolved problem, constantly lures mankind to study it again and again.

> (Quoted in Hamlin, 2001, p.544)

Goethe's hopes have been substantially fulfilled, as generations of critics during his lifetime and subsequently have been lured to study the play again and again. In line with Goethe's hopes, there has been general agreement that 'single masses' of the work are 'clear and significant', but there have also been frequent doubts expressed about the qualities of the work as 'incommensurable whole'.

The 'unsolved problem' of *Faust* is in fact part of a larger difficulty critics have had in trying to locate Goethe in relation to the main intellectual currents of his age: the Enlightenment, German cultural nationalism and Romanticism. Quite simply, *Faust* does not fit neatly into these broad movements, and indeed Goethe actively worked to resist being thus classified. However, although *Faust* in many respects exceeds these existing categories, the play has nonetheless been interpreted more than any other work as a distillation of the dominant issues in Germany and even Europe in the period 1780–1830. In these two units, we have therefore taken up Goethe's challenge to study *Faust,* thus joining a long tradition of readers who have grappled with the 'incommensurable' nature of the play.

References

Ashton, R. (1980) *Four English Writers and the Reception of German Thought, 1800–1860*, Cambridge, Cambridge University Press.

Beddow, M. (1986) *Goethe: Faust I* (Critical Guides to German Texts series), London, Grant and Cutler.

Berman, M. (1988) *All That Is Solid Melts Into Air*, Harmondsworth, Penguin.

Blackbourn, D. (1997) *The Fontana History of Germany 1780–1918: The Long Nineteenth Century*, London, Fontana.

Boyle, N. (1992) *Goethe: The Poet and the Age, Volume 1: The Poetry of Desire*, Oxford, Oxford University Press.

Boyle, N. and Guthrie, J. (eds) (2002) *Goethe and the English-Speaking World: Essays from the Cambridge Symposium for his 250th Anniversary*, London, Camden House.

Brown, J.K. (1986) *Goethe's Faust: The German Tragedy*, Ithaca and London, Cornell University Press.

Gearey, J. (ed.) (1986) *Goethe: The Collected Works, Volume 3: Essays on Art and Literature*, Princeton, Princeton University Press.

Hamburger, M. (1984) 'A perilous multiplicity', in E. Wilkinson (ed.) *Goethe Revisited*, London, John Calder and New York, Riverrun Press, pp.11–30.

Hamlin, C. (ed.) (2001) *Faust: A Tragedy*, 2nd edn, trans. W. Arndt, New York, Norton and Co.

Hauhart, W.F. (1966) *The Reception of Goethe's 'Faust' in England in the First Half of the Nineteenth Century*, New York, AMS Press.

Herzfeld, M. von and Melvil Sym, C. (ed. and trans.) (1957) *Goethe: Selected Letters*, Edinburgh, Edinburgh University Press.

MacDonald, R.D. (2002) *Goethe: Faust Parts One and Two*, London, Oberon Books.

Mason, E.C. (1967) *Goethe's 'Faust': Its Genesis and Import*, Berkeley, University of California Press.

Möbus, Frank, Möbus, Friedericke and Unverfehrt, G. (eds) (1995) *'Faust': Annäherung an einen Mythos*, Göttingen, Wallstein Verlag.

Muecke, D.C. (1970) *Irony* (The Critical Idiom series), London, Methuen and Co.

Schöne, A. (ed.) (1993) *Goethe: Faust Kommentare*, Frankfurt-am-Main.

Staël, A.L.G. de (1813) *Germany, Volume 2: On Literature and the Arts*, London, John Murray.

Wilkinson, E. and Willoughby, L.A. (1970) *Goethe: Poet and Thinker*, London, Edward Arnold.

Williams, J.R. (1987) *Goethe's 'Faust'*, London, Allen and Unwin.

Williams, J.R. (1998) *The Life of Goethe*, Oxford, Blackwell.

Wittkowski, W. (1997) 'Gretchen, Gretchen-Interpretation und neuer Hexenhaß', in *Kritische Fragen an die Tradition*, Stuttgart, Verlag Hans-Dieter Heinz, pp.287–309.

Further reading

Atkins, S. (1973) 'Motif in literature: the Faust theme', in P.P. Weiner (ed.) *Dictionary of the History of Ideas: Studies of Selected Pivotal Ideas*, vol.3, New York, Charles Scribner's Sons.

Boyle, N. (1991) *Goethe: The Poet and the Age, Volume 2: Revolution and Renunciation (1790–1803)*, Oxford, Clarendon Press.

Gearey, J. (1981) *Goethe's 'Faust': The Making of 'Part One'*, Yale University Press.

Hamlin, C. (ed.) (2001) *'Faust' by J.W. Goethe*, 2nd edn, trans. W. Arndt, New York, W.W. Norton.

Lamport, F.J. (1990) *German Classical Drama: Theatre, Humanity and Nation 1750–1870*, Cambridge, Cambridge University Press.

Sagarra, E. and Skrine, P. (1997) *A Companion to German Literature: From 1500 to the Present*, Oxford, Blackwell.

Watt, I. (1996) *Myths of Modern Individualism: Faust, Don Quixote, Don Juan, Robinson Crusoe*, Cambridge, Cambridge University Press.

Unit 28
Schubert's Lieder: settings of Goethe's poems

Prepared for the course team by Robert Philip

Contents

Study components

Weeks of study	Supplementary material	Audio-visual	Anthologies and set books
1	AV Notes Illustrations Book	Audio 6 Audio 7	Anthology II

Objectives

By the end of your work on Unit 28, you should:

- have learned about Schubert's place as a composer in early nineteenth-century Vienna;
- have learned about the place of Schubert in the history of German song and the development of Romanticism;
- be able to follow the words of songs by Schubert while listening to a recording, using parallel German and English texts;
- be able to comment on the relationship between words and music in Schubert's song settings.

1   Introduction

After studying the grand sweep of Goethe's most ambitious drama, *Faust*, we are going to spend this unit focusing on a form at the opposite extreme in scale: short poems in German set to music by Franz Schubert (1797–1828) for a single voice with piano, a genre known as 'Lieder' (the German for 'songs'). These are miniatures, but in Schubert's hands they become miniatures of an exceptionally concentrated kind. Their characteristic distillation of the emotional essence of a poem illustrates Romanticism at its most intimate. Schubert's Lieder, once they became widely known, influenced succeeding generations of songwriters through to the present day.

A selection of Schubert's settings of Goethe's poems is discussed in this unit, and recordings of all of them are provided on Audio 7, tracks 5 to 15. Details of the recordings are listed in the AV Notes corresponding to this unit. The poems, in German with parallel translations into English, are in Anthology II (pp.251–8) and the music scores of four of the song settings are in the Illustrations Book (Plates 28.3–28.6). You are not expected to be able to read the music, but even if you are not very familiar with musical notation, you may well find the scores useful in identifying what is happening in the songs. Plates 28.1 and 28.2 in the Illustrations Book also relate to this unit.

EXERCISE   Before you read on, play one or two of the songs on Audio 7, if you have not already done so, following the parallel text provided in Anthology II. It doesn't matter which ones you listen to: just get an initial impression of what sort of material this is.

---

2   Schubert and Vienna

If Goethe is regarded as the greatest German poet of his time, Franz Schubert (see Figure 28.1) is generally accepted as the greatest songwriter of the period. But their careers and experience could not have been more different. Unlike Goethe, who lived into his eighties, Schubert died at the age of 31. Goethe's writing career extended from the 1770s, when Enlightenment writing was at its height, to his death in 1832, by which time Romanticism was in full flood. Schubert's important work was concentrated into a period of 15 years at most. Goethe for many years enjoyed esteem and status beyond that of any literary figure in Europe. Schubert was, until long after his death, virtually unknown except to a circle of friends and connoisseurs in and around Vienna. The

Figure 28.1   Leopold Kupelwieser, Franz Schubert*, 1821, pencil drawing, State Museum of Vienna. Photo: © Museen der Stadt Wien.*

dominant musical figure in Vienna during Schubert's lifetime was Beethoven, who died in 1827, just one year before Schubert. Schubert greatly admired Beethoven, but probably never even met him, and was merely one of many young composers struggling to earn a living in his shadow. Many of Schubert's large-scale works – symphonies, piano sonatas, string quartets and other chamber works – remained unplayed and unpublished until half a century after his death. The only field in which he did achieve limited success was as a songwriter. A handful of his songs achieved local fame in Vienna during his lifetime, and some of them were modestly successful when published, selling five or six hundred copies while he was alive. But this hardly amounts to 'success' for a composer who has since come to be regarded as one of the major musical figures of the nineteenth century. And the songs published in Schubert's lifetime were only a small fraction of the more than 600 which are now to be found in the complete edition of his works.

Schubert's father was a schoolteacher, and Schubert earned a living as a young adult by working as an assistant teacher in his father's school. From 1818, when he was 21, until his death ten years later, he led a precarious existence as a professional composer, depending for income on friends and patrons, and the small amount he earned from publications of his works.

The Vienna in which Schubert lived in the early nineteenth century was full of domestic music-making. But the centre of musical activity had shifted somewhat since the late eighteenth century. Then it was the aristocracy who had supported Mozart and, at the turn of the century, the young Beethoven. By the time Schubert was active as a composer, the middle classes were taking over as the main musical patrons. This change is summed up by the Schubert scholar, Maurice Brown:

> Secular music was no longer the product and solace of the aristocratic patron; the prince and priest of the eighteenth century, whose establishments contained bands of musical servants hired to perform chamber and orchestral music, with a composer-servant at their head to provide that music – they were passing. Instead, the wealthy middle-classes were paying the piper, and they called the tune. The publishing-houses were pouring out the songs and dance-music and pianoforte pieces which they loved and asked for. The piano was the centre of this music-making, and in the large and comfortable houses of the merchants and lawyers and civil servants were held these musical evenings, often weekly, to which numbers of guests were invited, and at which part-songs and cantatas, songs, chamber-music, pianoforte duets and so forth were performed.

(1966, p.11)

It was at such gatherings, though occasionally at more public concerts, that Schubert's songs and small-scale instrumental pieces became known in well-to-do middle-class circles in Vienna. Some of his first contacts with these circles were made when he was still a teenager. In 1816 Schubert was asked by a group of law students to write a cantata for the name-day of their professor. The cantata was called 'Prometheus', and was reported to be a fine work, though it was lost after Schubert's death. One of the students who sang in the chorus, and whom Schubert met for the first time on this occasion, was Leopold von Sonnleithner, the son of a distinguished barrister, Ignaz von Sonnleithner. The Sonnleithners were one of those prominent families in Vienna who held weekly concerts in their house to a large audience of invited guests. They became Schubert's friends and supporters, his music was often played and sung at their concerts, and they helped to raise money to publish some of his songs. By the 1820s, several households, including the Sonnleithners, were devoting whole evenings to Schubert's works, and these gatherings came to be known as Schubertiads. The first report of such a gathering was made in January 1821:

> Franz [von Schober] invited Schubert in the evening and fourteen of his close acquaintances. So a lot of splendid songs by Schubert were sung and played by himself, which lasted until after 10 o'clock in the evening. After that punch was drunk, offered by one of the party, and as it was very good and plentiful the party, in a happy mood anyhow, became even merrier; so it was 3 o'clock in the morning before we parted.

(Quoted in Deutsch, 1946, p.162)

By 1825 Schubert's painter friend Moritz von Schwind was reporting, 'There is a Schubertiad at Enderes's each week – that is to say, Vogl sings' (quoted in Deutsch, 1946, p.401). Schwind names seven regular male members of the group, so even allowing for wives and other unnamed friends it was quite a small gathering. Another report of a Schubertiad at Enderes's the following year mentions that 'more than 20 people have been asked' (quoted in Deutsch, 1946, p.531), and several other gatherings were of similar size. The musical part of the evening was always followed by food and drink, and sometimes dancing, for which Schubert often played the piano. Afterwards some of the group would go on to an inn.

Johann Michael Vogl (1768–1840), mentioned above by Schwind, was a key figure in the success of Schubert's songs on such occasions. Vogl was a celebrated baritone at the Vienna Court Opera who met Schubert for the first time in 1817. He was aged 49, and reaching the end of a successful operatic career. He was renowned for his performances in both Italian and German opera, and three years earlier he had taken part in the première of Beethoven's *Fidelio*. Through the intervention of a friend, Vogl was persuaded to come to Schubert's lodgings to try some of his songs. Vogl sang three songs, including 'Ganymed', which Schubert had only just completed. His manner was haughty, and Schubert, as an unknown composer, was somewhat in awe of him. But Vogl was impressed, and soon became a great advocate of Schubert's Lieder, frequently performing them at private and public concerts, often accompanied by Schubert himself – though, since Schubert was not a pianist of the first rank, also by professional pianists on the more public occasions. Despite Vogl's grand manner, he and Schubert became friends. Several times they travelled together during the summer, and Schubert stayed with Vogl on visits to the singer's birthplace, Steyr in Upper Austria. On one trip in 1825, they travelled back via Salzburg, staying at a number of houses on the way and performing to private gatherings.

Schubert wrote a long letter to his brother Ferdinand describing this trip. At Salzburg:

> Through Herr Pauernfeind, a merchant well known to Herr von Vogl, we were introduced to Count von Platz, president of the assizes, by whose family we were most kindly received, our names being already known to them. Vogl sang some of my songs, whereupon we were invited for the following evening and requested to produce our odds and ends before a select circle; and indeed they touched them all very much, special preference being given to the 'Ave Maria' already mentioned in my first letter. The manner in which Vogl sings and the way I accompany, as though we were one at such a moment, is something quite new and unheard-of for these people.
>
> (Quoted in Deutsch, 1946, pp.457–8)

This was a partnership important to both of them: it did a great deal to spread Schubert's name as a song composer, and it gave Vogl a second career when he was too old to continue on the opera stage. Ironically, Vogl, already famous in his own lifetime, is now remembered only because of this later association with Schubert.

As Schubert's letter shows, he was delighted with the way Vogl performed his songs. Other writers confirm that he sang with mastery, but sometimes suggest a somewhat conceited and affected manner, as in the following two descriptions:

> On 11th November [1823] we had a Schubertiad at home, at which Vogl took over the singing ... V. was much pleased with himself, and sang gloriously; we others were merry and bright at table ...
>
> (Quoted in Deutsch, 1946, p.302)

> Vogl sang Schubert's songs with mastery, but not without dandyism.
>
> (Quoted in Deutsch, 1946, p.573)

Vogl had a habit of elaborating Schubert's vocal lines, as his surviving copies of the songs confirm. Nowadays, this would be considered shocking, though there is no report that Schubert objected to such liberties, and it is quite possible that this was a general habit among singers of the day. And he had a somewhat mannered habit of playing with his glasses while singing. But he was undoubtedly an important agent in getting Schubert's songs known, and he devoted much of his time to them once he had retired from the operatic stage. In 1823 (two years after Vogl's retirement), Schubert wrote in a letter: 'He is taken up with my songs almost exclusively. He writes out the voice-part himself and, so to speak, lives on it' (quoted in Deutsch, 1946, p.301).

EXERCISE   Plate 28.1 in the Illustrations Book is a famous sepia drawing by Moritz
von Schwind, a painter who was a close friend of Schubert. It shows a
Schubertiad at the house of Josef von Spaun. It was inspired by a
particular evening on 15 December 1826, at which Schubert and Vogl
performed more than 30 of Schubert's songs, but was not drawn until
1868. It shows Schubert at the piano, with Vogl sitting beside him
performing one of his songs. Figure 28.2 is a sketch of Vogl and Schubert
by Schwind, one of several preliminary studies for the complete drawing.
Figure 28.3 is a caricature drawing of Vogl and Schubert, with the
description, 'Michael Vogl and Franz Schubert setting out to fight and to
conquer'. It was drawn in about 1825, possibly by Franz von Schober,
the friend who first introduced Vogl and Schubert in 1817.

Study these three illustrations, and read the following contemporary
description of the same gathering, written by Franz von Hartmann, one
of those who attended. What do these different pieces of evidence

Figure 28.2   Moritz von Schwind, Schubert at the piano with the singer
Johann Michael Vogl, *1868, drawing, study for* A Schubertiad at Ritter
von Spaun's, *location unknown. Photo: AKG Images, London.*

Figure 28.3   Attributed to Franz von Schober, Vogl and Schubert Setting out to Fight and to Conquer, c. *1825, caricature, pencil, Historisches Museum der Stadt Wien, Vienna, Austria. Photo: AKG Images, London/Erich Lessing.*

suggest to you about the relationship between Vogl and Schubert, their audience, and the character of a Schubertiad compared with a modern concert?

> 15th December 1826: I went to Spaun's, where there was a big, big, Schubertiad. On entering I was received rudely by Fritz and very saucily by Haas. There was a huge gathering. The Arneth, Witteczek, Kurzrock and Pompe couples, the mother-in-law of the Court and State Chancellery probationer Witteczek: Dr. Watteroth's widow, Betty Wanderer, and the painter Kupelwieser

with his wife, Grillparzer, Schober, Schwind, Mayrhofer and his landlord Huber, tall Huber, Derffel, Bauernfeld, Gahy (who played gloriously *à quatre mains* [i.e. piano duets] with Schubert) and Vogl, who sang almost 30 splendid songs. Baron Schlechta and the other Court probationers and secretaries were also there. I was moved almost to tears, being in a particularly excited state of mind to-day, by the trio of the fifth March [Op.40 No.5, a funeral march for piano duet], which always reminds me of my dear, good mother. When the music was done, there was grand feeding and then dancing. But I was not at all in a courting mood. I danced twice with Betty and once with each of the Witteczek, Kurzrock and Pompe ladies. At 12.30, after a cordial parting with the Spauns and Enderes, we saw Betty home and went to the "Anchor", where we still found Schober, Schubert, Schwind, Derffel and Bauernfeld. Merry. Then home. To bed at 1 o'clock.

(Quoted in Deutsch, 1946, pp.571–2)

DISCUSSION   The main differences between this Schubertiad and a modern concert performance are obvious enough from the sepia drawing: the audience is small and crammed together very close to the performers. Most of the women are sitting in the front (there are three peering through the doorway on the left), and most of the men are standing behind them. It was an intimate, social occasion compared with most modern performances of Schubert's songs. It is important to remember, however, that the drawing was not done until 42 years after the event. It has a rather stylized appearance, with many of the figures drawn with exaggeratedly emotional poses. Vogl himself gazes at the ceiling, with his chest puffed out, and one hand extended towards the music on the piano, the other holding his glasses. The sketch is much more lively and down-to-earth, as sketches often are. Vogl sits in a more natural way, looking straight ahead, not at the ceiling. In one hand he holds his glasses, as in the finished drawing, but in the other he holds a single sheet of music, rather than extending his arm towards the music on the piano. Since Schubert, in the letter quoted earlier, describes Vogl as writing out the voice-parts of the songs, this is presumably the voice-part of the song he is singing.

In both the finished drawing and the sketch, Vogl is seated to sing, not standing as in the modern concert hall. This suggests not only a less formal relationship between performer and audience than we are used to, but also a more intimate style of performance than that of the modern Lieder singer. There is good evidence that the big, dramatic voices that modern singers are trained to produce are far larger in volume than the voices of the early nineteenth century were. Modern voices have been trained to carry in large opera houses and concert halls, and to be heard over the modern orchestra. In Schubert's day, orchestras were smaller, instruments (including the piano) were quieter than their modern counterparts, and voices had less to compete against. Vogl's singing was probably on a much smaller scale than most of the singing of Lieder to be heard today.

However, Figure 28.3 certainly suggests that Vogl was a character with a grand manner, as also do some of the descriptions of him. It caricatures the contrast between Vogl, the operatic star, and Schubert, the somewhat shy, diminutive and chubby composer. (His height was 157cm, less than 5ft 2ins, and he was known to his friends as 'Schwammerl', a kind of small mushroom.)

Hartmann's description of this Schubertiad makes it clear that the invited guests consisted of a mixture of musicians and artists together with prominent members of the middle classes and a smattering of minor nobility: lawyers, senior civil servants, and a baron. These were the people whose interest had to be aroused, and whose financial help had to be gained, if a composer was to succeed in Vienna in the early years of the nineteenth century.

Plate 28.2 in the Illustrations Book shows a smaller gathering at the castle owned by Franz von Schober's family at Atzenbrugg, 40 kilometres from Vienna. Schober was a lawyer, and an important member of Schubert's group of friends. It was at Schober's home in Vienna that the first reported Schubertiad (described on p.158 above) took place. Schubert stayed at the Schober family castle three summers in succession (1820–2) and this watercolour by another friend, Leopold Kupelwieser, dates from that period. It was Schober who introduced Vogl to Schubert, and he was himself described as rather a theatrical character. Kupelwieser's painting shows a game of charades being played. Schubert is seated at the piano, a dog by his side. He is reported to have improvised music for his friend's entertainments and dancing on such occasions.

3   Schubert and the Lied

Schubert set to music the words of a wide range of poets, from those who were internationally famous to others who were known only locally and were among his group of friends. Schubert was capable of making a first-rate song out of a mediocre poem, and often did so. But of all the writers he set, Goethe was the one who most consistently inspired him to write songs of startling power and originality. The first of his songs to be widely acclaimed as a masterpiece was his famous setting of Gretchen's song at the spinning-wheel from *Faust*, composed in 1814 when he was just 17 years old. 'Erlkönig' ('The Erl-king'), which rivals 'Gretchen' for the position of Schubert's most famous song, followed in 1815. 'Ganymed', one of the songs that so impressed Vogl in 1817, is also a setting of Goethe. In all, Schubert wrote more than 70 songs to words by Goethe – more than one in ten of his output.

As I mentioned in the Introduction, the songs that Schubert wrote for one voice and piano are known as Lieder, the plural of Lied. Lied is simply the German word for 'song', but it has come to be used specifically to refer to songs in German for voice and piano. Even in England, a concert of such songs is usually referred to as a 'Lieder recital'. These Lieder became increasingly popular in German-speaking countries in the second half of the eighteenth century. A number of factors encouraged this trend: the growth of the middle classes with an appetite for domestic music-making, the rise of the piano as an instrument in the home, and a growing fashion for songs in a direct and simple style, which developed partly as a reaction to the complexity and artifice of the Italian opera aria with its elements of display and its international star singers.

One important factor in this development was the influence of folk-song, an influence which was also important in Goethe's writing. As you learned in Units 26–27, one of Goethe's mentors as a student was Johann Gottfried Herder, who published two important volumes of folk-songs in 1778, and who encouraged Goethe to collect folk-songs himself. It was Herder who coined the term *Volkslied* (folk-song) – a word which, in English as in German, has become so commonplace that one hardly ever thinks about the assumptions and meanings that lie behind it. A number of other collections followed, which included examples from across Europe, English and Scottish examples being particularly valued. One of these collections, Brentano and von Arnim's *Des Knaben Wunderhorn* (*Youth's Magic Horn*, 1806–8), was dedicated to Goethe, and was described by him as an essential volume for any household. Something of the impulse underlying this interest in folk-song is shown by the preface to a collection by J.G. Naumann (1784):

> The times in which dazzling and forced styles found approval are past. Men who had a deeper feeling for the simple tones of nature quickly recognized those errors and took care to avoid the rocks of false taste.

(Quoted in Smeed, 1987, p.29)

Folk-song was not the only element encouraging writers towards simplicity. In 'Lieder *c.*1740–*c.*1800', James Parsons points out that German poets and composers throughout most of the eighteenth century emphasized the need for simplicity and naturalness in the writing of songs. The origins of this approach, Parsons argues, go back to a time before Herder's interest in 'folk-song', to the Neoclassicism of the 1730s. J.C. Gottsched, professor of poetry at the University of Leipzig in the 1730s, begins his treatise on the art of poetry (1730) with a quote from the Latin poet Horace's *Ars Poetica*: 'In short, everything you write must be modest and simple.' Gottsched instructs the song composer to strive for 'nothing more than an agreeable and clear reading of a verse, which consequently must match the nature and content of the words.' Later in the century, writers praised song that was devoted to 'the noble simplicity of unadorned expressions' (Johann Peter Uz, 1749) and 'the touching joy of unadorned nature' (Christoph Martin Wieland, 1766–7). This emphasis on classical simplicity, Parsons writes, is a counterpoint to the better-known promotion of classical virtues in the visual arts, exemplified by Johann Joachim Winckelmann's praise for the 'noble simplicity and quiet grandeur' of Greco-Roman sculpture (1755) (all quotations in this paragraph in Parsons, 2001, p.669).

But it is important not to be simplistic in our thinking about these calls for 'simplicity'. In what way is the simplicity of a folk-song like the simplicity of ancient Greek sculpture? Could one really describe the subtle and complex Latin odes of Horace as 'simple'? It does not take too much thought to realize that such appeals to old or rustic models were more to do with modern writers' perceptions than with the actual qualities of the models themselves. Writers and musicians of the late eighteenth and early nineteenth centuries sought inspiration in what they saw as the purity of the ancient past and of the unaffectedly rural.

From our perspective, it is easy to see that the ideas of 'classical' simplicity, the interest in folk-song, the emphasis on 'nature' and the direct expression of feelings, came together in an extraordinary way in the writings of Goethe and Schubert. But this was exceptional: the overwhelming majority of German songs were not the work of great composers, but pleasing and quickly composed settings turned out at high speed for the domestic market, by hundreds of largely forgotten composers, both professional and semi-professional. The sheer quantity of songs published in German-speaking countries reached an extraordinary climax in the late eighteenth and early nineteenth centuries. 'Has there ever been an age more prolific in song than ours?', wrote the editor of the *Allgemeine Musikalische Zeitung* in 1826 (quoted in Parsons, 2001, p.671). By that date, more than a hundred song collections per month were being published. It was a huge and successful market.

Schubert himself wrote over 600 Lieder. This is often cited as remarkable, and it is indeed a large number to have been written by a composer who lived only to the age of 31. But the sheer number is not the point. There were plenty of composers around 1800 who wrote many hundreds of songs, among them Reichardt and Zelter, both of whom were closely associated with Goethe (as Schubert was not). What is remarkable about Schubert's output is the range and quality of his writing, and the creative imagination which he brought to the musical setting of poetry. These qualities made his songs extremely influential on later composers. A succession of German composers wrote Lieder through the nineteenth and early twentieth centuries, including Robert Schumann, Johannes

Brahms, Hugo Wolf and Richard Strauss, and they all acknowledged Schubert as the pioneering master of the genre.

Ironically, the very quality of his talent limited his success during his lifetime. He composed songs with a great range of mood and complexity, from simple settings much like those of most other composers to highly dramatic and emotionally intense works, often very difficult to sing and to play. These were not suitable for the average amateur performer who regularly bought the latest monthly offerings of the publishing companies. While certain of Schubert's songs quickly became well known and were published soon after he wrote them, the great bulk of his work lay virtually unknown until after his death. This applies not only to songs, but also to his major instrumental works. The 'Great' C major Symphony, for example, now acknowledged as one of the most important works of the period, sat with most of Schubert's instrumental compositions in a trunk in the house of Schubert's brother Ferdinand, until the composer Robert Schumann visited him in 1839. Following this discovery, Mendelssohn conducted a performance of the work, in an abbreviated version, later that year in Leipzig. But when he attempted to rehearse it in London with the Philharmonic Society in 1844, they refused to play it. The same had happened two years earlier in Paris under the conductor François Habaneck. Many of Schubert's major works similarly suffered from decades of neglect and misunderstanding.

One particularly poignant fact is that Goethe knew nothing of Schubert's talent until it was too late to help him. In 1816 Schubert's friend Josef von Spaun gathered together two volumes of Schubert's Lieder to send to Goethe, hoping that the great man would help in promoting the publication of the young composer's works. The collection included three settings of Goethe's words, which are now among Schubert's most famous songs: 'Heidenröslein', 'Gretchen am Spinnrade', and 'Erlkönig' (all of which we shall be studying in this unit). The first volume was sent to Goethe, but he never opened it and it was returned to von Spaun. By this stage of his career, no doubt Goethe was inundated by requests from hopeful composers and writers, as famous authors always are. But it is a sad thought that, if Goethe had realized what the package contained, Schubert's career could have been quite different from that of a struggling, provincial composer with little recognition outside his immediate circle.

4   The songs

A note on the translations and scores

The German text and a parallel English translation of each of the songs we shall study in this unit are in Anthology II (pp.251–8). The styles of translation vary, depending on the style of the original poem. For poems without a regular metre and without a rhyming-scheme, a literal translation of the German is given so that you can follow the original word by word. For poems with regular metre and a strong rhyming-scheme, the translation follows the rhythm and rhyming as closely as possible, in an attempt to convey the impact of the original poem. Inevitably, there are some minor freedoms in these translations. The 'strict' translations are 'The Harper's Songs I', 'Prometheus' and 'Ganymede'. Freer versions are 'Wild Rose', 'Wanderer's Night Song II', 'Gretchen at the Spinning-Wheel' and 'The Erl-king'.

At the end of 'Gretchen' and 'Ganymede', Schubert repeats some of Goethe's lines. In 'Gretchen' these are indicated in brackets. In 'Ganymede', where the repetition is straightforward, the lines are not repeated in the printed text.

You will find in the Illustrations Book music scores for 'Wild Rose', 'Gretchen', 'The Erl-king' and 'Ganymede' (Plates 28.3–28.6). Although you are not required to be able to read them, you may find them helpful in identifying some of the musical points in the following commentaries and discussions.

'Heidenröslein' ('Wild Rose', 1815) and 'Wandrers Nachtlied' ('Wanderer's Night Song II', 1822)

The selection on Audio 7 begins with songs composed to two of Goethe's best-known poems (several composers other than Schubert wrote settings of them). Schubert's versions are both very short and simple. But they are simple in quite different ways.

EXERCISE   Listen to these two songs on Audio 7 (tracks 5 and 6). First read through the poem in English, and then follow the words in the parallel text (pp.251–2) as you listen to each song. You should find that, even if you have little or no knowledge of German, you will, with a little practice, be able to follow the German words as they are sung, and to keep an eye on the meaning through reference to the English translation. Without attempting any detailed analysis, consider in general terms the main differences in character between the two poems and the two songs.

DISCUSSION   In the following and subsequent discussions I will offer you my analysis of the question I have posed. If you have not had much experience of trying to analyse music, I realize that you are unlikely to think of everything I suggest. But don't be disheartened by this. If you find it more helpful, you could read through my discussion before attempting the exercise, and then set yourself the task of recognizing and

understanding my comments. Or you could work through the exercise
on your own before seeing what I have made of it.

There are a number of features of the poem 'Heidenröslein' which make
it very like a folk-song: the simple rhyme-scheme (AB-AAB-CB) which is
repeated in each verse, the repeated refrain of the last two lines, and the
mock-innocent story of the boy plucking the rose, which is obviously not
just about roses.

Schubert's setting is also simple, and does not distract from the folk-song
style of Goethe's poem. He adheres to the pattern of three verses,
repeating the same music for each verse (the musical term for this
method of setting is '**strophic**'). In the manuscript (see Figure 28.4) he
just writes the music out once, with the words of the first verse placed
underneath the voice-part, and verses 2 and 3 given at the bottom of the
page (as in a modern hymn-book). In the published edition, the words
of the three verses are all fitted under the voice-part, making it easier to
follow words and music together. The piano part consists of a regular
pattern of chords, continuing until the singer has finished each verse,

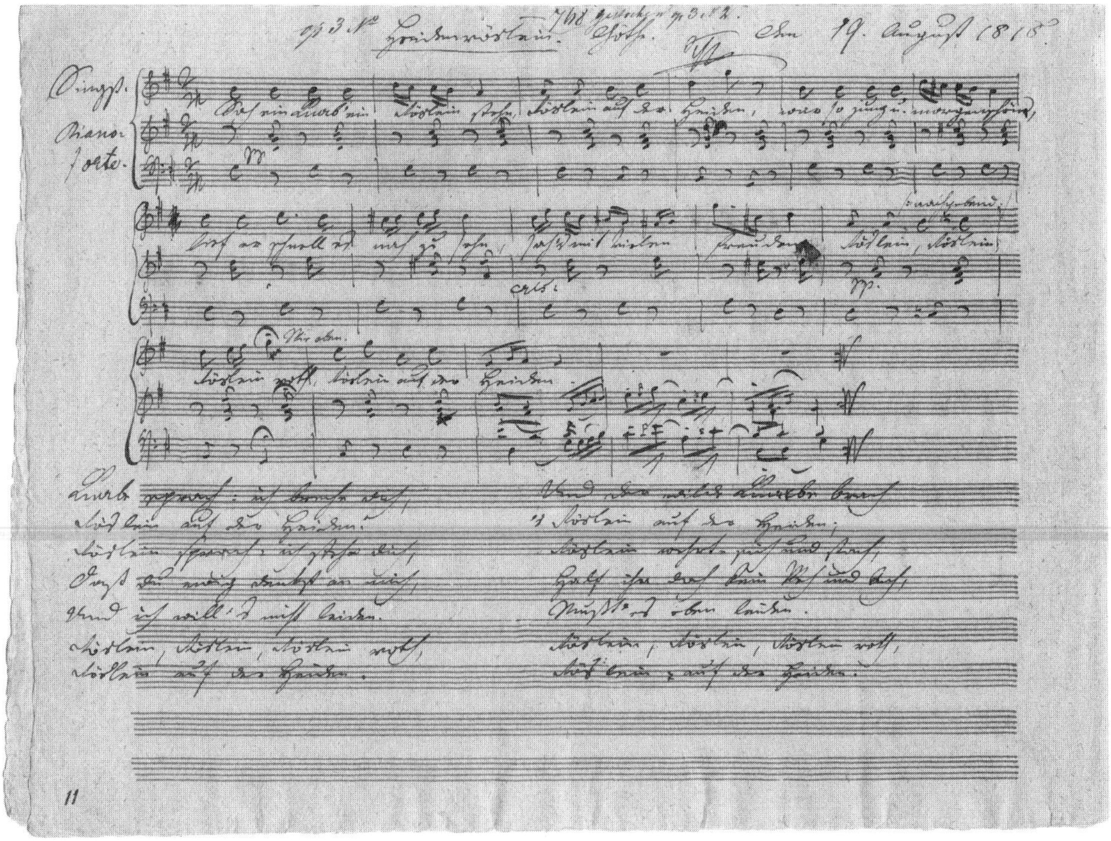

Figure 28.4   Franz Schubert, Heidenröslein, *autograph score, 1815. Photo: courtesy of
Lund University Library, Sweden.*

and then rounding off the verse with a slightly varied repetition of the singer's last phrase. There are subtleties in Schubert's choice of chords, the most noticeable effect of which is that lines 3–5 of each verse seem to 'run through' without any sense of coming to rest until the end of line 5 ('Freuden' in verse 1). This helps to emphasize Goethe's verse structure, in which lines 2 and 5 rhyme.

'Wandrers Nachtlied' is simple, but not in the way that 'Heidenröslein' is. The poem has none of the feel of a folk-poem. It does rhyme, but the rhyming pattern is not as regular as in a folk-poem: it goes AB-AB-CD-DC (the rhymes in the German are full rhymes; the translation has resorted to half-rhymes for some lines – 'still/feel, breeze/peace'). There is no division into verses. The relationship between rhyming and rhythm is subtle: the first four lines rhyme AB-AB, but Goethe undermines any sense of regularity by varying the lengths of the lines and by running the sense over from line 4 to line 5.

I think you'll agree that Schubert's setting of 'Wandrers Nachtlied' does not sound in the least like a folk-song. It is very slow, with long vocal lines that need the resources of a trained singer to sustain them. The piano part is quiet and deep throughout, with low bass notes emphasizing the profound calm and darkness of the poem. It sounds almost like a hymn, but one of great solemnity.

One fundamental difference between these two songs is that 'Heidenröslein' is a narrative about a boy, though incorporating some dialogue. 'Wandrers Nachtlied' is not a narrative: it is sung by the wanderer himself. When he sings that peace will come soon, he is comforting himself. So the contrast is between, in the first song, a simple story, simply set like a folk-song and, in the second, a song which encapsulates a single moment of reflection, evoking a particular emotional state for its own sake, not as part of a story. We can imagine that there might have been a story, but we have to make it up for ourselves. 'Wandrers Nachtlied' is in that sense more Romantic in spirit than 'Heidenröslein'. It is an example of art directly expressing emotional experience.

The idea of a wanderer expressing his or her own thoughts became a very popular theme in early nineteenth-century poetry and Lieder. A number of composers wrote 'song-cycles' using this idea – sequences of songs to be performed continuously, meditating on a journey. These were, in the more subtle examples of the genre, to be understood as analogous to the journey through life, and a meditation on the human condition. The most famous is Schubert's *Winterreise* (*Winter's Journey*), written in the last year of his life – a cycle of songs with a predominantly melancholy, and increasingly bleak, character, which can have an overwhelming impact in a good performance.

Simplicity and complexity

As we have already discovered, the concept of 'simplicity' is not a simple matter. We saw earlier in the unit that the simplicity of folk-song is not the same as classical simplicity, though both influenced the taste of Lieder writers. 'Heidenröslein' and 'Wandrers Nachtlied' are simple in quite different ways, both in their poetry and in their music. Many other songs by Schubert are much longer, much more complex, and treat the poetry with much greater freedom. This aspect of Schubert's style, which is now so much appreciated, did not always please his contemporaries.

Goethe himself preferred composers to take a direct approach to setting his poems – direct in the sense that he wanted them to stay close to the structure of his text, and not to indulge in free fantasy and repetition, nor to overlay it with too heavy a piano accompaniment. Poetry and song were closely linked in Goethe's mind – he envisaged the songs in his plays and novels actually being sung, not just spoken, and some were originally published with simple musical settings – and he had clearly-stated views on how such songs should be set to music. The composers with whom Goethe worked, and of whom he approved (notably Reichardt and Zelter), took a direct and simple approach to his poems, leaving their structures more or less unchanged, and restricting the piano part to a fairly straightforward accompaniment. This straightforward approach to what German Lieder should be like was shared by many writers of Schubert's time, and for that reason the more subtle and complex of Schubert's settings were not always appreciated by contemporary commentators. Even in the last year of his life, 1828, the publication of a new collection of his songs provoked a reviewer to sum up Schubert's strengths and weaknesses in the following way:

> Herr S. knows how to choose poems which are really good (in themselves and for musical treatment) and have not yet been used up either; he is capable and usually succeeds in discovering in each what predominates emotionally and therefore for music, and above all he places that into his generally simple melody, while he allows his accompaniment, which however is very rarely mere accompaniment, to paint this further, and for that purpose he is fond of using images, parables or scenic features in the poems. In both he often shows originality of invention and execution, sound knowledge of harmony and honest industry: on the other hand he often, and sometimes very greatly, oversteps the species in hand, or else that which should by rights have been developed in such and such a piece; he likes to labour at the harmonies for the sake of being new and piquant; and he is inordinately addicted to giving too many notes to the pianoforte part, either at once or in succession.

> (Review in the Leipzig *Allgemeine Musikalische Zeitung*, 23 January 1828, quoted in Deutsch, 1946, p.718)

The essence of this rather verbose exposition is an oft-repeated view in the period of Schubert, as it was through the second half of the eighteenth century: that the German Lied requires straightforwardness and simplicity, and that introducing too much complexity, as Schubert was said to do, goes against the spirit of the genre. But Schubert's approach varied considerably throughout his career, and to demonstrate the point we shall now look at two settings by Schubert of a single poem, and compare them with a setting by Goethe's favourite song composer, Carl Friedrich Zelter (1758–1832).

'Harfenspieler I' ('The Harper's Songs I'): three settings

This poem comes from Goethe's novel, *Wilhelm Meister's Apprenticeship*. It is one of a number of songs scattered through the book, some sung by the tragic young heroine, Mignon, others, like this one, sung by the mysterious harper, who at the end of the novel is revealed as Mignon's father. He is an old man living on the fringes of society, in a garret on the edge of the town, slipping in and out of a madness caused by his guilt for his incestuous relationship with his sister. The first edition of the book included simple musical settings of these songs.

Wilhelm, the hero of the book, visits the harper in the hope that his music will bring him comfort. As he climbs the stairs to the old man's room, he hears the sweet sound of a harp coming from inside, 'heart-moving, plaintive tones, accompanied by sad and mournful singing. Wilhelm crept into the room, and the good old man recited a sort of fantasy, and repeated more than once a few verses, partly singing and partly reciting'. Wilhelm asks him to sing another song: 'The old man looked upon the strings; and after touching them gently, by way of prelude, he tuned and sang' (Goethe, 1998, pp.227–8).

This song, 'Wer sich der Einsamkeit ergibt' ('He who gives himself to solitude') is the song the harper now sings. (It is known in the catalogue of Schubert's works as the first of the Harper's Songs, even though it is the second song he sings in the novel.)

Audio 7 contains three settings of this famous poem. The first (track 7) is by Zelter. The second and third (tracks 8 and 9) are by Schubert, the first dating from 1815, the second from the following year. Listening to these settings one after the other will enable us to compare Schubert's approach with that of Goethe's favoured composer, and to hear how varied Schubert's own settings of the same poem could be.

EXERCISE   Read the English translation of the poem (Anthology II, p.252). Then listen to the three settings, following the German words as they are sung. Try to summarize what each setting does to the poem and the main differences between them. Are they 'strophic' (with the music repeated at each verse) or '**through-composed**' (without repetition at each verse)? What distinguishes Schubert's approach from Zelter's? And how different are Schubert's two settings from each other?

DISCUSSION

Zelter's setting stays closest to the shape of Goethe's poem. The poem is written as two verses, and the music keeps to that pattern, repeating both the vocal line and the piano part almost note for note. This is another strophic setting, like Schubert's 'Heidenröslein'. Zelter takes very few 'liberties' with the poem: he runs lines 5 and 6 together, giving the word 'einmal' ('once') several notes. This has the effect of slightly obscuring the rhyme-scheme at that point, so that one does not notice the repetition of '-al' very clearly. In the penultimate line he emphasizes the word 'Grabe' ('grave') by giving the first syllable three notes. Zelter's piano accompaniment is simple: it consists of little more than a succession of chords, and it would have no interest at all if one were to play it on its own without the voice. Its function is simply to support the voice. The piano part is almost the same in the second verse as in the first, except that Zelter gives extra intensity to the climax on 'die Pein' ('suffering') by using a more poignant chord at that point.

Schubert's first setting seems at first to be strophic, and almost as straightforward as Zelter's, but it is more complicated and subtle than it might appear. One of its most striking features is the way that Schubert deals with the join between the first and second verses. The first verse ends ('... nicht allein'), and the piano repeats the last phrase by way of a short interlude between the verses. Then the second verse begins: or does it? Instead of repeating the music of the first verse, Schubert sets the beginning of the second verse to new music, and comes to a halt at the end of the second line ('Ob seine Freundin allein?'). Only then does he return to the music of the beginning, at the words 'So überschleicht ...'. The effect is to make a new verse start there. Schubert has lifted out the first two lines of the second verse and put them on their own, giving them a hesitant, questioning character. Before the last line of the poem, Schubert pauses again, and then he repeats the last line twice, to give it extra poignancy. Finally, the piano echoes the last phrase of the singer. So this is a rather subtle adaptation of the strophic form.

There are other subtleties. The first verse begins in one key (A minor) and ends in another (F major). There is no reason why you should have been aware of this, but perhaps you might have felt that the end of the first verse sounded inconclusive, and that the song could certainly not have ended like that. If so, the change of key is the reason. Schubert goes through the same change of key in the second verse, but then uses the repetitions of the last line to work his way back to the home key of A minor.

Schubert's final setting is an altogether more ambitious reworking of Goethe's poem. It is through-composed, with no suggestion of separate verses, and lasts about twice as long as his first version (and Zelter's). It begins haltingly, with several pauses before reaching the end of the fourth line ('... seiner Pein'). Then it sets off in a great, sweeping melody, right through to the end of the poem without interruption, with the piano keeping up a constant flow of rhythm to underpin the vocal line. The setting is highly dramatic: in the last three lines Schubert instructs the singer to sing very quietly, and then to burst out *fortissimo* at 'Da lässt sie mich allein' ('Then they will leave me alone'). Then he repeats the whole of those three lines, this time quietly right through to the end, and the piano adds a postlude, descending back to the same, deep chord which ended the prelude at the beginning of the song.

This setting treats Goethe's text much more freely than the other two. But there is one way in which it might be considered closer to Goethe. If you look back at the description of Wilhelm's visit to the harper, which I quoted before this exercise, you may be struck by the way in which Schubert's final setting echoes some of that description. The spread chords of the piano introduction evoke the impression of the old man looking at the strings and 'touching them gently, by way of prelude'. Goethe describes the harper's singing of the previous song, which Wilhelm hears as he enters the room, as 'partly singing and partly reciting', with verses repeated. In Schubert's setting of this song, the hesitant opening lines have something of the effect of an improvised recitative (the musical setting of speech-rhythms, which you encountered in *Don Giovanni*). And Schubert repeats the final three lines of the song. Graham Johnson, a pianist who specializes in Schubert's Lieder, plausibly conjectures that perhaps when Schubert wrote his shorter, first setting, he had not yet read Goethe's novel but had come across the poem on its own. Then when he did encounter the novel, he was struck by the description of Wilhelm's visit to the harper, and incorporated some of it into his setting (see Johnson, 1991, vol.10).

Voice and accompaniment

One thing that is clear from the Lieder we have already considered is that Schubert's writing for the piano is a crucial element of his skill as a songwriter. Sometimes, and throughout his career, he wrote very simple accompaniments, as in 'Heidenröslein' – the approach favoured by Goethe and many other writers of the time, who considered that the German Lied should not overload the poem with too much elaboration. Schubert's later version of the 'Harper's Song' is more complex, with an introduction and a postlude in the piano, and a more varied style of accompaniment throughout the song.

In many of his Lieder, Schubert uses a device which, though not new, he made particularly his own. This consists of taking a rhythm, or a little melodic phrase (motif), and repeating it in the piano part throughout the song to give it a strong and coherent character. Schubert's particular gift was to find rhythms and motifs which seem to encapsulate some essence of the poem and its mood. His two most famous songs do this: 'Gretchen am Spinnrade' ('Gretchen at the Spinning-Wheel'), and 'Erlkönig' ('The Erl-king').

'Gretchen am Spinnrade' ('Gretchen at the Spinning-Wheel', 1814)

This celebrated song was Schubert's first setting of a poem by Goethe. Written when he was only 17, it was one of the few songs to be sold in quite large numbers during Schubert's lifetime – though he made little money out of it. Robert David MacDonald's translation, taken from his version of *Faust*, conveys not only the meaning of Goethe's words, with a few liberties, but also the rhythm and something close to the rhyming-scheme of the original. The six concluding lines are in brackets because they are repeated in Schubert's song but not in Goethe's original poem.

The poem and its translation appear in Anthology II (pp.253–4) and the music score of this song is in the Illustrations Book (Plate 28.4).

EXERCISE   Before you play the song, find this scene on Audio 6 (track 12) and play that first. Then play the song on Audio 7 (track 10), following the translation, and consider what Schubert has done to Goethe's poem. In what ways has he remained faithful to the rhythm and structure of the poem, and in what ways has he changed or adapted them?

DISCUSSION   The poem is short and simple. The lines are short, and Gretchen conveys her feelings directly and forcefully.

Is Schubert similarly direct and simple? Yes and no. In one essential way Schubert does remain faithful to the rhythm of the poem. Each line of the poem is very short; it is partly the constant repetition of this rhythm in the poem itself that conveys Gretchen's sense of obsession, of being taken over by her feelings for Faust, of knowing that she cannot escape. Schubert's phrases are also short. Each line of the poem is set to a separate phrase, and even at the climax of the song those phrases are short. In this way Schubert has preserved the detailed structure of each verse of the poem; the short phrases of music, rising twice to a climax, add to the impression of breathlessness which is already in Goethe's poem.

However, Schubert's extra repetition of some of the words alters the broader structure of the poem in fundamental ways. Goethe repeats the opening verse twice, to form a recurring refrain, but he does not return to it at the end. Goethe's original ends with 'Vergehen sollt'!' ('sink and die'). Schubert repeats Goethe's final verse, so extending the climax of the song, and then, after the piano part has quietened, repeats Goethe's refrain one last time. This final repetition of the refrain is made especially poignant by the fact that Gretchen does not complete it: she sings only the first two lines. This has the wonderful effect of making the song sound unfinished – it does come to an end, but the feelings hang in the air, heightening the impression that Gretchen can never escape from them.

Schubert intensifies the effect of this refrain with an internal repetition which is not so obvious. In line 3 of the first verse, he repeats 'Ich finde', and he does this each time the refrain occurs. This might seem a small point, but it has the effect of creating a longer phrase than at any other time in the song. Every other phrase in the song is two bars long. Those phrases often form pairs, four bars long, like a pair of lines in the poem. But lines 3 and 4 of the first verse are moulded into one continuous, longer phrase, five bars long (or six, if you count the bar that the piano plays at the end of it). It is not important to know how many bars long the phrases are, though you may like to check my analysis on the score. What is important is the yearning emphasis this continuous, longer phrase throws on those lines: 'I'll find it never, nevermore'. Because Gretchen comes back to it twice, it seems like the heart of the song. And then at the end, when she fails to reach it, this intensifies the feeling of something unfinished and ongoing.

The other striking feature of Schubert's song is the piano part. Goethe's stage instruction specifies that Gretchen is at her spinning-wheel. In the performance of *Faust* on Audio 6, Gretchen is accompanied by the sound of a real spinning-wheel, and you can hear how Goethe must have intended its rapid, bumpy rhythm to add to the impression of Gretchen's agitation, like a racing pulse. Schubert's accompaniment does not literally sound like a spinning-wheel: the rhythm is quite different. But he has created a musical analogy, with a whirling pattern of rapid notes which repeats constantly, changing pitch and key as the song progresses, but never changing its basic pattern and rhythm. If you look at the piano part in the score, you can see that, in the right hand, the pattern of six notes is repeated throughout the song, only very occasionally being varied. There is also a regular pattern through most of the left hand. This generates not only an effect suggestive of a spinning-wheel, but also a sense of something that cannot be escaped. Indeed, as often in Schubert's songs, it almost seems wrong to talk of the piano part as an 'accompaniment'. You could equally well say that it is the piano which determines the mood and the structure of the piece, and the voice sings an 'accompaniment'.

There is one obvious, basic difference between the song and the poem. The song has an enormous emotional range, beginning softly and rising twice to great climaxes. At the first climax, at 'Und ach, sein Kuss!', the music stops abruptly after the high note on 'Kuss' ('kiss'), and then restarts quietly and hesitantly. This gives the impression that Gretchen is getting the spinning-wheel going again; but it also conveys a sense of hopelessness, as she realizes that her overwhelming passion has doomed her to a sense of loss. The final climax is even higher and more sustained, with the climactic phrase repeated to the words 'Vergehen sollt'!' ('sink and die'), and then the climax dying away as the spinning-wheel slows down, and Gretchen sadly reiterating her half-finished refrain.

But is it right to say that the song has a greater emotional range than the poem? Certainly the singer of the song is asked by Schubert to encompass a massive range of volume, from *pianissimo* at the beginning to *fortissimo* at the climax, and from low notes at the start to high notes at the climax. Readers of the poem, whether in the context of the play or not, would never do that. It is easy to imagine how ridiculous it would sound if the actor playing Gretchen were to speak or sing it with massive climaxes, as in Schubert's song. But does that mean that the poem is less emotional than the song? Music certainly has its own emotional structures and dynamics, and one of the hallmarks of Romantic music is the use of greater freedom and more extreme contrasts than were used in the time of Mozart.

'Gretchen' is a song sung by a female character in Goethe's *Faust*. Although nineteenth-century singers often sang Lieder which seem intended for the opposite sex, only women are reported to have sung this song in Schubert's lifetime. There is no record, as far as I know, of Vogl singing it. A number of women singers were important in promoting Schubert's songs specifically for women. Among them were the much-loved actress Sophie Müller, who sang his songs 'most touchingly', sometimes with Schubert himself accompanying (Deutsch, 1946, p.403), and a pupil of Vogl, Anna Milder, for whom Schubert wrote the lovely song with piano and clarinet, 'The Shepherd on the Rock'.

'Erlkönig' ('The Erl-king', 1815)

EXERCISE   Before continuing with the unit, read the English translation of 'Erlkönig' (Anthology II, pp.254–5). The translation attempts to stay close to the rhythm and rhyming-scheme of Goethe's poem, and should therefore give you a fairly good idea of the character of this famous ballad.

Schubert wrote 'Erlkönig' only a year after 'Gretchen'. Schubert's friend Josef von Spaun left a description of how he wrote 'Erlkönig' on 16 November 1815, after reading Goethe's poem:

> We [von Spaun and Johann Mayrhofer] found Schubert all aglow reading the 'Erlkönig' aloud from a book. He walked to and fro

several times with the book in his hand; suddenly he sat down, and in no time at all the wonderful ballad was on paper. We ran to the *Konvikt* [the school where they had both been pupils] as Schubert had no piano and there, the same evening, the 'Erlkönig' was sung and wildly acclaimed. Old Ruzicka [Schubert's music teacher at the school] then played through all the parts himself carefully, without a singer, and was deeply moved by the composition. When one or two of the company questioned a recurring dissonant note [at the boy's cries of 'Mein Vater'], Ruzicka played it on the piano and showed them how it matched the text exactly, how beautiful it really was and how happily it was resolved.

(Quoted in Fischer-Dieskau, 1976, pp.48–9)

The Schubert scholar Maurice Brown argues convincingly that this story must contain some elements of myth. It is well established that Schubert did have a piano, so there would have been no need to rush to the school (nearly an hour's walk away). And even if the song had completely formed itself in Schubert's mind, it would have taken him a long time to write it all down sufficiently clearly for his teacher to examine it in detail (a slightly longer song, composed in the same year, has a note on the manuscript that it took Schubert five hours to write). Brown suggests that the story is probably constructed from separate events which have been brought together – finding Schubert pacing up and down with Goethe's text, the completion of the song, and the showing of it to Ruzicka (1966, pp.46–7).

Whatever the truth of Schubert's writing of 'Erlkönig', it scored an immediate success, and is one of the few of his songs that became well known during his lifetime. It was already one of Goethe's best-known poems, and several composers had set it to music, including Goethe's associates Reichardt and Zelter. Goethe took an old German legend about an evil goblin that abducts children, and wrote it in the style of a Scottish ballad. Ballads were one of the forms of folk poetry that Goethe's mentor, Gottfried Herder, helped to make popular in Germany. One of the inspirations for this fashion was Bishop Percy's *Reliques of Ancient English Poetry* (1765), which included one of the most famous old Scottish ballads, 'Edward' (of uncertain origin). Herder had translated 'Edward', and Schubert set that translation as a song too.

Goethe's 'Erlkönig' was always intended to be sung, and it occurs in his play *Die Fischerin* (*The Fisherwoman*, 1782). The stage direction reads:

Scattered under tall alder trees at the edge of the river are several fishermen's huts. It is a quiet night. Round a small fire are pots, nets and fishing-tackle. Dortchen sings at her work: 'Wer reitet so spät ... '

(Quoted in Fischer-Dieskau, 1976, pp.48–9)

The actress who played the part of Dortchen at the première wrote her own simple eight-bar melody, which she repeated for each verse. The effect must have been somewhat like that of Patti Clare, who plays Gretchen in the recording of *Faust* on Audio 6 (track 6), humming 'A king of a Northern fastness' as she undresses. Goethe stated his own view on the realization of such songs where they occur in his dramas:

> The singer has learned it somewhat by heart and recalls it from time to time. Therefore these songs can and must have their own, definite, well-rounded melodies which are attractive and easily remembered.

(Quoted in Fischer-Dieskau, 1976, pp.48–9)

Schubert has lifted the song completely out of this original dramatic context, setting the drama of the ballad itself with extraordinary power.

EXERCISE Listen to 'Erlkönig' in the two recordings on Audio 7 (tracks 11 and 12), one sung by a man, the other by a woman. Follow the poem and its translation as you listen. Then consider the following questions:

1 How does Schubert use the piano part to conjure up the scene?

2 How does Schubert distinguish between the three speakers – the father, the child, and the Erl-king? Consider, in particular, the lengths of the phrases that they sing, and the pitch at which they sing them.

DISCUSSION 1 As in 'Gretchen', it is the piano that sets and maintains the scene vividly. The right hand hammers away relentlessly at repeated notes, and continues to do so through most of the song. (From the second bar onward, diagonal strokes through the stems of the notes indicate that the pattern of bar 1 is to be repeated – a conventional abbreviation.) A little rushing figure in the bass is also repeated again and again. Even before the mention of horse-riding in the first line of the poem, a feeling of urgency, perhaps even fear, has already been established. This is typical of Schubert's way of establishing tone and atmosphere: he takes an element of the poem, in this case the rhythm of a horse galloping, and uses it to create a motif which vividly establishes the mood of the poem, and provides a sense of unity through the whole of the song.

2 This is more difficult to answer, because of the way that singers add characterization of their own to what Schubert has written. Naturally a singer will tend to sing the father's passages in a solid, manly way, the child's part in a lighter, more childish tone, and the Erl-king in a wheedling and spooky manner. It also makes a difference whether it is a man or a woman singing it. Since all the characters in the song are male, a male singer tends to give more sense of actually impersonating the characters, particularly the father. A woman singer

inevitably tends to give more the impression of telling the narrative, with less sense of actually being the different characters. Nowadays it is more often sung by a man than by a woman, though both male and female singers performed the song in Schubert's lifetime, and of course Goethe originally intended the ballad to be sung by an actress on the stage. And it was a woman, Wilhelmine Schröder, who sang it to Goethe after Schubert's death and persuaded him that it was a great song (too late to benefit Schubert, alas). There is even a report of Schubert taking part in a performance with three singers while he and Vogl were staying with a musical family on a visit to Steyr: Schubert sang the part of the father, Vogl that of the Erl-king, and the 18-year-old daughter of the family that of the boy. Figure 28.5 is a

Figure 28.5   Ferdinand Georg Waldmüller, Schubertiad, *with Franz Schubert, Josefine Fröhlich and Johann Michael Vogl at the piano, 1827, drawing, from* Grimschitz Katalog, *Albertina Graphic Collection, Albertina Museum, Vienna. Photo: with permission from Albertina Museum, Vienna.*

drawing of just such a scene at a Schubertiad, with Schubert and Josefine Fröhlich seated at the piano, and Vogl standing behind. They might even be performing 'Erlkönig', though the drawing does not specify the song.

After that preamble, how does Schubert's music distinguish between the father, the boy, and the Erl-king, quite apart from how the singers characterize them? The most striking difference between them is that the Erl-king is the only one of the three who gets a real, continuous melody. And, until the very end of his part, where he threatens force, his melodies stay in major keys. By contrast with the Erl-king, the boy and the father have only short, disjointed phrases, almost always in minor keys. The Erl-king's smooth melodies sound sweet and agreeable, and in the context of the song, that is what makes them sinister. He sounds at ease, and his very fluency suggests that he is the one in control of the situation. The Erl-king's lines are also the only parts of the song where the hammering of the piano part relents, switching to a more easy-going rhythm. You can see this in the score: at 'Du liebes Kind', in the right hand of the piano, Schubert leaves out the first of each group of three notes, and has the bass playing a short note on each beat, as if the horse has settled into a comfortable rhythm. At the Erl-king's next entry, 'Willst, feiner Knabe', the right hand of the piano stops its hammering altogether, and plays easy-going **arpeggios**, up and down, giving almost the lulling effect of a cradle-song. And the third time the Erl-king sings, the bass of the piano remains static, playing long notes, while the right hand continues its hammering, but *pianissimo*. This gives a great sense of tension, which then bursts out at the boy's final cries of 'Mein Vater', where Schubert gives the marking *fff* (even louder than *fortissimo*).

It was the Erl-king's lines that most struck contemporary listeners to the song:

> The cradle-spell that speaks from the melody, and yet at the same time the sinister note, which repels while the former entices, dramatizes the poet's picture.

(Deutsch, 1946, p.254)

The German novelist Jean Paul Friedrich Richter (known as Jean Paul) was reported to be particularly moved by the Erl-king's passages in the song: 'the premonition of secret bliss, suggestively promised by the voice and the accompaniment, drew him, like everyone else, with magic power towards a transfigured, fairer existence' (quoted in Deutsch, 1946, p.511).

The father's short phrases are pitched quite low in the singer's voice, and that adds to the impression of a man who is at least trying to remain calm, and cannot see what his son can see. If he is alarmed, he is certainly not going to show it. The boy's phrases are also short, but they are higher in pitch, and they get higher as the tension mounts. His cries of 'Mein Vater, mein Vater' are pitched a step higher each time: up to E flat the first time, F the second time, and G flat the third and last time, the highest note in the whole song. Each time this phrase occurs, it clashes discordantly against the relentlessly hammered-out notes in the right hand of the piano part (the touch that Schubert's teacher Ruzicka is said to have admired). And each time the phrase is exactly the same. This, together with the rising pitch, the dissonance and the sudden return to the hammering of the piano, gives a vivid sense of increasing desperation.

The ending of the song is dramatic in a subtle way. After the climactic cries of the terrified child, and then the father's accelerating gallop, they finally reach home. The climax of the story is delivered quietly and simply: the boy was dead. The extremely 'undramatic' setting of this line is extraordinarily effective. Goethe has already given the clue to it, by switching for the first and only time in the poem to the past tense. If he had written 'the child *is* dead', it would have had quite a different effect. By writing 'the child *was* dead', the narrator steps out of the story, as if closing the book and saying, 'I don't have to tell you the rest. Of course the boy was dead.' Schubert's underplayed setting of this ending enhances that effect.

Schubert wrote several drafts of this song before arriving at the version which is now always performed. (This in itself counts against von Spaun's story of Schubert dashing the perfected song down at one sitting.) Most of the others are different in fairly small ways. In all of them, the beginning is marked *pianissimo*, whereas in the final version it is *forte* from the start so that the song begins straight away with the emphatic pounding of the horse's hooves. One version has a more fundamental difference, and the first page of Schubert's manuscript of it is shown in Figure 28.6. As well as having the soft opening, it simplifies the ferociously difficult piano part, giving the right hand only two notes per beat instead of three. This easier version is never played nowadays. But it is in this form that Schubert himself used to play it (he was not a great virtuoso pianist, unlike Beethoven), and it was this version that was sent to Goethe in the package that the poet never looked at. The opening bars of this simplified version of the piano part are played on Audio 7, track 13. This would be a good point at which to listen to it.

This manuscript also shows that Schubert used a shorthand to save time when writing. As in the final version of 'Erlkönig', the repeated notes in the right hand of the piano part are written out only at the beginning. After that, he writes a succession of minims (long notes) with a diagonal stroke through them, to indicate that each note is to be subdivided in four, as in the first bar. Does this make it more likely that Schubert's first draft could have been ready 'in no time at all'? Perhaps.

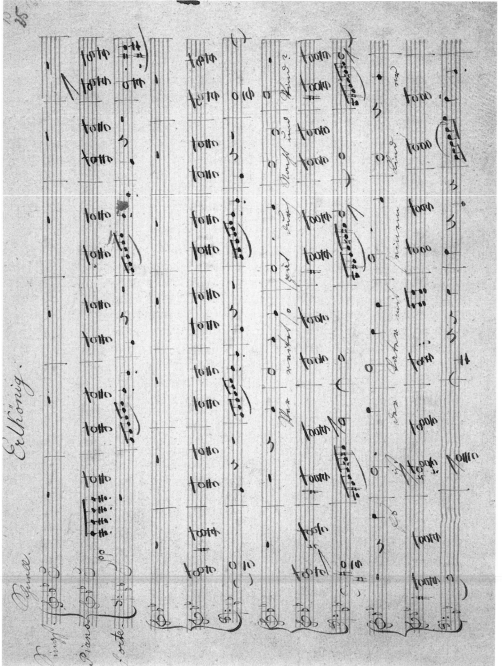

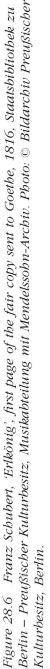

Figure 28.6   Franz Schubert, 'Erlkönig', first page of the fair copy sent to Goethe, 1816, Staatsbibliothek zu Berlin – Preußischer Kulturbesitz, Musikabteilung mit Mendelssohn-Archiv. Photo: © Bildarchiv Preußischer Kulturbesitz, Berlin.

This figure also shows the simplified piano part that Schubert himself played.

'Erlkönig' was the first song by Schubert that Vogl sang at a public concert, in a theatre in Vienna in 1821. Schubert accompanied him at the rehearsal, and was asked by Vogl to add a few bars in the accompaniment so that he had enough time to breathe. It is not clear whether these extra bars were incorporated into the published version that we now know. Vogl's performance at the concert was a great success, and was encored. A review reported that '[s]everal successful passages were justly acclaimed by the public' (quoted in Deutsch, 1946, p.166), which suggests that the audience applauded during the performance, more like a modern jazz audience than the silent audience at 'classical' concerts. (Many reports during the nineteenth century indicate that this was quite normal in concerts of the time.)

Two mythological songs: 'Prometheus' (1819) and 'Ganymed' (1817)

Goethe's poem 'Heidenröslein', with which we began, is a mock folk-song; 'Erlkönig' is a mock ballad along the lines of Scottish models. They are, so to speak, poems in fancy dress. 'Prometheus' and 'Ganymed' are songs on subjects from ancient Greek myth, but they are in no way imitations of ancient classical models. In these two poems Goethe has taken myths and created modern meditations on them of startling, but quite distinct, kinds.

'Prometheus'

Both the poem and the song are quite different from the others considered in this unit. The poem does not rhyme, and its rhythmic patterns are irregular. It is more like an extract from a drama than a conventional poem – and indeed it comes from a play that Goethe began writing in 1773 and never finished.

Prometheus was, in ancient Greek mythology, one of the Titans, who created the human race out of clay. Zeus, the king of the gods, tried to destroy humanity by denying them access to fire. Prometheus saved them by stealing the fire back. For this offence Zeus condemned him to be chained to a mountain-top, where his liver was pecked out each day by an eagle and regrew each night. The myth of Prometheus attracted a number of writers and musicians of the late eighteenth and early nineteenth centuries. Shelley wrote a verse drama on the subject; Beethoven wrote music for a ballet called *The Creatures of Prometheus*. Schubert wrote a substantial cantata on Prometheus in 1816, which had several successful performances during his lifetime, but was lost after his death (this was the cantata written for the name-day of a law professor, and which gave him his entrée to the Sonnleithners' weekly concerts).

In Goethe's drama, Prometheus delivers this speech in his smithy. Schubert's song is like a miniature cantata, or perhaps a scene from an opera. It takes the form of a short, dramatic monologue – a form which is often referred to by musicians by the Italian term *scena*.

EXERCISE Read the poem 'Prometheus' (Anthology II, pp.256–7). How would you describe the substance and tone of what Prometheus is saying? Then play the performance (Audio 7, track 14) and follow the words. In what way is Schubert's setting like a scene from an opera? How does he characterize each section of the poem?

DISCUSSION The predominant tones of the poem are defiance and revolt. But Prometheus does not merely defy the king of the gods: he views him and the other gods with disdain, declaring that they survive only because credulous fools continue to believe in them. He glories in the fact that he has achieved what he has without the help of the gods, and he ends by extolling the full range of human experience, from suffering to joy.

This is a poem of defiance against the rule of gods, and in praise of human accomplishment and human emotional experience. It is very much in tune with the anti-religious sentiments of much Enlightenment writing, and it places a Romantic emphasis on the primacy of the emotions. Its emphasis on striving for freedom, and its portrayal of Prometheus as a creative hero, align it with the *Sturm und Drang* movement described in Units 26–27.

Schubert's setting sounds somewhat like a scene from an opera because much of it is written in recitative, the operatic style which you encountered in *Don Giovanni*, in which the freedom of the vocal line comes close to the rhythms of speech. If you imagine it accompanied by orchestra rather than piano, it is close in style to the *accompagnato* recitative that Mozart uses from time to time.

Schubert's *scena* has no obvious formal structure. Though it is in sections, they do not repeat – it is through-composed. It has the character of a psychological drama, emphasizing the emotional force of each part of the poem as it occurs. But the song nevertheless falls into distinct and contrasted sections. As in 'Gretchen' and 'Erlkönig', it is the piano which both sets the tone and drives the song forward. The assertive rhythm which begins the song punctuates the opening section from time to time, giving a coherent sense of defiance to a passage which would otherwise seem like nothing more than a piece of speech set to music. Schubert continues this section through to the first two lines of the second verse in the original, so shifting the break by two lines. Then, at 'Ihr nähret kümmerlich' ('Meagrely you nourish ...'), the tone changes completely. The sliding harmonies in the piano give the passage a smooth, almost creepy character, perhaps intended to be ironic.

At 'Da ich ein Kind war' ('When I was a child ...') the piano adopts a walking tread, giving a sense of narrative. The voice reaches up at the description of the young boy gazing up at the sun, and the 'ear to listen' and the 'heart to pity' are set to high, plaintive phrases. This is abruptly interrupted by fierce chords at 'Wer half mir' ('Who helped me ...'), returning to the mood of the opening. Then the pace increases at 'Ich dich ehren?' ('I honour you?'), with an impatient-sounding, lurching rhythm in the piano. And the scene ends magnificently, with Prometheus's final shout of defiance, at 'Hier sitz' ich' ('Here I sit ...'), punctuated by forceful chords, like a yet fiercer version of the rhythm with which the song began.

Unusually, the song ends in a different key from its beginning. After the opening bars, the music settles into G minor for the first entry of the voice. The final section, from 'Hier sitz' ich', is in C major. This absence of any formal structure of keys adds to the impression of a song which proceeds freely from one mood to the next.

This unusual informality of structure is something that Schubert exploits to even more striking effect in the last song we shall consider, 'Ganymed'.

'Ganymed' ('Ganymede')

'Ganymed' is another through-composed setting of a poem inspired by ancient Greek mythology. Ganymede was a boy of exceptional beauty, and Goethe's poem describes the feelings of the young lad as he is transported up to heaven by Zeus to become cup-bearer to the gods.

Like 'Prometheus', this is a freely written poem, with no consistency in the length of lines nor any formal metrical scheme. There is only one rhyme ('Nachtigall' and 'Nebeltal' in lines 18–19), and there are only occasional suggestions of half-rhymes (in the first verse there are 'Liebeswonne', 'Wärme' and 'Schöne', which have enough similarity to sound associated).

EXERCISE   Read the poem 'Ganymed' and its translation (Anthology II, pp.257–8), and then listen to the song on Audio 7 (track 15). What has Schubert done to Goethe's poem? Does the combination of words and music suggest further similarities with 'Prometheus', or with the other songs you have studied?

DISCUSSION   Perhaps the most obvious similarity to 'Prometheus' is that the poem is written in the first person. The two poems/songs are expressions of personal feelings. But unlike Prometheus, who is raging against the gods because of past events, Ganymede is expressing his feelings while the most important event of his life is actually taking place. In this sense, he has more in common with Gretchen at her spinning-wheel (though even she is describing her feelings about what has already happened).

Another feature which 'Prometheus' and 'Ganymed' share is that the music, like the poems, is extremely free. About 'Prometheus' I wrote that Schubert's setting has no obvious formal structure and that it has the character of a psychological drama, emphasizing the emotional force of each part of the poem as it occurs. The same applies to 'Ganymed'.

As in several of the songs we have discussed, Schubert has been rather free in the pacing of 'Ganymed', dividing up Goethe's verses where they are continuous, and continuing where they are divided. The first eight lines are continuous, as in Goethe, and Schubert emphasizes the effect of 'Unendliche Schöne' ('Infinite beauty') by drawing the phrase out, giving several notes to a syllable for the first time in the song. In the poem, the next two lines ('Dass ich dich ...') stand on their own, separated from what follows. But Schubert ignores this, carrying straight on for four lines to a gap at 'Lieg ich, schmachte'. Then he introduces a gap after another two lines ('... an mein Herz'), another gap three lines later (after '... Morgenwind'), and another, coinciding with the end of Goethe's verse, at '... aus dem Nebeltal'. Schubert has used these gaps in the vocal line to emphasize the sense of ecstatic calm in the poem, as if Ganymede is looking around him, drinking everything in. There is a charmingly naïve touch just before the mention of the nightingale, where, during the pause which Schubert has introduced in the vocal line, the piano plays trills to suggest the bird's song.

From 'Ich komm ...' the character of the piano part changes: the rhythm becomes insistent and staccato, and Schubert gives the instruction '*un poco accelerando*' ('accelerating slightly'). There is a distinct sense of 'We're off'. The song drives through, reaching two climaxes. The second climax is achieved by repeating the last seven-and-a-half lines of the poem, and then repeating again the final cry of 'Alliebender Vater!' ('All-loving father!'). This repetition is certainly taking liberties with the poem, but the changing character of the music is, one could argue, simply a response to what is already in the verse, as the lines and phrases become shorter and more urgent towards the end of the poem.

As in several of the songs we have studied, it is the piano which sets the mood, the pace and the rhythm as the events unfold, with the voice, so to speak, floating on top of the piano part – almost as if the voice is the 'accompaniment', as in 'Gretchen'. A big difference between 'Ganymed' and 'Prometheus' is that, whereas 'Prometheus' falls into distinct and contrasted sections, 'Ganymed' does not. It all flows smoothly on, and even when the voice pauses, the piano continues. This helps to convey the impression of events unfolding which are not within Ganymede's control – the piano, like Zeus, sweeps him away.

As in 'Prometheus' and 'Gretchen', we are not told the story in the poem. It is as if the poet and composer have thought 'What would it be like to be Ganymede/Prometheus/Gretchen in this situation?', and have sought to convey that directly, assuming that the audience would know the stories from which these characters come (and Goethe and Schubert could assume some knowledge of classical myths in the well-educated circles to whom their work was principally addressed). This is very different from the narrative of 'Erlkönig', in which the song tells the whole story, as well as conveying the feelings of the characters in it.

Schubert ends the song with six bars of the piano, rising higher and higher, *pianissimo*. Like the song of the nightingale earlier, this has an effect which is both powerful and naïve: it conveys both a strong sense of mystery and the suggestion of Ganymede physically disappearing up into heaven.

More than in any of the other songs we have discussed, I would say that, by the end of 'Ganymed', we have the sense of having travelled a long way since the song began. There is one particular musical reason for this: as in 'Prometheus', the song ends in a different key from the beginning. It starts in A flat major and ends in F major. (In the recording on Audio 7, Olaf Bär sings the whole song at a lower pitch, but the effect is the same.) During the song, the music progresses through a variety of keys so gradually that the listener is not necessarily aware of how far from the original key it has travelled. But if you replay the beginning of the song immediately after listening to the ending, you will hear the contrast between the F major of the ending and the A flat major of the beginning.

5   Conclusion

Robert Wilkinson wrote in Units 24–25 that Romanticism in the end became 'the dominant view of art in Europe, and we are to this day its heirs'. This is nowhere truer than in song. Even if you have never encountered German Lieder before, you may have been struck by how the emotional directness of Schubert's writing seems like something familiar from much more recent times. The attempt directly to express emotional experience in poetry and in song, often without explanation or narrative, is characteristic of Romantic writers and composers. Of course, poetry and music had sought to express emotions for centuries before Goethe and Schubert. There have, for example, been love-songs and love-poetry since ancient times. But concentrating solely on the essence of the moment is a characteristically Romantic thing to do, and in the field of music it was to be one of the central features of song-writing through the nineteenth century into the twentieth. One could go so far as to say that the modern popular love-song, from American writers of the 1920s and 1930s such as Cole Porter and George Gershwin through to rock and pop songs of the twenty-first century, are later developments from this intense fusion of poetry and music that was created in the early nineteenth century.

An important element in the drive towards directness and 'simplicity' in song was the interest in what Goethe's mentor Herder called 'Volkslied' ('folk-song'). In the Introduction to this unit I said that this term is now so commonplace that we rarely consider its underlying implications. The concept of a 'folk-song' suggests that the words and music have come from 'the people' rather than from an author and composer. The anonymity of folk-song is taken to be a virtue in itself, as if it has sprung from the soil. Of course, music and poetry do not actually arise like that; someone, sometime, thought up the words and the tune (though it is characteristic of folk-songs that they are passed down through oral tradition, and different versions often result). The idea that simplicity and naturalness in music and the arts generally were to be preferred to the elaborate and artificial has connections with Enlightenment ideas about nature and the concept of the 'noble savage'. But by the end of the eighteenth century this elevation of the simple and the natural was taking on a new dimension that can be seen as Romantic, because of its association with individual feeling and experience. In England Wordsworth was its chief exponent, especially in his *Lyrical Ballads* (1798). In Germany Goethe's supremacy in this field helped to fuel the association of ideas of purity, truth, nature and simplicity with German nationalism, an increasingly powerful force through the nineteenth century. The simpler kinds of Lieder, which Goethe preferred, remained close to the model of folk-song. Schubert sometimes wrote Lieder like that throughout his career (as in 'Heidenröslein'), but he also stretched the concept of the Lied in highly adventurous and imaginative ways.

I used the term 'psychological drama' to describe Schubert's settings of 'Prometheus' and 'Ganymed' (a description that could already be applied to Goethe's poems). One particular example of this approach is 'Erlkönig', which is both a ballad and a horror story. Horror stories in various guises became very popular in the early nineteenth century. The fascination with the 'Gothic novel', often with medieval settings and evoking the supernatural, reached a peak in England in the early nineteenth century. Mary Shelley's *Frankenstein* was written in 1818, three years after Schubert's setting of 'Erlkönig'. In opera, Weber's *Der Freischütz* (1821), a story involving the devil and magic bullets, set a fashion for operas with a supernatural element. Of course, this idea was not entirely new: Mozart's *Don Giovanni*, as you know, culminates in the spectacular intervention of the dead Commendatore from beyond the grave. Goethe's *Faust*, similarly, is a modern reworking of a medieval story of a pact with the devil.

Schubert's particular contribution to this field was to create Lieder that drew out with extraordinary intensity the emotional situation of those overtaken by supernatural forces. In another famous song, 'Der Doppelgänger' (1828, to a poem by Heinrich Heine, one of the most important German Romantic poets), a man visits the house of his former sweetheart at night, to be confronted by his own ghost. Schubert makes of this a song of terrifying power.

Even when not dealing with the supernatural, Schubert is frequently grappling with the inner struggles and resolutions of the human mind. The defiance of Prometheus, the ecstasy of Ganymede, the anguish of Gretchen, the bitter loneliness of the Harper, the calm resignation of the Wanderer, all are expressed in music so subtle and expressive that one has a sense that it is not merely beautiful, but is somehow conveying insights into the human condition.

An important Romantic element of Schubert's method is his freedom with traditional musical forms and procedures. The 'rules' of setting verse have always been flexible in practice. Goethe's preference for adherence to the structure of the poem only went so far, as the settings of Zelter demonstrate. Composers before Schubert, notably Beethoven, stretched the conventions of word-setting. But Schubert went further than any previous composer in giving his imagination free rein, moulding the possibilities of the words in ways that sometimes take them far from their original structure as poems. It was not only in his songs that Schubert did this. His way of writing large movements in his instrumental works is extremely free. Some of his late works, such as his last String Quartet in G major and the second Piano Trio in E flat, had to wait until the second half of the twentieth century before their extraordinary qualities were fully appreciated. Before that time they were often described as 'curate's eggs', works with marvellous music in them, but too long and somewhat disorganized in their construction.

All of this marks Schubert out as a composer with strongly Romantic elements in his music. By comparison, Mozart, with whom this course began, was a composer of the Classical period, whose way of writing was moulded by eighteenth-century aesthetics. The sections of *Don Giovanni* that you have studied have shown you that, however powerful the emotional impact of the music, the structures of individual numbers are always very clear, whether in the more simple items such as 'Batti, batti' or in longer and more complex arias such as 'Il mio tesoro' and 'Or sai chi l'onore'. The sense of balance, between one phrase and the next, between one section and the next, and in the overall shape of a piece of music, is very strong in Mozart. This is not to say that there are no surprises in his work: the sense of the music of *Don Giovanni* following the dramatic developments is also very strong, and there could be nothing more surprising and powerful than the Statue's entry at dinner. Even this striking moment, however, is a carefully balanced repetition of music heard right at the opening of the opera.

Mozart never wrote anything remotely as free in structure as 'Ganymed'. The music seems guided solely by imaginative recreation of a developing psychological situation. It is not written according to any classical conventions. It is a song as free as any in Romantic music. And yet Schubert has Classical elements too. He, like Beethoven, is often described as straddling the Classical and Romantic periods, and combining both tendencies. 'Erlkönig' and 'Gretchen am Spinnrade' are beautifully structured songs. The way they are constructed out of very little material, and the way their refrains are repeated, give them a structural integrity which is as strong as in Classical composers such as Mozart and Haydn. But the way Schubert uses these structural devices to create gradually increasing emotional intensity is thoroughly Romantic, and puts him at the beginning of a musical line that was to lead to the full-blown Romantic orchestral works of Liszt and operas of Wagner.

References

Brown, M.J.E. (1966) *Schubert: A Critical Biography*, London, Macmillan.

Deutsch, O.E. (1946) *Schubert: A Documentary Biography*, London, Dent.

Fischer-Dieskau, D. (1976) *Schubert: A Biographical Study of his Songs*, London, Cassell.

Goethe, J.W. von (1998) *Wilhelm Meisters Lehrjahre*, book 2, chapter 13, *Werke*, vol.7, München, Deutscher Taschenbuch Verlag.

Johnson, G. (ed.) (1991) *The Hyperion Schubert Edition, Complete Songs*, vol.10, London, Hyperion Records.

Parsons, J. (2001) 'Lied', section III: 'Lieder *c*.1740–*c*.1800', in S. Sadie (ed.) *The New Grove Dictionary of Music and Musicians*, 2nd edn, 29 vols, London, Macmillan.

Smeed, J.W. (1987) *German Song and its Poetry*, London, Croom Helm.

Further reading

Brown, M.J.E. (1966) *Schubert: A Critical Biography*, London, Macmillan. A fascinating and thoughtful study, which explodes many of the 'romantic' myths about Schubert's work.

Capell, R. (1957) *Schubert's Songs*, 2nd rev. edn, New York and London, Duckworth. Still the best study of Schubert's songs.

Deutsch, O.E. (1946) *Schubert: A Documentary Biography*, London, Dent. This was the first, and remains the most important, collection of documents relating to Schubert. A book to dip into for insights into Schubert's life and work in Vienna.

The Hyperion Schubert Edition, Complete Songs (1988–), 37 volumes, London, Hyperion Records. A series of CDs which includes all of Schubert's 600 Lieder. The series is masterminded by the pianist Graham Johnson, whose notes for the CD booklets are scholarly and highly informative. A book on Schubert's songs by Graham Johnson is to be published by Yale University Press (currently in press, 2004).

Units 29–30
Byron, *Childe Harold III*

Prepared for the course team by Nicola J. Watson

Contents

Study components

Weeks of study	Supplementary material	Audio-visual	Anthologies and set books
2	AV Notes Illustrations Book	Video 4	Anthology II

Objectives

By the end of your work on Units 29–30, you will have:

- further developed your skills in reading and analysing poetry through tackling a long narrative poem via the concepts of **persona**, **voice**, **imagery**, and **genre**;

- analysed some of the elements that make this a 'Romantic' poem;

- improved your understanding of how to relate a text both to other earlier texts and to biographical and historical context in an appropriately nuanced and cautious way;

- a grasp of the way in which Byron, perhaps above all his contemporaries, came to epitomize the idea of a Romantic genius through a conflation in the public eye of his life and his writing, and of how Romantic genius came to be powerfully associated with torment and transgression through him;

- taken a retrospect across the years we've already covered in the course, seeing how the French Revolution and the Napoleonic empire were viewed after Waterloo.

1   Introduction

Over the next two weeks, we're going to be studying one of the most celebrated poems by one of the most celebrated poets of his day, George Gordon, Lord Byron (1788–1824) (see Figure 29.1). Byron was recognized by his contemporaries as in some sense the epitome of the Romantic Poet. This was a heroic role in which he was himself heavily invested, and which he consciously inaugurated, elaborated, and fine-tuned in his poetry. His poetry was stupendously successful, outselling any other poet in Europe (and that includes those poets whom you have already met in this course, Wordsworth and Goethe), and exerting a massive, instantaneous, and long-lasting effect upon nineteenth-century culture in Britain, Europe and America alike.

Childe Harold's Pilgrimage was the poem that first shot Byron to bestsellerdom and overnight celebrity; and, for his contemporaries, it was probably his most important poem. It was published in four 'cantos' at irregular intervals. Cantos I and II, drafted in 1809 and 1810 respectively, were published together in March 1812; the volume went through five editions in that year alone, not counting the first American edition. Byron commented that he 'awoke and found myself famous' (*Works*, vol.7, p.vi); John Murray, his publisher, who had purchased the copyright outright from the author, awoke to find himself well on the way to riches. Combined with the smash-hit successes of his next publications, 'oriental tales' of forbidden love, notably *The Giaour, The Bride of Abydos,* and *The Corsair* (all published between 1813 and 1814), this poem made Byron into the literary lion of Regency high society and, incidentally, helped him into the beds of a number of prominent women. Byron's poetry conjured far-off places, wild passions, and fatal secrets; these poems supplied, from one point of view, up-market bodice-ripper pleasures calculated to appeal to well-heeled women readers. (This is the point of the satirical sketch *c.*1820 entitled *Byron Mania* – see Figure 29.2.) In April 1816, however, ostracized from London society on account of his stormy and scandalous separation from his recent bride, Annabella Milbanke, and sped by well-founded rumours of his incestuous liaison with his half-sister Augusta Leigh, Byron left England. Behind him he left two little girls: his unacknowledged daughter by Augusta, called Medora, and his daughter by Annabella Milbanke, called Ada.

As it turned out, he had left both them and England behind forever. Refused a passport for France because he was politically suspect as a possible sympathizer with the disgraced Napoleon, he travelled through Belgium down the Rhine to Switzerland to arrive in Geneva. (For a map of his route, see Figure 29.3 (p.198); for a detailed map of Lake Geneva and its environs, see Figure 29.4 (p.199)). There, comfortably accommodated in the lakeside Villa Diodati (see Plate 29.1 in the Illustrations Book), famous enough to be a tourist-sight himself as he sat on the terrace, spied on through the telescopes of the paparazzi, he

Figure 29.1   George Harlow, Byron, *from* Thirty Illustrations of Childe Harold, *1855, Bodleian Library, University of Oxford (shelfmark 17078 d.389(1)).*

Engravings such as this (after the 1814 Philips portrait George Gordon Byron, 6th Baron – *see Plate 29.7 in the Illustrations Book) made Byron's likeness widely and cheaply available, contributing to his celebrity.*

Figure 29.2   Olivia de Ros, Byron Mania, *c.1820, sketch. Photo: courtesy of the Marquess of Salisbury.*

This satire depends upon the contrast between the fashionable, leisured and luxurious setting of the lady, and the sentiments drawn from Byron's poetry (at the bottom) in which she is indulging herself. Note the engraving of Byron at top left, balanced by an engraving of Almack's on the right. Almack's was an exclusive club for the aristocracy.

drafted the last sections of *Childe Harold's Pilgrimage III*. The poem was published in London in December to great acclaim, the sales helped along by Byron's widespread notoriety. Canto IV was drafted in 1817, and was published the following year; it deals with Byron's further travels in Italy, most especially to Venice and to Rome. We are going to confine ourselves, however, to the study of Canto III, because although it is one of a series, in many ways it is also a free-standing poem. It represents one of the most influential of Byron's many mature styles and modes, and one of his most ambitious quasi-autobiographical poetic experiments. It also achieves a number of other closely interwoven things which make it an especially illuminating text within the context of this course's cross-disciplinary preoccupations:

1   It provides a retrospect on Enlightenment intellectual history from a post-Revolutionary, post-Napoleonic stance.

2   It defines a particularly potent and timely mood of post-Waterloo melancholy and disillusion, and rethinks it as Romantic alienation for all subsequent writers in the nineteenth century. (In this context, 'alienation' means a glamorized sense of being out of kilter with the times owing to a particularly acute and refined **sensibility**.)

3   It invents Byron as a prototype for the Romantic author-celebrity still familiar to us today. (This is the idea of the writer as 'mad, bad, and dangerous to know' in Lady Caroline Lamb's famous bon mot, whose own life experiences fuel their poetry and make it especially potent.)

4   It delineated a whole new kind of subjectivity, the Byronic, to which people, both real and fictive, longed to assimilate themselves for the next 50 years or so. Such people included Stendhal (Henri Beyle), whose acquaintance you made in Units 7–8.

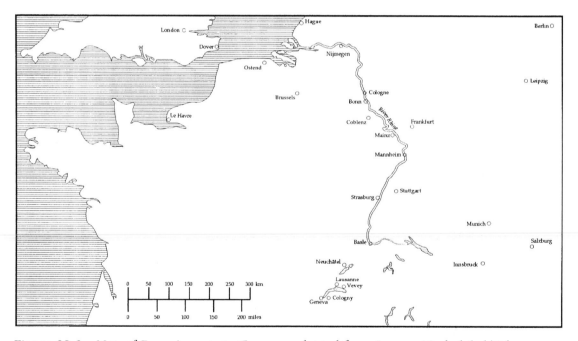

Figure 29.3   Map of Byron's route to Geneva, adapted from Jeanne Moskal (ed.) The Novels and Selected Works of Mary Shelley, *vol.8, Pickering & Chatto (Publishers) Ltd, 1996.*

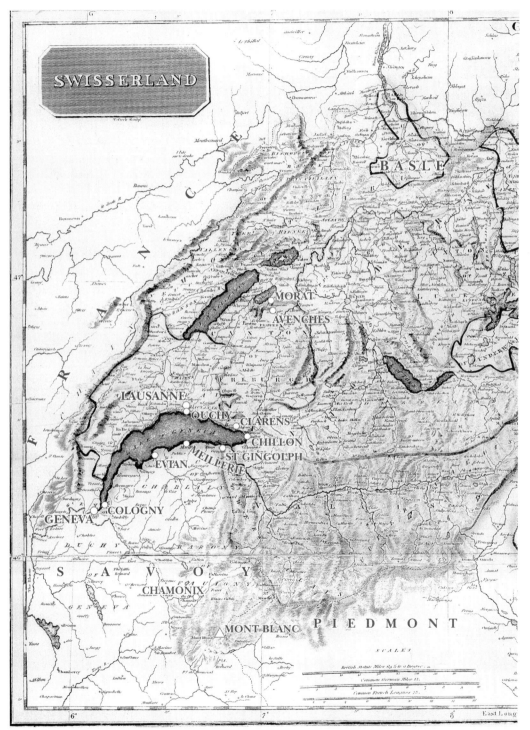

*Figure 29.4   Map of the environs of Lake Geneva, detail of map 28: 'Swisserland',
in John Thompson,* A New General Atlas, *1817, Bodleian map room 2027a.160,
University of Oxford.*

2   Starting to read the poem

The title

Let's start by asking ourselves what *sort* of poem *Childe Harold's Pilgrimage, Canto III* is, or, at any rate, what sort of poem its title claims it to be. The original readers had one especial advantage over you when they picked up this book in 1816, because they had (at the very least) heard of *Childe Harold's Pilgrimage* in the shape of the two preceding cantos, and they had certainly heard of, even if they hadn't read, Byron's poetry beforehand. Still, the title gives brand-new readers quite a lot of clues as to what to expect.

EXERCISE   Take a moment to consider the title. What sort of expectations does it rouse in you? You will find a good dictionary useful here. (Most local libraries will keep the Oxford English Dictionary. Alternatively, if you have Internet access, you might like to experiment with *The Oxford English Dictionary Online.* For information on how to do this, see section 11 of the Course Guide.) Try looking up 'childe' and then 'pilgrimage', for a start.

DISCUSSION   The first thing that strikes me as worthy of note is that the poem is apparently going to be about someone called 'Childe Harold'. *The Oxford English Dictionary* notes that 'childe' can mean 'a youth of gentle birth: used in ballads and the like, as a kind of title', and further remarks that it was a term used in the thirteenth and fourteenth centuries to denote 'a young noble awaiting knighthood'. This suggests to me a number of hypotheses about the poem. First of all, the central personage is going to be 'noble'. The spelling of 'childe' is consciously archaic in the early nineteenth century, so perhaps the language of the poem will be deliberately archaic, too. If we look at the examples of modern usage that the *Oxford English Dictionary* gives, they include quotations from Edmund Spenser's *Faerie Queene* (1591–6), a famous snippet sung by the Fool in Shakespeare's tragedy *King Lear* (1606): 'Childe Rowland to the darke Tower came', thought by the most up-to-date scholarship to be a quotation from a much older ballad, and the last comes from an important late eighteenth-century scholarly collection of ballads, Bishop Percy's *Reliques of Ancient Poetry* (1765). This title, then, already conjures up Spenser's long pseudo-archaic narrative poem and old ballads: both tell stories, so the chances are that this poem will tell a story, too, and that it will probably be set in the past.

In fact, the story seems to be likely to be his 'pilgrimage'. As the *Oxford English Dictionary* makes clear, the primary sense of this word is of a journey undertaken to some sacred place as an act of devotion, but it has two interesting secondary senses: the first, more generally a journey or wandering, and the second, its figurative sense as a metaphor for life's journey, and the homelessness of the spirit on this earth.

Taken together, this evidence begins to suggest that the poem will have a flavour of medieval **quest-romance**. The hero's 'pilgrimage' may be in the nature of the sort of quest that would-be knights typically undertake in romances by Italian authors such as Ariosto (1474–1533) or Tasso (1544–95) before becoming worthy of their spurs. Such quests are physical (they cover a lot of often ambiguously imaginary or magical territory) and they are spiritual (they involve often enough a process of growing-up, religious enlightenment, and sexual initiation). The suggestion of romance is supported also by the use of the 'canto' as an organizational structure for the poem, perhaps most famously used by Spenser in his *Faerie Queene* and signalling a long, even an epic, romance. (*The Faerie Queene*, even in the unfinished form in which Spenser left it at his death, runs to six and a bit books of a proposed 12 or 24; each book consists of a number of cantos.) Indeed if we had been readers of the original volume of *Childe Harold* (containing Cantos I and II) we would also have been aware that the poem was originally subtitled 'A Romaunt'.

What we can deduce from the title is also borne out by the verse-form of the poem.

EXERCISE   Choose a stanza from early in the poem, which begins on p.261 of Anthology II. Count the number of lines in it. Then analyse the rhyme-scheme: call the first rhyme 'A', the second 'B', and so on. Finally, read the lines aloud, and see if you can work out where the line makes you stress individual words or syllables. Mark these heavy stresses with a line above the syllable.

DISCUSSION   The poem (for the most part) is constructed as a series of nine-line stanzas. The rhyme-scheme typically runs ABA-BBC-BCC. The metre is basically iambic pentameter, that is, five two-syllable 'feet' stressed on the latter syllable, as follows:

> | The mórn | is úp | agáin, | the dé | wy mórn. |

(Stanza 98, line 1)

(Note: if your scansion didn't work, don't panic, as poets often depart from orthodox scansion so as to introduce variety within the poem. Try choosing another line instead, and have another go.) The last line of each stanza, however, typically has *six* stresses.

This stanza form is the Spenserian stanza, so-called because this is the form that Spenser used in *The Faerie Queene*.

In fact, in 1812 Byron had prefaced Cantos I and II with a discussion of his aesthetic choices, which usefully amplifies (and complicates) our conclusions so far.

EXERCISE   Read Byron's 'Preface' to Cantos I and II of *Childe Harold's Pilgrimage* (Anthology II, pp.303–5) and, as you do so, make some written notes in answer to the following questions:

1   What do you take to be the selling-point to Byron's original audience of 'the scenes which [the poem] attempts to describe'?

2   What is the relative importance of the central character of Childe Harold?

3   What is distinctive about Harold as a hero?

4   What reasons does Byron give for adopting the Spenserian stanza?

5   Which of the conventions of romance we've been discussing does Byron seem to be planning to exploit?

DISCUSSION   One of the things that may have escaped you in this age of the mass package holiday is that Byron is relying on exotic locations in the south and the east to sell his poem. Childe Harold himself is described as merely a convention or an occasion to connect the poem's landscape set-pieces. This disclaimer is belied, however, by the denial that Harold is a self-portrait and by the long discussion of Harold's rather dubious moral character in the 'Addition to the Preface' supplied in 1813; both suggest that the figure of Harold was perceived as rather more important than here suggested. (In fact, the Childe was instantly taken to be a very thinly-disguised self-portrait.) Harold is clearly peculiar as a romance hero – for one thing he seems an 'anachronism', and for another he is of a 'very indifferent character'. This, along with that rather curious remark that his hero might have done more and expressed less, suggests that he is an **anti-hero**, that is to say, an unheroic character who nonetheless fills the place and function of the hero in the story to comic or ironic effect.

Byron clearly adopts the Spenserian stanza as consciously archaic ('the old structure of versification') and as especially hospitable to waywardness and mercurial shifts of tone; this is of a piece with the preface's earlier insistence that the cantos are 'experimental' and make 'no pretension to regularity'. This is a characteristically Byronic standpoint; his aesthetic is (famously) always consciously desultory and even aggressively amateur, as befitted an aristocrat.

Overall then, we have certain aspects of romance flagged up – in particular, its verse-form and its 'looseness' – and we are provided with the spine of the narrative, an aristocratic protagonist upon a journey or unspecified quest.

We will come back rather later to the question of whether the title's promise to deliver 'romance' is actually fulfilled. Meanwhile, let us start reading the poem itself. But just before we start, a word of advice if you are anxious about reading poetry, as many people are. The important thing to remember is that if reading poetry seems more difficult than reading most types of prose, this is because it is often highly compressed. Compression may result in unusual syntactical constructions, and is fundamental to the use of **metaphor**. Therefore, there are two useful rules for reading poetry. The first is to sort out the *grammar* of the statement which is being made in each stanza. Ask yourself – who or what is the subject? Where is the main verb? Who or what is the object? (In other words, who or what is doing what to whom?) Each of Byron's stanzas typically make an opening statement which is then investigated, elaborated, and qualified – so make sure you know what the *argument* of each stanza is. (Byron's contemporaries would have read this poem out aloud to one another in the drawing room – this isn't a bad idea if you're having trouble working out the meaning of a stanza, since it slows you up, and helps you decide where the stress should fall to make sense of the sentence. Find a friend to be an audience! The accompanying video has sections of the poem read aloud especially to help you here.) The second rule is related to my first observation because Byron typically uses a sequence of metaphors to investigate, elaborate and qualify his argument. (Metaphor, to remind you, is simply an *implicit* comparison between one thing and another – it's a simile if an *explicit* comparison is made.) Make sure, therefore, that you know who or what is being compared to what in each metaphor, and then ask yourself what the relationship between each metaphor in the string might be. But if you remain baffled by the odd line or lines, don't worry – eminent academics regularly conduct spirited arguments about the possible meanings of obscure lines. I advise you to pass over lightly when you've done your best. Now, let's turn to look in detail at the opening stanzas.

The apostrophe and opening

This poem begins with an **apostrophe**. This is a formal term for an opening of a poem that directly addresses another person, whether friend, lover, child, parent, god, or muse, as though they were present or as if the poem was a letter.

EXERCISE   Now read stanza 1 (Anthology II, p.261) and answer the following questions. Who is the poem addressed to? Where is the poet? And what is the story so far? (You may find it useful to recall my opening remarks in the unit.)

DISCUSSION   The poem is addressed to Ada, the poet's young daughter. The poet 'awakes' from what seems to have been a dream-vision of the face of his smiling young daughter, so like her mother's, to reality in the shape of waves and wind. We are encouraged to infer therefore that he is at sea, and this is confirmed by the word 'depart' and located by the phrase 'Albion's lessening shores'. Put crudely, he's offshore on a ship, watching the English shoreline fade away, thinking of his wife and daughter, leaving for he knows not where, and apparently in a state of depression induced by a parting without 'hope' which has entirely displaced any ordinary sadness or pleasure at travelling away from home.

This paraphrase doesn't really do justice, though, to the sheer drama of this stanza. It begins like a play, with the direct and impassioned address to Ada, breaks the line at line 5 to dramatize the poet's awakening, and with it recapitulates the severance of relationship with the child, and by disorienting us as readers, dramatizes the poet's own momentary disorientation and his dreary recall of the situation – 'I depart'. I hope you admired, too, the economy of this stanza – just compare how many words I've had to use to describe the meaning and effect of this stanza with the number Byron uses!

EXERCISE   Now read stanza 2. Bearing in mind what we've already discovered about the dramatic qualities of this verse, describe the ways in which the poet's mood seems to have changed. You will find it useful to think about the metaphors he deploys.

DISCUSSION   The poet now shifts gear from depression and regret to revelling in a familiar pleasure, that of travel. We know it's familiar because of the metaphor the poet uses: 'the waves bound beneath me as a steed/That knows his rider', and we know that he is revelling in it from his cry of 'welcome'. The poet begins in a state of self-dramatizing delight at being forced on into the future by the rising waves and wind – he imagines himself as the ship riding out the storm – and then, with a sudden diminution of both heroism and euphoria, as seaweed torn from its rock. Indeed, as the stanza progresses, the change of metaphors suggests that the poet comes to imagine himself as having less and less control over his circumstances.

What our detailed discussion of the opening of the poem already suggests is that we have on our hands not so much a story about things happening as the dramatization of a state of mind as it fluctuates. If you hold onto this insight as you read the poem, it will help you not to get lost or baffled. I might as well warn you now that it would be possible to say that nothing much 'happens' in this poem.

Let's carry on a little looking at the opening moves of the poem.

EXERCISE   Now read stanza 3 through to stanza 7 (pp.261–3). Bearing in mind that this is in some sense an autobiographical poem, and remembering what you know about Byron's life and career to this point, make a summary of the narrative of these stanzas, and outline the poet's description of his current state of mind.

DISCUSSION   Stanza 3 begins by recapitulating the story so far. When he was younger ('in my youth's summer') he wrote the two first cantos about Childe Harold ('I did sing of One,/The wandering outlaw of his own dark mind'), and now he's going to write the next canto ('Again I seize the theme'). Looking back, he describes the early cantos as seeming now to the older poet to be the traces of previous, now vanished, thought and emotion ('furrows' and 'tracks' of thought and 'dried-up tears'). The question that seems to hang over the last two rather difficult lines is whether the 'Tale' can be reclaimed from sterility, whether new life can be breathed into it. Stanza 4 continues to ponder this problem. Have age and unhappiness changed or weakened him as a poet, he asks ('perchance my heart and harp have lost a string,/And both may jar'), or will the exercise be good for him, weaning him 'from the weary dream/ Of selfish grief or gladness'? Stanza 5 effectively sets out a story of the suffering poet who turns to the magic of memory and imagination described as 'lone caves, yet rife/With airy images, and shapes which dwell/Still unimpair'd, though old, in the soul's haunted cell.' The very famous stanza 6 lays out Byron's theory of why a poet writes at all. Writing enables him to live more intensely because what is imagined by the poet invigorates and empowers him, and even supplies him with feeling, despite his emotional numbness ('feeling still with thee in my crush'd feelings' dearth'). Stanza 7 describes the state of mind that will dominate the poem hereafter and does it in metaphors that will resonate throughout the poem. The poet has been 'poison'd' by the wildness of his youthful emotion, and moreover, he is irrevocably changed by age and sadness. 'Phantasy and flame' are now to be replaced with silent endurance of the 'bitter fruits' of his youthful unwisdom, which remains rather unspecified.

Now that we have made a start on techniques for taking apart the verse of *Childe Harold III*, I'd like to change gears and talk in more general terms. Something that has already become apparent is that the poem seems to be both voiced by and 'about' a poet-narrator, as well as 'about' Childe Harold himself. This narrator's fluctuating sensibility structures the poem as episodic and associative, although by stanza 8 he is claiming that the poem will (at long last!) be about 'long absent HAROLD'. In the next section we're going to consider the relation between Harold and the narrator.

Three voices

Harold is at once a 'character' and a 'voice'. As a 'character', this jaded voluptuary has a past, a personal history, supplied by Canto I and alluded to again in Canto III, stanzas 8–16. Canto I had provided this curriculum vitae for its hero:

> For he through Sin's long labyrinth had run,
> Nor made atonement when he did amiss,
> Had sigh'd to many though he loved but one,
> And that loved one, alas! could ne'er be his.
> Ah, happy she! to 'scape from him whose kiss
> Had been pollution unto aught so chaste;
> Who soon had left her charms for vulgar bliss,
> And spoil'd her goodly lands to gild his waste,
> Nor calm domestic peace had ever deign'd to taste.
>
> And now Childe Harold was sore sick at heart,
> And from his fellow bacchanals would flee;
> 'Tis said, at times the sullen tear would start,
> But Pride congeal'd the drop within his ee:
> Apart he stalked in joyless reverie,
> And from his native land resolved to go,
> And visit scorching climes beyond the sea;
> With pleasure drugg'd, he almost long'd for woe,
> And e'en for change of scene would seek the shades below.
>
> The Childe departed from his father's hall: ...
>
> (Canto I, stanzas 5–7)

Canto III reiterates much of this with more sophistication in stanzas 8–16.

EXERCISE   Take a careful look at stanzas 8–16 (pp.263–5), and jot down some notes describing the flashback history of Harold's state of mind. As you're doing this, also note what sort of metaphors and images Byron is using.

DISCUSSION   This Harold, the poem claims, is older and more experienced, but no less tortured and restless. He still carries with him some secret torment, described excitingly and mysteriously in a metaphoric language of extremes, as 'wounds which kill not, but ne'er heal' (stanza 8, line 68), 'a chain/Which gall'd for ever, fettering though unseen' (stanza 9, lines 77–8). Did you notice how often the poem calls up the idea of inescapable and perpetual doom through the words 'ever', 'never', and evocations of death? If you didn't, take a look at lines 67, 68, 76, 78, 81, 94, 124 and 140. Over this secret torment without apparent source or solution, he has bound a self-protective 'guarded coldness', a proud and disaffected self-isolation 'as one, might 'midst the many stand unheeded'. But he has fallen prey to temptations – 'the ripen'd rose', 'beauty's cheek', 'Fame' – or love and ambition. He has been briefly seduced back into 'the giddy circle', but this turns out to have been temporary because he is too proud and too exceptional 'to herd with Man'. With more than a touch of Milton's Satan or of Mary Shelley's ambitious scientist Victor Frankenstein, 'He would not yield dominion of his mind/To spirits against whom his own rebell'd;/Proud though in desolation; which could find/A life within itself, to breathe without mankind' (stanza 12, lines 105–8). Though Nature (disconcertingly Wordsworthian in places, as when he abandons books for 'Nature's pages' – stanza 13, line 117) provides an intermittent palliative, his state is akin to the rather grandiosely blood-stained would-be escapee falcon in stanza 15. The important thing about this torment is that although it seems to be partly a matter of the human condition in a fallen world ('this clay will sink/Its spark immortal', lines 123–4), it also seems to be in some sense self-generated and, moreover, seems to be the imprimatur of an especially great and uncommon soul; it inspires a divine restlessness which results in the 'self-exile' and wandering at the beginning of stanza 16.

You may, of course, find this all very faintly silly (the satirical novelist Thomas Love Peacock, friend of Keats and Shelley, would have agreed with you, as we'll see, so you'd be in good company), or all very sexy (Lady Caroline Lamb, who fell in love with the poem and so into bed with the poet must have found it so), or even downright pernicious (that's what the right-wing periodical *The Anti-Jacobin* thought). Still, it's glorious rolling verse and sounds well read aloud, which (as I've already remarked) is what most of Byron's admirers would have done of an evening in the drawing room.

The other moment when Harold makes a substantial appearance in the poem is at the centre point of the canto in what is usually referred to as the Drachenfels lyric (four separately numbered stanzas), together with the preceding four stanzas (stanzas 52–5).

EXERCISE   Turn to stanzas 52–5 and the following four stanzas (pp.277–80). Take a
few moments to try to decide what differentiates the Drachenfels lyric
from the rest of the poem. You might want to consider the rhythm of the
inset poem, its rhyme-scheme, its speaker, and its addressee.

DISCUSSION   The Drachenfels lyric is distinguished from the main body of the poem
first of all by its system of numbering. More important is the change in
the verse-form. Looking at the poem on the page you can readily see
that there is one extra line in each stanza. It is also the case that the lines
are shorter; if you read it aloud, you'll discover that the line has fewer
stresses. So, we would scan the first line of the Spenserian stanza like
this:

   | 'And hé | had léarn'd | to lóve, | – I knów | not why' |

and the last line of the stanza, which is rather longer, like this:

   | 'In hím | this glów'd | when áll | besíde | had céased | to glów' |

But the lyric scans like this:

   | 'The cástl | ed crág | of Drách | enféls' |

That is to say, the Spenserian line has five stresses in it, unless it's the last
line, in which case it has six, while the lyric has only four stresses
throughout. The immediate effect of this is a lighter, more spontaneous,
speedier, and more naïve line, suitable to an effusion of 'absent
greetings' from a lover. The rhyme-scheme, too, of the lyric is lighter and
less sophisticated. The Spenserian stanza's rhyme-scheme can be
described as ABA-BBC-BCC. It makes it suitable for carrying an extended
thought throughout (via the rhyme B), pivoting after the first four lines if
liked, and clinching the thought with the final couplet. Perhaps it is
needless to say that if you get interested in this and trawl through the
poem you will discover that Byron blithely breaks every rule of rhyme,
rhythm and pacing at one point or another – he was a master of
versification. (For an example, look at the last line of stanza 47, where
Byron manages the stresses so as to get a particularly heavy and slow
effect compounded by the flamboyant use of **alliteration**.) By contrast,
the lyric's rhyme-scheme is simpler and more varied: the first two verses
are the same, but the last two are each different. The lyric's more free-
floating form is like a ghost of the more sophisticated form. It is worth
pausing on the effects Byron gets out of the final couplet, aided by the
convenient rhyme of 'Rhine' with 'thine' and 'mine'. In three out of the
four stanzas, the stanza begins with landscape description, and comes
back to the addressee in the couplet. The overall effect is to insist that
the landscape is incomplete without the ability to share the experience
with the absent woman.

The Drachenfels lyric is the last moment when we see Harold. He then, disconcertingly, vanishes. But he has always had a rather strange relation to the poet-narrator or minstrel. After all, it is definitely a slight shock at the beginning of stanza 52, when after apparently attending to the poet-narrator's thoughts on the Rhine castles for a couple of pages, Byron simply sums them up casually with 'Thus Harold inly said, and pass'd along' (stanza 52, line 460). I am unable to distinguish anything in the preceding stanzas that seems calculated to characterize their meditations as peculiarly Harold's. If their consciousnesses seem to blend seamlessly, so do their life-stories. Harold seems just as well supplied with transgressive and scandalous love-interest as the poet-narrator (stanza 55), and there's even a suggestion of a baby: 'he had learn'd to love, [...]/ The helpless looks of blooming infancy,/Even in its earliest nurture' (stanza 54, lines 478–81). The narrator's torment and alienation are also brought about in roughly the same way as Harold's – 'untaught in youth my heart to tame,/My springs of life were poison'd' (stanza 7, lines 59 and 60).

Harold, in short, seems to double and to distance the poet-narrator's own **psychodrama** of guilt and alienation. While these two voices and characters are imperfectly distinguished, there is another highly distinctive voice, a voice that earths the poem – the voice of the editor. After all, what *are* all those footnotes doing in this poem?

EXERCISE Now glance through the poem, pausing at Byron's footnotes.[7] (I know this is an odd way of doing it – reading the footnotes before you've read the poem, but I think you'll find it illuminating.) Try to do two things:

1 Write out a summary of what is characteristic about the voice of Byron's footnotes.

2 See if you can make a list of the sort of effects produced by the juxtaposition of that voice with the main body of the poem.

DISCUSSION What I noticed first of all is that the editor is clearly identified as the same person as the poet-narrator. Their experiences are the same, and the notes comment on occasion on the aesthetic choices made and the literary allusions chosen. After that, my list of the editor's characteristics runs as follows: pedantic, well-read, well-travelled (see the note to stanza 30), invested in historical and topographical detail, and in the documentary detail (see the note to stanza 67), the complete tourist and souvenir hunter (see the note to stanza 63), a conventional first-person travel-writer dealing in the authority of the personal anecdote (see the notes to stanzas 58 and 71, and others), even a flavour of the journalist (see the note to stanza 30). The editor is committed to a viewpoint in the historical present.

[7] Notes marked with an asterisk are Byron's own.

My list of effects was much harder to compile, but it looks like this:

- This voice is necessarily discontinuous, by which I mean that it doesn't carry the main burden of narrative address, and only appears occasionally.

- It is apparently contingent to the main narrative, by which I mean it is parasitical and explanatory of the main body of the poem.

- But, although the first two points suggest that the notes are secondary to the main text, the notes powerfully qualify the effect of the poetry. Here, we might cite the long note to stanza 30 in which Byron is guided round the topography of the field of Waterloo. Its interest in the eye-witness evidence of the guide, in the fast-vanishing physical evidence of the solitary trees and the remains of a shallow grave makes a striking end-piece to the celebrated flight of imaginative empathy with which Byron conjures up the interrupted ball in Brussels to strenuous immediacy on his reader's pulses – 'Did ye not hear it?' (stanza 22, line 190). We descend from the epic grandeur of 'Battle's magnificently-stern array' (stanza 28, line 248) to the comparatively banal. The note also qualifies the patriotic romance elements of the depiction of the battle with one sly clause waiting in ambush: 'As a plain, Waterloo seems marked out for the scene of some great action, though this may be mere imagination: I have viewed with attention those of Platea, Troy, Mantinea, Leuctra, Chaeronea, and Marathon; and the field around Mont St Jean and Houguomont *appears to want little but a better cause* ... to vie in interest with any or all of these ... ' (italics added). A similar effect of the degeneracy of the modern by comparison to the heroics of the past is produced by the note to stanza 63, in which 'Morat! the proud, the patriot field!' appears in the note in the shape of a destroyed chapel, and a few bones which the Swiss are in the habit of using as knife-handles and Byron removes as souvenirs. These notes thus serve to ironize the sentiments of the main text; others are even more purely ironical, operating as mere disruption. Even as the verse solicits imaginative identification with the state of Romantic alienation and deprivation at the centre of the poem, and we are swooning into the deliciousness of the Drachenfels lyric, we are blandly interrupted at the very first line with a piece of lack-lustre and entirely irrelevant guidebook information: 'The number of castles and cities along the course of the Rhine on both sides is very great, and their situations remarkably beautiful.'

Overall, the multiple consciousnesses that the poem boasts have the effect of dislocating the reader's experience of the poem. To put it another way, you never quite know where you are with the poem. The poem is full of deliberate traps and surprises to unnerve the unwary reader – some of them we've already noted above, but there are many others. One of the more celebrated is the very first stanza. If you look again at this stanza and notice the tenses, you'll see the sophisticated games Byron is playing with us. It seems to start with an address to his daughter Ada, who, it is suggested, is present; then it slips into flashback of the memory of the previous parting, then into a memory of the latest parting, and then all of this turns out to be in some sense a dream and the poet awakes mid-Channel. Another surprise effect is brought into play at the end of stanza 16 when we're brought up sharp by direct apostrophe and prohibition: 'Stop! – for thy tread is on an Empire's dust!' (stanza 17). It's a startling moment, because it suddenly incorporates us as readers into the poem's fictional world – it suddenly makes us visible and accountable.

This characteristic of the poem – its tendency to disjuncture – is one of the things that identifies it as subscribing to a Romantic aesthetic. In fact, it might well remind you of the discussion in Units 24 and 25 of the idea of Romantic irony. Disjuncture draws attention to the limitations of the poem as a work of art.

Let's briefly recapitulate. So far our investigations have suggested that the poem offers a psychodrama. Byron's multiple-voicing produces an effect of fracturedness and discontinuity. I'd like to suggest as a provisional hypothesis to bear in mind as you read further that this fracturedness is meant to be construed as a rendition of a universal modern state of mind – a state of alienation. The poem, then, might be built not so much out of an accumulation of content but rather out of the disjunctions and thresholds between its many modes, between apostrophe, narrative, description, meditation, confession, and conversation. As you read on, you'll find yourself alternating abruptly and dizzyingly between animated energy and descriptive calm, between emotional introspection and mini-narrative, between an apocalyptic poetic vision of fragmentation and failure and a faintly smug set of footnotes. (You might recall here from Units 24–25 that Romantic irony was designed to prevent the reader from becoming mentally too comfortable!) All this discursive drama is, however, held together by variants of **first-person narration**, and this results in the reader's identification with the **implied author**, 'Byron'. It is a sort of seduction, and readers then and now have been seduced. I hope you will be, too.

Overview

We are now going on to tackle a series of short episodes in the poem one by one. Only towards the end of your studies will I be asking you to read the poem in its entirety. However, I think at this stage you will find it useful to have a sense of the overall structure of the poem, and so overleaf is a chart that gives an overview of what 'happens' over the course of the poem, and keys it to stanza numbers.

Stanzas 1–2	The poet-narrator leaves his home, family, and England by boat.
Stanzas 3–7	Analysis of the poet-narrator's state of mind and resolution to take up the poem about Childe Harold where it was left off.
Stanzas 8–16	Analysis of Harold's state of mind and his departure from England.
Stanzas 17–20	Harold (and the poet-narrator) visit the field of Waterloo, within a year of Wellington's victory and Napoleon's defeat, and meditate upon the meaning of the defeat of Napoleon and the current peace.
Stanzas 21–9	Evocation of the battle of Waterloo.
Stanzas 30–4	The poet-narrator considers the bereaved and the state of bereavement.
Stanza 35	Waterloo considered in relation to the verdict of history.
Stanzas 36–45	Fall of Napoleon considered and analysed, leading to a general meditation on the fate of ambitious men throughout history.
Stanzas 46–61 (including the Drachenfels lyric)	Harold and the narrator embark on the Rhine (a hard-fought border, in Napoleon's time, between the French and the Prussians) and travel by river along one of the most famous stretches of picturesque scenery in Europe at the time, from Drachenfels Castle (near Bonn), past Coblenz, down to Ehrenbreitstein, and so on towards present-day Switzerland. Meditations upon nature and history, punctuated by further analysis of Harold's state of mind and his love-letter (the Drachenfels lyric) back home to his estranged and anonymous love.
Stanzas 62–8	Journey through the Alps, taking the only possible route to the city of Geneva along a chain of lakes via the battlefield of Morat and the Roman ruins at Avenches. The narrator (now mysteriously unaccompanied by Harold) meditates upon the banks of Lake Geneva (also known rather confusingly by its French name, Lac Leman). (See Figures 29.3 and 29.4, pp.198–9.)
Stanzas 69–75	Meditation upon the narrator's state of mind and the possible comforts that nature may offer.
Stanzas 76–81	Consideration of the career and importance of Jean-Jacques Rousseau as political theorist.
Stanzas 82–4	Meditation upon the failure and legacy of the French Revolution.
Stanzas 85–98	Evocation of Alpine landscape around Geneva, culminating in a set-piece storm.
Stanzas 99–104	A visit to local sites along the shore of the lake, Clarens, and Meillerie, prompts further consideration of Rousseau's career, this time as autobiographer and novelist.

3   Byron in post-Napoleonic Europe

Although we've begun to dip into the detail of Byron's poem, we haven't touched upon some of the most important and celebrated sections of the poem as yet. These include the sections on Waterloo and Napoleon, on Rousseau, and on the Alps, and we're going to devote our attention to them now. In so doing, we will find ourselves investigating how Byron transforms the political, historical, fictional, poetical, and aesthetic monuments and sights of Europe into a highly personalized experience, and discovering how a report on the political, physical and spiritual state of post-Napoleonic Europe can be dramatized as a state of mind.

Waterloo

The first tourist site that Harold and the poet-narrator happen upon is the field of Waterloo. This was geographically almost inevitable if you made the Channel crossing from Dover to Ostend; but it was also inevitable that Byron and his poem should make a stop there in 1816 (the fact that he says it was his carriage breaking down that delayed him long enough to make the visit seems almost beside the point). The battle of Waterloo was a landmark in the political, cultural, and imaginative European landscape of the time; and unsurprisingly it had particular meanings in Regency Britain. This was not simply because it brought to an end 20 years of war (a lifetime for Byron); it was because how it was construed determined the public perception of the whole period since 1789 (Bainbridge, 1995, p.136). As the defeat and downfall of Napoleon, it provided the dramatic moral catastrophe to the great social experiment of the French Revolution embodied in the emperor's career. On the other hand, the outcome of Waterloo also delineated the contours of the political future: restored hereditary monarchy across Europe. On the whole, then, Waterloo appeared to the British and their European allies as a great and decisive event; as we shall see, however, Byron has a rather different view.

The story of Waterloo always was the stuff of high drama. As you have already read in Stendhal's account, the defeated Napoleon escaped from his exile in Elba in the spring of 1815, landed in the south of France with a thousand men, and marched up over the Alps and so to Paris, collecting support fast the further north he went, most crucially from the army, which had been his own creation. The Bourbon king fled Paris, and Napoleon took power again without a shot fired. He was to rule for a hundred days, until his final defeat at Waterloo, a village close to Brussels, by the Duke of Wellington and Marshal Blücher (commanding the Prussians) on 18 June. Wellington was caught by surprise by Napoleon's full-frontal attack (hence his presence at the ball at Brussels on the eve of battle from which the officers departed hurriedly), and the battle was a very close-run thing – as Wellington himself remarked.

Napoleon's last campaign had immense mythical power in the British popular imagination: the war-weary Allies wrangling over the shape of the new Europe at the Congress of Vienna were astonished and horrified to see Napoleon, as it were, rise from the dead with apparently renewed vitality, and the confrontation between him and the Duke of Wellington, between two national heroes, had the flavour of an epic duel. As one contemporary writer put it, echoing the report in *The Times* a week after the news broke:

> In the Annals of Ancient and Modern history, a parallel to the BATTLE OF WATERLOO is sought for in vain ... ages may roll away before the talents of a Wellington, a Blücher, and a Napoleon, shall be combined at once in so tremendous a contest!
>
> (*Description*, c.1817, p.iii)

With the news of victory, Britain went Waterloo-mad. There were victory balls, and a special day of celebrations in the parks on 1 August. Entrepreneurs set up grand 'panoramas' in London and Liverpool of the battle. (A panorama was a round room into which you went and found yourself in the Regency equivalent of Imax. Like Imax, a panorama could rise spectacularly high, curved round the viewer so that the image filled the peripheral vision – the result is a sense of total immersion in the experience. You bought a key and explanatory notes, and then stood in the middle of a circle of huge action-paintings – the figures in Liverpool's 'Grand Historical Peristrephic Painting' were life-size likenesses. After your visit you could buy their equivalent of a postcard in the shape of little engravings.) There was a scale-model of the field set up in London's Regent Street. Catering for the more highbrow end of the market, the British Institution set up a competition for the best depiction of Waterloo designed as 'a national commemoration of the moral and political effects of this great victory'; the winner was 'The Battle of Waterloo, in an Allegory' by James Ward, RA, in oils on the heroic scale of 35 ft by 21 ft (Ward, 1821, p.4).

From the first, London was flooded with eye-witness accounts of the battle by officers and soldiers, accounts of visits to the field shortly afterwards, and engravings and aquatints to suit every pocket depicting the sites of the battle, celebrated episodes, fallen heroes, and even Bonaparte's guide, John de Coster. There were biographies of Blücher and Wellington, broadsheet ballads such as 'The White Flag, or Boney done over', and a score or so of patriotic poems of every type from ballad through ode (with notes) written by everyone from a baronet to 'William Jordan of the 33rd Regiment'. All sorts of souvenirs and relics of the battle were in circulation, so much so that a museum was set up in Pall Mall, which exhibited a variety of weapons, including 'the Sword of the heroic and ever to be lamented Duke of Brunswick, picked up in the field the day after the fall of the gallant hero' (*Catalogue,* 1815, p.3), torn and battered articles of clothing and armour (cuirasses), saddles, knapsacks, cooking apparatus, a fiddle 'taken from a French drummer killed in the action' (*Catalogue,* 1815, p.5), two shells, and a large selection of Bonaparte memorabilia, together with a number of affecting paintings of the action. The most spectacular souvenir of all, Napoleon's carriage, captured on the field, was exhibited with all its solid gold fittings at the London museum. The general sentiment in Britain is well summed up in the *Guide to the Grand Improved Model of the Battle of Waterloo*:

> The grand results of the triumph of Waterloo will show to the world and to posterity, that England's sons are invincible in battle, and that they are capable of the mightiest exertions of every kind. It is England alone that has held out, without any interval of faultering, and entirely escaped degradation.

> (*Guide, c.*1815, p.2)

(This last sentence was a jibe at the Prussians, who arrived late, through no fault of their own, though this was not the view adopted by contemporary British propagandists.)

Nor was this interest in Waterloo confined to the first flush of victory in 1815; plenty of poems were written in the next few years invoking the battle as a way to defuse the post-war political panic that gripped Britain in 1816, driven by the consciousness of the vast cost of the war and the problem of the many returning discharged and disaffected soldiers, often disabled, and unable to find work. As the author of *The Battle of Waterloo, A Poem, with Notes* (1817) revealingly remarked in his Preface:

> The Author of the following lines offers them to a kind and generous Public, under the firm conviction, that they may have at least a trifling effect in dispelling the clouds which have for some time past enveloped our political hemisphere, in consequence of those unavoidable distresses, which the expenses of the late tedious and protracted war necessarily occasioned.

Waterloo remained an important subject for many years, although inevitably the inflection changed: of these depictions certainly one of the most famous was David Wilkie's *Chelsea Pensioners Reading the Waterloo Despatch* (1822), commissioned by the Duke of Wellington himself (see Plate 29.2 in the Illustrations Book).

Byron, then, was just one of a flood of inquisitive British tourists who made their way to the Continent to see for themselves, and to bring back their own souvenirs, sketches and accounts. He was by no means the first of these tourists, nor was he the only famous poet who came, saw, and composed a lucrative work. Both Sir Walter Scott and Robert Southey produced their own important pieces on the occasion of their visits to Waterloo, respectively, *The Field of Waterloo* (1815) and *The Poet's Pilgrimage to Waterloo* (1816). Although neither Scott's nor Southey's poem became as celebrated as *Childe Harold*, we can identify what was relatively conventional about Byron's treatment of Waterloo, and what was highly distinctive, by comparing some extracts both from these poets' letters and from their poems. Let's start with their letters.

EXERCISE   Turn to Anthology II (pp.306–9 and 312–14) where you will find (i) an extract from Sir Walter Scott's letter to the Duke of Buccleuch describing his visit to the field (August 1815), and (ii) an extract from Byron's letter to Hobhouse on his visit to the battlefield (May 1816).

Start by comparing Scott's letter with Byron's and with the footnote to stanza 30 of *Childe Harold's Pilgrimage* (pp.270–1). What similarities between these three pieces of prose can you identify? Can you put your finger on any critical differences?

DISCUSSION   As you will have realized from Scott's letter, he is an earlier visitor than Byron to the scene, arriving in August 1815. (Lockhart, Scott's biographer, claimed that he was 'among the first civilians who hurried over' (1893, p.314), and certainly his use of military escort would suggest that was true.) Even so, he was not early enough to have arrived before much of the clear-up, at which he seems perhaps a little disappointed. Although he makes a token bow to epic grandeur (the scene is 'now [forever] consecrated to immortality'), his letter is clearly more interested in the way in which the aftermath of battle is commercial enterprise: though the field is littered with 'relics', they are the ones that won't fetch a price. However, 'there is a mart established' for the showier souvenirs, and he is quick to lay down his money for his share of the spoil (which, to this day, you can see handsomely displayed in Scott's home at Abbotsford on the Borders). His letter also suggests the marketability of the experience – he sends his patron the Duke of Buccleuch a sketch of the battle, an eye-witness account of the topography, and a detailed account of the information he obtains from Bonaparte's own guide, John de Coster, in the reasonable expectation that the letter would be circulated more generally among the Duke's intimates. The journalistic detail of sheer mess and stink (other eye-witness accounts frequently remark on the stench, too) replaces grand or pathetic meditations upon the scene; documentary detail seems anything but heroic, as in the description of the meeting of the cuirassiers and dragoons as making a noise 'not unaptly compared to the tinkering and hammering of a smith's shop.' There is an excitement and an affectation of manliness that is striking.

Byron visited the field on 4 May 1816. From the evidence of his letter to Hobhouse, Byron, like Scott, seems to get a buzz from vicarious military glory (he gallops across the field on a warhorse several times), and buys his souvenirs ('a quantity of helmets, sabres, etc.') in much the same way. From the evidence of the footnote to stanza 30, he also takes a guide across the field of Waterloo – in fact, the same guide that Scott used (Bainbridge, 1995, p.166). What strikes me, however, even allowing for the later date of Byron's visit, is how dismissive and brief his letter is. Turning to his footnote, what strikes me is the way it downgrades the 'cause', and its peculiar insistence in rating Waterloo as a *future* 'celebrated spot' – it wants 'that undefinable but impressive halo which the lapse of ages throws around a celebrated spot' (footnote to stanza 30). Such aestheticization of the battlefield into a sort of historical picturesque rather noticeably displaces patriotic effusion. You might also have noticed the way that the footnote insists on inserting Byron himself into the foreground of the picture as a relative of Major Howard, in the guise of chief mourner.

Scott had visited Waterloo with the express intention of writing a poem, and turned it out there and then (Lockhart, 1893, p.316). He was the first major poet to deal with the subject, and consequently this establishment piece, dedicated to a member of the royal family and sold to raise money for the Waterloo fund for widows and orphans, had by 1816 set a norm for mainstream poetry about Waterloo; one symptom of this is the frequency with which it is quoted in the handbooks that accompany panoramas, sometimes as the occasion for the depiction, for example (see the *Description*, c.1817, p.26).

EXERCISE   In Anthology II (pp.317–34) you will find reprinted Sir Walter Scott's poem *The Field of Waterloo* (1815). Read it and make notes identifying (i) its main events; (ii) its mood(s); and (iii) its governing imagery. Try to avoid becoming bogged down in fine detail.

DISCUSSION   Scott's poem starts with a visit to the site, and contrasts the apparent pastoral which a naïve observer would register with the realities of war that are in fact graven into the landscape; the two collide in the metaphor of harvest. (So influential was this poem that it probably dictates the increasing tendency in pictures of the battle to emphasize the trampling down of the ripe wheat in the fields. For depictions, see Broadley, 1905.) The poem then provides a heroic narrative of the battle as a confrontation between Wellington and Napoleon, chronicles Napoleon's loss of nerve and flight, depicts him execrated by his soldiers, speculates on his future conversion to humility, praises Wellington, and pays 'tribute' to the dead generally, providing elegies for the famous dead more particularly, before concluding roughly that there is patriotic compensation for the slaughter in 'fame'.

Scott's poem established what would become standard subject matter. As Simon Bainbridge has noted, the vast majority of Waterloo poems would include a set number of features:

1   condemnation of Napoleon and his crimes;

2   Waterloo as appropriate retribution, featuring Britain as Europe's saviour;

3   praise for Wellington as the hero of the hour (often at the expense of admitting any involvement on the part of Blücher and others);

4   tributes to the dead, usually the Duke of Brunswick, Picton, Ponsonby and Shaw, the ex-pugilist Guardsman;

5   some sort of acknowledgement of the bereaved, often citing De Lancey, one of the dead officers who had only been married a few weeks;

6   description of the battle, concentrating on the French cavalry charges against the British squares and, less usually, the desperate battles around Hougoumont and the farm at La Haye Sainte;

7   comparison of Waterloo to previous historic English victories against the French, notably Cressy, Agincourt, and Blenheim;

8   a heroic, hyperbolic, and declamatory style (see Bainbridge, 1995, p.158).

In short, the prevailing mode was one of patriotic celebration tempered here and there with a softening note of elegy.

EXERCISE   Now read *Childe Harold's Pilgrimage III*, stanzas 17–35 (pp.265–72), and compare and contrast the two poems. Does Byron follow Scott's basic narrative schema? To what extent does he use the same imagery as Scott? Is the prevailing mood the same?

DISCUSSION   Clearly there are similarities; for example, both poems start as meditations upon the site after the event. Both poets import the reader directly into the scene after the event *(CH, stanza 17, line 145, FW,* stanzas 4–6) and make a claim to interpret it by way of narrative. But where Scott begins by revivifying the scene with a rousing narrative of the battle (*FW, stanza 8*), and goes on to provide tribute and elegy in about equal proportions, filling the canvas of the poem with animated figures, Byron initially insists that the scene is not only empty, but should remain so. Stanza 17 begins by giving meaning to the rural landscape – it's not earth we're treading on but 'an Empire's dust' (line 145); the rather unremarkable landscape hides the sublime of history: 'An Earthquake's spoil is sepulchred below!' (line 146). This sublime, however, is invisible; there's neither colossal bust nor 'column trophied for triumphal show' (line 148). The scene is not memorialized by monuments. Provocatively, given that Byron must certainly have been aware of plans and subscriptions being got up to fund the monuments that were raised a few years later (see Figure 29.5), he goes on to insist that the lack of monuments is appropriate because, he argues, the battle has *not* been a world-historical event. It has merely reinstated pre-1789 monarchy, 'the patch'd up idol of enlighten'd days' (stanza 19, line 168). Byron twists Scott's metaphor of harvest round – here, the battle has

Figure 29.5 Anonymous, fifth plate, Waterloo Monuments, *from* Vues de Bruxelles et Souvenirs de Waterloo, *1825, Bodleian Library, University of Oxford (shelfmark 20471 c.5).*

Engraving of the Waterloo monuments with the remains of the tree under which Major Picton died in the foreground.

been merely a horrid fertilizer. Unlike Scott, who pays tribute to male heroism and comradeship (stanza 12) with a blow-by-blow account of the day, Byron summarizes the course of the battle in half a stanza (stanza 28, lines 246–52). Although he too memorializes the Duke of Brunswick and Major Howard, he doesn't do much by way of heroizing them as gallant. His account concentrates principally on the way war destroys the social, breaking up love affairs, and is elegiac in its language throughout, equally lamenting, so it seems, the sepulchring of 'an Earthquake's spoil', 'the grave of France', and the deaths on the British side. Victory is hollow, death is the reality heralded by the 'knell' of line 189, the 'deadlier' echo of line 197 that is heard by Brunswick's 'fated chieftain', and by the wood of Ardennes which already knows that the soldiers are 'the unreturning brave' (stanza 27, line 238). When Scott does turn to count the cost of the battle in stanzas 20–2 he does his best to find a patriotic compensation:

> And ne'er beside their noble grave
> May Briton pass and fail to crave
> A blessing on the fallen brave
> Who fought with Wellington!
>
> (Stanza 22)

By contrast, Byron insists that 'Fame' is no compensation. He takes over the mourning of the many bereaved, and couches it not in Scott's public patriotic oratorical language of tribute (as in *FW*, stanza 20), but in a language that is already familiar to the reader in conjunction with the 'Byronic' apparently impregnable but silently broken heart (see especially stanzas 32 and 33 with their vocabulary of withering, wreck, ruins, and imprisonment). By stanza 34, he has inserted himself into the ranks of the bereaved and appropriated their grief to his state of alienation so successfully as actually to dismiss the deaths of the men in battle as less dreadful than living on:

> There is a very life in our despair,
> Vitality of poison, – a quick root
> Which feeds these deadly branches; for it were
> As nothing did we die; but Life will suit
> Itself to Sorrow's most detested fruit ...
>
> (Stanza 34, lines 298–302)

Finally, and most tellingly, Byron is absolutely silent on the matter of Wellington's heroism. Indeed this section of the poem, along with the whole poem's characteristic mode of gloomy misanthropy, questions the viability of the heroic mode in a post-Waterloo world.

What I have been trying to highlight here is a crucial difference in the politics of the two poems. Scott sees the battle as a costly victory; Byron sees it as a hollow victory '... is this all the world has gain'd by thee,/ Thou first and last of fields! king-making Victory?' (stanza 17, lines 152–3). In fact, Byron's treatment of Waterloo was essentially conceived as a riposte to Scott's poem: *CH*, stanzas 27 and 28 were first composed for and written in the autograph album of the wife of the guide whom both Scott and Byron used. They are written under the lines that Scott had written in from *The Field of Waterloo*. Byron's remark 'Their praise is hymn'd by loftier harps than mine' (stanza 29, line 253) directly refers to Scott. In due course, Scott was to review *Childe Harold's Pilgrimage* – you will find this review excerpted in Anthology II (pp.337–44). His comments on the Waterloo stanzas reinforce the argument that I have been making for Byron's radical stance on the matter of Waterloo. He laments that Byron shuns to celebrate the victory of Waterloo and that as a result 'we have lost that note of triumph with which his harp would otherwise have rung over a field of glory such as Britain has never reaped before.' In particular he notes the omission of Wellington, though he insists that 'If his lofty muse has soared in all her brilliancy over the field of Waterloo without dropping even one leaf of laurel on the head of Wellington, his [Wellington's] merit can dispense even with the praise of Lord Byron.'

EXERCISE   At this moment I suggest you watch Video 4, band 1: *In the Steps of Childe Harold*, Part 1, which is entitled 'On the Field of Waterloo', and do the exercises in the accompanying AV Notes.

Napoleon

Of course, as I've already suggested earlier, much of the 'meaning' of Waterloo hinged on what you thought about the extraordinary and unprecedented phenomenon of Napoleon. You have already learned something of the ways in which Napoleon controlled his own representation within the French empire; it won't surprise you to know that there was a vast body of other representations of 'Boney' in circulation in the country that was at war with all he represented for the best part of 20 years.

What may surprise you, however, is that over the course of the wars British intellectuals and writers were by no means universally hostile to Napoleon. This is particularly true of those in opposition to the government, known as the Whigs, of whom Byron was a prominent member. Byron himself had a lifelong engagement with the figure of Napoleon. As Bainbridge remarks, 'Napoleon dominated Byron's imagination ... both satisfying and frustrating his characteristic craving for the heroic' (1995, p.135). For the admiring Byron, Napoleon was the child of the French Revolution and the working-out of its democratic and republican principles, although he was bitterly disappointed in his hero, who failed to live up to being a hero in 1814 by tamely surviving instead of committing suicide. In common with his contemporaries, Byron was unaware that Napoleon had indeed attempted a suitably Roman suicide by poison after his first abdication in 1814, and seems to have contemplated it again after his second abdication. To the world, and Byron, Bonaparte's instinct for survival had seemed to resurface again after Waterloo, and caused the same disappointment. As William Thomas Fitzgerald put it in his obscure poem *Wellington's Triumph: or, The Battle of Waterloo* (1815):

> Had he, when Fortune vanish'd from his side,
> Amidst his guards, like English Richard,[8] died!
> In death one trophy had adorned his head,
> A tyrant living, but a hero dead!
> There where Ambition's cruel race was run,
> His end had dazzled like the setting sun!
> And half his crimes o'ershadowed by his fate
> Had left his name, though execrated, great!

(p.14)

Napoleon as a man of action governed Byron's own rather anxious self-projections as a failed man of action, a mere writer of verse; he was, after all, to dub himself grandly but self-mockingly in *Don Juan* 'the grand Napoleon of the realms of rhyme' (*Don Juan*, XI, 55, 8). Nor was this simply a private affair between Byron and Napoleon; contemporaries too perceived a congruence between the grandiose and theatrical ways in which both men presented themselves. On 4 December 1821, Byron wrote to John Murray:

> By extracts in the English papers ... – I perceive that the 'two greatest examples of human vanity in the present age' are firstly 'the Ex-Emperor Napoleon' – and secondly – 'his lordship the noble poet etc.' – meaning your humble servant – poor guiltless I – Poor Napoleon! – he little dreamed to what 'vile comparisons' the turn of his wheel would reduce him.

(Quoted in Marchand, 1976)

In many ways, this public perception had been produced by Byron's early poetry in which he developed the Byronic hero. 'Masterful, moody outlaws, haunted by some secret consciousness of guilt, these heroes act as a focus for contemporary fantasies. Not the least element of guilty complicity about them is that they echo the French cult of Napoleon: they are fictional equivalents of David's handsome idealized portrait of the French emperor on a white charger surmounting the Alps' (Butler,

---

[8] The reference here is to Richard III.

1981, p.118).[9] In 1816, moreover, Byron rather grandiosely saw a parallel between his own overthrow, disgrace and exile, and Napoleon's fall and exile; Byron's friend Thomas Medwin recalled that Byron 'used to say there were three great men ruined in one year, [Beau] Brummell, himself, and Napoleon!' (quoted in Lovell, 1966, p.72). Given that Beau Brummell was the great London dandy and wit just fallen from royal favour for one final, unforgivable piece of impertinence, the tone of this remark, in this instance at any rate, is surely mock-heroic. Yet Byron conspicuously registered and reinforced this parallel with Napoleon by leaving England for his journey across the Continent in a travelling carriage which was a replica of Napoleon's on display down the road, down to the initials 'N.B.' emblazoned on the door which ambiguously identified 'Noel Byron' with 'Napoleon Bonaparte'.

Byron's personal investment in the figure of Napoleon was, however, conditioned by the ways of representing Napoleon in circulation in the wider culture. Of these, by far the two most important for Romantic writers of all political persuasions were the parallels commonly drawn between Napoleon and Milton's depiction of Satan in *Paradise Lost*, on the one hand, and between the emperor and the Greek dramatist Aeschylus's version of Prometheus, on the other. Both these ambitious figures transgress in the eyes of the powers that be (Satan aims at God's throne, Prometheus steals fire to aid humanity), and both are punished frightfully (Satan being chained on the burning lake, Prometheus chained to a rock on which daily he is condemned to endure the torments of an eagle plucking out his liver), but, as the instigator of original sin, Satan is much the more clearly criminal of the two in human eyes. Conservative caricaturists tended to associate Napoleon with the Devil and hell, most especially in his resurgence in 1815 and his meteoric fall after Waterloo (caricatures put out in 1815 included 'The Devil to Pay, or, Boney's Return from Hell (Elba) Bay' and 'Boney's Return from Elba, or, the Devil among the Tailors' – see Ashton, 1884). This modulated in one of the most famous treatments to depicting Napoleon as Milton's fallen Satan, which, though clearly hostile, also pays tribute to Napoleon's second fall both as a world-historical event and as epic tragedy (see Figure 29.6). In *The Poet's Pilgrimage to Waterloo* (1816), Robert Southey, the then Poet Laureate, explicitly compares the resurgent Napoleon with Milton's Satan at the moment that he resolves to ruin Eden:

> Such was the danger, when that Man of Blood
> Burst from the iron Isle, and brought again,
> Like Satan rising from the sulphurous flood,
> His impious legions to the battle plain:
> Such too was our deliverance, when the field
> Of Waterloo beheld his fortunes yield.

> (*Poet's Pilgrimage*, I, i, 4)

---

[9] See Plate 9.8 in the Illustrations Book.

Figure 29.6   George Cruikshank, Boney's Meditations on the Island of St Helena, or, The Devil addressing the Sun, *1815, coloured engraving, British Museum, London. Photo: © The British Museum, London.*

Napoleon's words echo those of Milton's Satan after his fall. The names radiating from the Sun (the Prince Regent) are of heroes of Waterloo.

Southey transforms the Napoleonic wars into a Miltonic epic struggle, and Waterloo into the providential triumph of good over evil. Let's now look at how Byron represents the fallen Napoleon.

EXERCISE

Now read stanzas 36–45 (Anthology II, pp.272–5), a famous passage which analyses Napoleon's character. Make some notes in answer to the following questions:

1   What connections does Byron see between Napoleon's character and his fate?

2   Byron's verse often works by **antithesis**: moving between opposites. Where can you see this at work in this passage?

3   What similarities does Byron suggest between himself and Napoleon?

DISCUSSION

1   Napoleon's character is responsible both for his meteoric rise and for his downfall: uncurbed and uncurbable, he is driven by a chronically reckless ambition and lust for conquest until finally he overreaches himself. His public abilities as commander and skill in manipulating kingdoms and men are matched and even enabled by a crippling inability to discipline or understand himself. He is nonetheless the heroic incarnate, a god-like figment not only of his own imagination and his own publicity, but looming large in the imagination of the culture at large. His fall is analogous to that of Milton's Satan (this is the allusion underlying the reference to 'hell' in stanza 42, line 370), who also suffered from fatal ambition, and who also is condemned to enduring inaction in the end.

2   Byron employs a number of antitheses to characterize the fallen emperor: notably, greatness and badness (line 316), mightiness and littleness (lines 318–19), conqueror and captive (line 325), bravery and cowardice (lines 334–5), and victory and defeat (lines 336–7). These are not simple opposites because they are 'mixt', and their complicated, even tormented, relationship is mirrored in the snaky movement of the verse that couples them line after line as the argument twists and turns upon itself – by comparison, Scott's verse is remarkably straightforward.

3   Byron starts to generalize Napoleon's fate by stanza 43, and makes his own identification with him explicit in lines 380–2 of this stanza, when 'Conquerors and Kings' are coupled with 'Sophists, *Bards*, *Statesmen*' (italics added) as 'unquiet things' which infect the generality with a madness of ideas. As with his treatment of the field of Waterloo, where the emphasis in the end fell not upon a triumphalism but upon the alienated, mourning, spectating and reflecting 'I', Byron turns Napoleon himself into a version of the Byronic, so giving 'the misanthropy and duality of the Byronic hero a

specific historical and political dimension' (Bainbridge, 1995, pp.181–2).

If Napoleon is the first of these relocations for the Byronic, he is not the last; counterpoised against the fallen man of action and child of Revolution who animates the field of Waterloo is the writer and philosopher who dreamed up revolution in the first place, Jean-Jacques Rousseau (see Plate 5.1 in the Illustrations Book). Arriving in Geneva, Byron found himself in the birthplace of Rousseau, certainly one of its most celebrated citizens, and this afforded him the excuse to meditate upon Rousseau, as pretty much every visitor to that city did in their travelogues. It was not coincidental that Byron's friend Shelley, and the girl who had eloped with him, Mary Godwin, were alternating visits to Byron at the Villa Diodati with rereading Rousseau.

EXERCISE   Now would be a good moment to view the second part of Video 4, band 1, 'Geneva'. You should also look at the corresponding AV Notes.

Rousseau: revolution and writing

Although Napoleon's 'adventure' was to conquer the world and Rousseau's 'adventures' had been a matter of thinking and writing, the one is intimately connected to the others. If Napoleon was the 'child of Revolution', embodying and enacting its principles, Rousseau, as the author of *The Social Contract* (1762) and *Discourse on Inequality* (1755), was, in the minds of British writers of all political complexions from the 1790s onwards, its instigator.

EXERCISE   Now read stanzas 81–4 (pp.289–90). Byron is here talking about Rousseau's thought in relation to the French Revolution. Make some brief notes on the following questions, paying especial attention to Byron's imagery:

1   What influence does Byron attribute to Rousseau?

2   What view does Byron seem to have of the French Revolution itself?

3   How does Byron build the idea of revolution into his own personal mythology?

DISCUSSION   1   Byron is broadly conventional for his period in his assessment of Rousseau's influence on world history – although Byron had deep-rooted misgivings about the power of writing in the real world, here he makes Rousseau the origin of the ideas and, more interestingly, *of the type of discourse* that generates revolution. Rousseau's writing 'set the world in flame,/Nor ceased to burn till kingdoms were no more' (stanza 81, lines 763–4); as surely as Napoleon, therefore, he overthrew kings – indeed, he overthrew kingship. Byron's language converts Rousseau from enlightened rationalist and political philosopher to something much more 'Romantic' and mythic. Rousseau's writings are turned into a 'voice' likened to that of the inspired prophetess of the Pythian oracle.

2   Roused up by Rousseau's writings to revolution, the French 'made themselves a fearful monument' of 'the wreck of old opinions' so old that they are described as organic ('grew', 'breathed', associated with the 'birth' of time). Byron describes the Revolution as apocalyptic; this is the point of his allusion to the New Testament account of Christ's death upon the Cross and the revelation to the Centurion that he is indeed the Son of God: 'the veil was rent in twain from the top to the bottom', as Matthew has it.[10] It is an event that makes a new heaven and new earth, or should have done so; with a characteristic Byronic backtracking twist, the verse reverses and claims that though all was laid in 'ruins', the ground-plan and the materials remained to hand 'to rebuild/Upon the same foundation' (stanza 82, lines 775–6).

Byron offers the conventional radical apologia for the Revolution familiar from the writings of radical intellectuals as early as 1796: that the scale of oppression had set the scale of the ensuing violence (stanza 81, line 769); that oppression had itself produced the brutality of the French mob that had dishonoured and brought down noble enlightened ambitions: 'they,/Who in oppression's darkness caved had dwelt,/They were not eagles, nourish'd with the day;/What marvel then, at times, if they mistook their prey?' (stanza 83, lines 784–7). But unlike the earlier optimists, he sees that after Waterloo the Revolution has been defeated for the moment.

3   Stanza 84 is chiefly remarkable for melding a political vision of future revolution – 'It came, it cometh, and will come' – with a peculiarly personal language that recalls more straightforwardly autobiographical stanzas, a language of 'wounds', scars, the heart, disfigurement, defiant endurance of suffering, and a sense of injury and coming vengeance. It is the backing and filling of Byron's verse, twisting and turning, that makes it so engaging, and so personalized; this is, and isn't, a political manifesto; political it is, but it is a statement of politics as lived out in pulsing feeling.

---

[10] Matthew 27:51 (Authorized Version).

Byron's analysis of Rousseau's thought is in the terms of passion; unlike the thought of Rousseau's contemporaries Voltaire and Gibbon, which Byron characterizes as 'daring doubts' aiming to overthrow heaven, fools, and thrones, Rousseau's thought is not a product of enlightened rationalism and materialist scepticism. Rousseau features as a madman, 'phrenzied by disease or woe,/To that worst pitch of all, which wears a reasoning show' (stanza 80, lines 759–60). Here Byron collapses the conventional antithesis between madness and reason; Rousseau's philosophy *was* a sort of madness. This analysis was also conventional, and depended not upon a reading of either *The Social Contract* or a *Discourse upon Inequality* but upon Rousseau's extraordinary autobiography, the *Confessions* (completed 1770, published posthumously in 1782 and then in translation in England, going through many editions by the end of the century).

Rousseau: Romantic confessions

It would be hard to overstate the importance of the *Confessions* to writers from Wordsworth to Goethe and through to Stendhal. Each reacted in their own fashion to this work of autobiography. It is characterized by Rousseau's devastating frankness about incidents in his life, couched in terms of a personal story of innocence and fall. They include episodes in which he exposes himself to young women, betrays and abandons a friend struck down by an epileptic fit in the street, receives and possibly makes homosexual advances, is seduced by a married woman of the world, lives in a sentimental *ménage à trois* with an older woman, abandons his five children by his live-in mistress to the Foundling Hospital, makes violent love to a married woman already attached to another lover, and apparently succumbs increasingly to paranoia about his friends, including the Encyclopédistes Diderot and Voltaire, at the same moment that he is drafting proto-revolutionary writings such as his *Discourse upon Inequality*. The whole is characterized by an extraordinary depth of psychological analysis of self and others, by the freshness and brilliance of tiny memories, by an identity apparently built upon a sense of deep-rooted guilt and a masochistic desire for exposure and punishment, and by a repeated cycle of desire followed by disappointment should that desire be attained.

The *Confessions* are important to Byron's poem in two ways. First, viewing Rousseau's politics as rooted in his personal experience, even in his illness, produces a particular view of history as driven not so much by the progress of ideas (an Enlightenment view) but by individual men and their desires. If Napoleon looked like a man of destiny driven by his own ambition, Rousseau looked like a man blown on the wind of passion. Both made history, but history thus seems potentially accidental and contingent. Because the *Confessions* thus makes over the political philosopher into something much more like the Romantic impotent that Byron and many of his generation felt themselves to be, Rousseau's autobiographical strategies and personae lie powerfully behind Byron's poem.

Second, Rousseau's autobiographical experiment tried to pin down the meaning of his life, and to describe and account for his inward nature. His spectacular and exhaustive self-portrait turns into a string of confessions, and a general self-justification in the face of his supposed enemies and detractors. Although Byron does not quite lay himself open in this way, inclining more to hinting at dark and sexy secrets hidden behind a mask of gloomy endurance, he certainly shares Rousseau's constant (if not entirely convincing) insistence on himself as a man whose affections have been cruelly slighted and disappointed, and whose sensibility is mismatched to the harshness of the world. Although the occasional structure of *Childe Harold* offers autobiographical snapshots rather than a feature film, the *Confessions* powerfully conditions the Byronic mode of confession and his self-projection as at once guilty, wronged, and misanthropic.

EXERCISE Read the extract from Rousseau's *Confessions* (Anthology II, pp.334–7), and then read *Childe Harold III*, stanzas 76–9 (pp.288–9), for which this passage is the source. What does Byron take from his source? What does he add?

DISCUSSION Clearly this passage from the *Confessions* delineates a Rousseau who is indeed 'self-torturing' as Byron puts it, to whom emotional 'affliction' and misfortune seem native, and for whom sexual emotion is profoundly bound up with memories of frustration, and ultimately with the imagination (stanza 77, lines 725–6). His love thus becomes in Byron's formulation 'passion's essence' (stanza 78, line 734), that is to say, ideal rather than actual or physical, and indeed principally realized in a performance of 'eloquence' designed to seduce the reader at second-hand rather than the lover herself into emotional or physical reaction: '... words, like sunbeams, dazzling as they past/The eyes, which o'er them shed tears feelingly and fast' (stanza 77, lines 732–3). This is sex sublimated as writing and reading. Rousseau's vocabulary of passion also finds its echo in Byron's verse: 'this devouring but barren flame by which ever since my childhood I had felt my heart to be consumed in vain' (p.335) is transformed elegantly into Byron's figure of Rousseau '... as a tree/On fire by lightning; with ethereal flame/Kindled he was, and blasted, for to be/Thus, and enamour'd, were in him the same' (stanza 78, lines 734–7) and into his conceit of Rousseau's 'burning page' (stanza 78, line 742). For Byron, Rousseau is a poet of 'ideal beauty', whose poetry realizes itself both in life and in fiction, in his enforcedly platonic passion for Sophie d'Houdetot, and in the creation of her double Julie, the heroine of his novel *Julie: ou La Nouvelle Héloïse* (1761).

Rousseau: fiction and landscape

If Rousseau's *Confessions* dictates something of Byron's self-presentation, his novel sets the agenda for Byron's visits, recorded both in his poem and his journal and letters, along the lakeshore to Clarens, Vevey and Meillerie, the settings Rousseau chose for his fiction.

Clarens, Meillerie and their environs were already an established site of pilgrimage for the literary tourist, and it is worth citing the accounts of another visitor to the site for the purposes of comparison with Byron's own take on the experience. In the mid-1790s, the celebrated British radical poet, historian, travel-writer and novelist Helen Maria Williams had escaped Robespierre's prisons and come to Switzerland. Part of her travels included a visit to this 'classic ground', on which she commented:

> It would be hopeless to attempt a new sketch of these enchanting regions after the glowing description of Rousseau, which has already been so often detailed by the hundred sentimental pilgrims, who with Héloïse in hand, run over the rocks and mountains to catch the lover's inspiration.
>
> (1798, vol.II, p.179)

Interestingly, after this confession of inadequacy in the face of Rousseau's prose, she goes on to remark that his description is no longer pertinent in the face of the hard political facts of despotism:

> All in nature is still romantic, wild and graceful, as Rousseau has painted it; but the soothing charm associated with the moral feeling, is in some sort dissolved. The soft image of the impassioned Julia no longer hovers round the castle of Chillon; which is now converted into a Swiss Bastille, and guarded by a stern soldiery. The tear of sensibility which has so often been shed over this spot for the woes of fiction, may now fall for sorrows that have the dull reality of existence. It is not the imaginary maternal shriek that pierces the ear, it is the groan of the patriot rising from the floor of his damp dungeon that rends the heart.
>
> (1798, vol.II, p.179)

In the same setting Rousseau chose for his heroine to save her son from drowning, Williams sees political oppression. The radical Williams displaces Rousseauesque sentiment with (admittedly sentimental) politics; let's see by contrast what Byron does with the problem of Rousseau.

EXERCISE   Read stanzas 99–104 (pp.295–8) and the accompanying footnotes. Start by summarizing Byron's argument in the poetry. Once you've done that, turn to the note to stanza 104 and consider how it relates to the main body of the poem.

DISCUSSION Briefly, Byron's verses contend that Clarens and its environs are the 'birthplace', 'couch', and 'throne' of 'Love', a classical god here who has retreated there into a pastoral fertility, and that Rousseau's choice of it for a setting has not conferred meaning upon it, but, rather, had more or less plagiarized its archaic meanings: 'he found/It was the scene which passion must allot/To the mind's purified beings' (stanza 104, lines 969–71). The note to line 927 (pp.295–6), however, tells a slightly different story. Although it reiterates the argument of the poem, it turns out that Byron has taken over Rousseau's language from *La Nouvelle Héloïse* and has visited the environs in order to check out the verisimilitude of Rousseau's descriptions: 'as far as my own observations have led me in a not uninterested or inattentive survey of all the scenes most celebrated by Rousseau in his 'Héloïse', I can safely say, that in this there is no exaggeration.' He insists that 'if Rousseau had never written, not lived, the same associations would not less have belonged to such scenes', but promptly admits to pleasure in having inhabited Rousseau's fiction to the extent of nearly being wrecked in just the same way as Rousseau's lovers (see Figure 29.7). And he is surprisingly critical of the destruction of the 'Bosquet de Julie' and the rocks of Meillerie, the destruction of 'souvenirs', memories, given his position that these are not really 'memories' of anything. One possible way of thinking about this disjunction is to remember that Byron was in the business of remaking in his own image the landscape through which he travels; here, he seems to fail. Clarens and its environs were and remained Rousseau's territory.

Byron's heroic version of Rousseau was not universally shared. It doesn't do to think that everyone in the period subscribed to what we would think of as Enlightenment values, let alone Romantic ones. We can frame Byron's verse by turning to the very different account of one Thomas Raffles, a well-connected Evangelical clergyman who set out from Liverpool on his travels in 1817, hard on Byron's heels, and arrived in Geneva clutching a copy of *Childe Harold III* as his tour guide. Raffles's view of Rousseau could not have been more vehemently different from Byron's. Of Meillerie, 'famous as the residence of Rousseau', he remarks:

> This name [of Rousseau], which I am well aware, would excite the eulogies of many a pen, and impart to the surrounding scenes, a charm more powerful than any their own romantic beauties could create, has, I must acknowledge, a far different influence on me. I cannot but connect it with the pestilential principles – the blasphemous productions – and the deep sensuality, of the infidel that owned it. Who, that has any respect for the honour of revelation, or the happiness of mankind, but must regret, that ever so great a name was lent to so base a career, or that such lovely scenes should have been polluted by the breath of such depraved and prostituted genius.

(1818, p.252)

Figure 29.7 Jean-Michel Moreau (the Younger), Julie and Saint-Preux in the Storm, from Jean-Jacques Rousseau, Collection complète des Oeuvres, 1774–83, Bibliothèque nationale de France, Paris.

In taking as his two most important figures Rousseau and Napoleon, Byron sets up an important relation between them that structures the poem. First of all, the two serve as book-ends to the figure of Byron himself, as the lines 'Conquerors and kings/Founders of sects and systems ... Sophists, Bards, [or] Statesmen' (stanza 43) suggest. The poem lines up Napoleon and Rousseau as 'incomplete developments of a Byronic ego' (Christensen, 1993, p.169). Both Napoleon and Rousseau, for all that one is a man of action and the other a man of feeling, are possessed by a sort of divine madness, 'madmen who have made men mad/By their contagion' (stanza 43, lines 379–80). Embodiments of restless, insatiate desire, both have 'quick bosoms' and so are equally doomed to 'hell' and tortures of their own making:

> But quiet to quick bosoms is a Hell
> And *there* hath been thy bane; there is a fire
> And motion of the soul which will not dwell
> In its own narrow being, but aspire
> Beyond the fitting medium of desire;
> And, but once kindled, quenchless evermore,
> Preys upon high adventure, nor can tire
> Of aught but rest; a fever at the core,
> Fatal to him who bears, to all who ever bore.

(Stanza 42, lines 370–8; italics in original)

These madmen are also connected with each other and with the figure of Byron through a **metaphorics** of fire (a metaphorics is a system of interconnected metaphors); in the stanza above, this manifests itself as the fire of the second line, the conceit of 'kindling' in the sixth, and the heat of the 'fever' in the penultimate line.

EXERCISE   Before you go on to the next section, I'd like you to work your way through the stanzas on Napoleon and Rousseau again, picking out metaphors of fire or fiery figures (lightning, for example). What meanings does fieriness typically carry?

DISCUSSION   You should have found a great number of examples, and if you searched the other stanzas of the poem, you would find that this metaphorics is an essential feature of the poem. You've probably discovered that fire is connected both with life and vitality and with death and destruction, often at the same moment. For example, the 'quickness' (meaning vitality) of the bosom in the stanza cited above turns first of all into a 'fire' and then a 'fever' which is by the last line not life-giving but 'fatal'.

The Alps

When Byron left Basle for Geneva, he travelled down a string of lakes cloven between the Alps. You can see very little of the Alps from Basle – they are very much in the distance, and the same was and is true of Geneva, which is 60 miles or so from the vale of Chamonix, from which, like Byron and later the Shelleys, you still ascend to view the Mer de Glace and Mont Blanc. Yet the imaginative pull of the alpine mountains was such by the early nineteenth century almost to overcome their distance and regular invisibility in cloud. As you discovered in your study of the Lake District earlier, landscape is never simply natural, but is always culturally constructed – that is to say, the culture 'sees' landscape in accordance with its ideas about landscape, which are themselves tied up often enough with complicated and sometimes incompatible ideas about class, agriculture, God, beauty, and the self. In the next section, I'm going to alternate between telling you a little about the meanings that the Alps had accrued over the course of the eighteenth century, and looking at which of those meanings condition Byron's poem.

If Lake District scenery supplied the sublime available to English travellers at home, the Alps embodied the sublime of which the Lake District was just a pale, if pretty, copy. Throughout the eighteenth century, the Alps were felt to be the antithesis to Enlightenment, the underside to complacent illumination with its strong belief in reason and progress, representing the deeps of the irrational – disorder, terror, danger, mortality, ruin, chaos, catastrophe, violence. In practice, Enlightenment travellers sophisticated this into a sort of aesthetic experiment upon the senses, what they typically described as 'delightful horrour'. The principal difference between the Alps as the location of the Enlightenment sublime and Romantic alpine sublimity was probably a new emphasis on the strife between the frightening impersonality and immensity of the inimical mountains and the Romantic imagination vaulting to conquer them. The metaphor of conquest that I'm using here is not fortuitous; this notion of imaginative conquest was intimately linked with the vocabulary of Napoleonic empire-building.

EXERCISE   To see this vocabulary deployed by Byron, turn now to stanza 62 (pp.282–3). Make a list of the metaphors that Byron employs here.

DISCUSSION   The Alps are described as buildings, as royal or even imperial 'palaces' with walls, pinnacles, and halls. They are also, fleetingly, **personified** (that is to say, they're imagined as people) in the phrase 'their snowy scalps'. They are the thrones of 'Eternity', associated with the throwing of 'thunderbolts' and so with pagan gods. In a characteristic Romantic sentiment, their sublimity both expands and appals the spirit, inspiring human imaginative ambition while pointing up its 'vanity'.

For Byron and his contemporaries the Carthaginian general Hannibal's crossing of the Alps on elephants was a type of the confrontation between ambitious man and nature. Hannibal's exploit had, of course, been doubled and outdone by the feat of another passage across the Alps, Napoleon's. As David's painting (see Plate 9.8 in the Illustrations Book) interestingly suggests, Napoleon conquered the Alps, outdoing both Hannibal and Charlemagne to conquer Italy; indeed, he crossed them not once but twice, the second time on his return from Elba. But where the propagandist David's painting therefore flatteringly fills its frame with the figure of Napoleon and leaves the Alps to be inferred from the snow, the British painter Turner elected to show Hannibal dwarfed by the storm (see Plate 29.3 in the Illustrations Book). The date of this painting, 1812, the year of the retreat from Moscow, surely cannot have been fortuitous. Simon Schama has suggested, noting that 'at the very compositional centre of this gathering calamity, seen in minute silhouette against the horizon, is a tiny figure', that the painting is a commentary on Bonaparte's overweening ambition, and that 'the Lilliputian generalissimo, astride his micropachyderm, may be the most devastating image of Napoleon ever executed' (Schama, 1995, p.462).

Although the Alps had their 'sublime' political meanings, they also have in *Childe Harold III* a more 'beautiful' pastoral side, as a place of Rousseauesque retreat and healing solitude, a version of mountain landscape for which he borrowed heavily from Wordsworth. Byron told his friend Medwin some time after that 'Shelley, when I was in Switzerland, used to dose me with Wordsworth physic even to nausea' (quoted in Lovell, 1966, p.194). Nor was this lost on Wordsworth, who rather enviously insisted that 'the whole third canto of Childe Harold's founded on his style and sentiments – the feeling of natural objects, which is there expressed not caught by B. from Nature herself but from him, Wordsworth, and spoiled in the transmission' (Moore, 1830, vol.1, p.355).

Stanzas 68–75 (pp.285–8) show Byron in full Wordsworthian mode. Particularly Wordsworthian are the images of the lake in a reciprocal mirroring relationship with sky and mountains (stanza 68, lines 645–7) and the sense that the individual sensibility is in a passionate relationship with the landscape, to the point of becoming 'portion of that around me' (stanza 72, line 681) and in which 'High mountains are a feeling' (stanza 72, line 682). The Alps and the lake are described as a potential refuge from the 'herd' of 'man' to an empowering 'loneliness' which will allow the poet 'to look through/With a fit mind the might which I behold' (stanza 68, lines 48–9). Renouncing 'the hot throng' and all its madnesses of adventure and ambition, fleeing the 'torture' of 'human cities' and 'the crushing crowd', the poet imagines the solace of nature to the extremes of dissolution, becoming after death 'the Spirit of each Spot' (stanza 74, line 705). Byron toys with the idea of renunciation of the world, of living the simple life contemplating nature, and so piercing through to some sense of the divine.

4   Thinking about the poem as a whole

We are now ready to tackle the poem as a whole, and this requires some consideration of **genre**, that is to say, the conventions that the poem obeys or alludes to. We'll start with romance, which we have already discussed briefly in relation to the title.

Romance

Romance was arguably the most important poetic genre of the first two decades of the nineteenth century in Britain. It derived from what has been called 'one of the great scholarly achievements of the Enlightenment, the recovery of medieval literature as embodied in its romances' (Curran, 1986, p.129), conducted by important antiquarians such as Bishop Thomas Percy, Thomas Warton, Bishop Richard Hurd, and Joseph Ritson, amongst others. Deeply nostalgic in temper, strongly invested in the celebration of the national, the revival of interest in romance (including especially an interest in *The Faerie Queene*) led ultimately to its rewriting. Romance resurfaced in the late eighteenth-century forgeries of Thomas Chatterton (whose early suicide, supposedly out of despair at lack of recognition, was to make him a type of the Romantic poet) and Macpherson (who sold the poetic fiction of the bard 'Ossian' to an enraptured audience), and triumphed in the experimental romances of the first decade of the nineteenth century. Now largely and unjustly forgotten, these last were what made the reputation (and the fortune) of poets such as Sir Walter Scott and Robert Southey. Such romances had a certain number of features in common:

- They were long poetic narratives, generally sub-divided into cantos.
- They often used experimental and consciously archaic poetic form.
- They preferred what Warton called, referring to Spenser, 'the careless exuberance of a warm imagination and a strong sensibility' over neoclassical symmetry (1762, p.21). As such, romance was an experimental form, permitting a certain looseness or license.
- They dealt with the 'far-away', whether in time, place or culture (they characteristically summon up nostalgia, although typically at the same time they reflect critically from a modern perspective upon the escapist lure of romance).
- They are structured as a hero's quest, geographical and/or spiritual.
- They typically have a 'broken structure' – that is to say, there may be more than one narrator or an **unreliable narrator**, there may be a 'gap' in the work's supposed documentary historical record, or the narrative may be fractured by flashbacks; there is often a 'modern' **frame-narrative** that exists in a slightly questionable relation to the main body of narrative; they are frequently deeply embedded in thickets of astonishingly erudite and lengthy footnotes, which

typically act in an uncomfortable way as another **voice,** usually more 'modern' or more 'realistic', which unsettles the status of the main narrative of the poem proper.

- The narrator is typically a 'minstrel' of isolated sensibility and self-regarding genius – often the last embodiment of a failing culture.

- They are deeply invested in the idea of the nation; this is especially true of the romances of Walter Scott. His important *Lay of the Last Minstrel* (1805), after all, contains the famous lines which single-handedly defined a sort of British intrepidness against the threat of Napoleonic invasion:

> Breathes there the man, with soul so dead,
> Who never to himself hath said,
> This is my own, my native land!
> Whose heart hath ne'er within him burn'd,
> As home his footsteps he hath turn'd,
> From wandering on a foreign strand!
> If such there breathe, go, mark him well;
> For him no minstrel raptures swell;
> High though his titles, proud his name,
> Boundless his wealth as wish can claim;
> Despite those titles, power, and pelf,
> The wretch concentred all in self,
> Living, shall forfeit fair renown,
> And, doubly dying, shall go down
> To the vile dust, from whence he sprung,
> Unwept, unhonour'd and unsung.
>
> (*Lay of the Last Minstrel*, 6, 1)

By the end of the opening decade of the nineteenth century, Scott was the acknowledged master of British poetry, and his mode was that of the romance (Curran, 1986, p.140). Invoking romance, Scott prefaces his important poem *Marmion* (1808) with this stanza which calls up the spirit of 'Chivalry':

> ... well may we then,
> Though dwindled sons of little men,
> Essay to break a feeble lance
> In the fair fields of old romance;
> Or seek the moated castle's cell,
> Where long through talisman and spell,
> While tyrants rul'd and damsels wept,
> Thy Genius, Chivalry, hath slept:
> There sound the harpings of the North,
> Till he awake and sally forth,
> On venturous quest to prick again,
> In all his arms, with all his train,
> Shield, lance, and brand, and plume, and scarf,

Fay, giant, dragon, squire, and dwarf,
And wizard with his wand of might,
And errant maid on palfrey white.

(*Marmion*, Introduction to Canto I)

By setting himself up as a writer of a 'Romaunt', Byron was deliberately
entering into competition with this sort of verse by Scott; famously, he
succeeded in dethroning Scott (who went on to yet greater things as a
novelist under the pseudonym 'the Author of Waverley') to become
himself the next decade's acknowledged virtuoso of British poetry. In
Canto IV he would eventually pay tribute to Scott, singling him out as
the master of romance:

Scott, the minstrel who call'd forth
A new creation with his magic line,
And, like the Ariosto of the North,
Sang ladye-love and war, romance and knightly worth.

(Stanza 40, lines 357–60)

The contemporary reader would therefore have opened this volume
prepared to settle down into a particular form of supposedly escapist
pleasure led by 'golden-tongued Romance, with serene lute!/Fair pluméd
syren, queen of far-away', as Keats put it in his poem 'On sitting down to
read *King Lear* once again' (composed January 1818). Something of this
is typically registered in later illustrations to the poem. You have two
examples here: one from 1838 which shows Harold in Canto I at home,
prey to *ennui*, and one from 1855 which shows Harold leaving England
(Figures 29.8 and 29.9).

If you look carefully at the figure of Harold you'll see that the artists
have dressed him in rather unspecified historical fancy-dress – the first
does him all-purpose Tudor-cum-Jacobean, and the second goes for all-
purpose medieval. In both of them, he is costumed for the never-never
land of romance.

EXERCISE   Now read the poem in its entirety for the first time. This should take you
a fairly long time, perhaps as much as two or three hours. Make sure you
read Byron's notes; you should also consult the explanatory notes
carefully. Once you've finished this read-through I'd like you to make
some notes about what would qualify this poem as a 'romance' in the
terms laid out for you above. Take a note, also, of what about the poem
might seem surprising in the light of this generic claim.

DISCUSSION   The poem qualifies as a romance on certain counts: it is long, it is
organized into cantos, and it uses an archaic poetic form (the Spenserian
stanza). It has a noble hero and it also has a minstrel in the shape of the

Painted by E.T. Parris.   Engraved by F. Bacon.

HIS HOUSE, HIS HOME, HIS HERITAGE, HIS LANDS,
THE LAUGHING DAMES IN WHOM HE DID DELIGHT,
WHOSE LARGE BLUE EYES, FAIR LOCKS, AND SNOWY HANDS,
MIGHT SHAKE THE SAINTSHIP OF AN ANCHORITE,
AND LONG HAD FED HIS YOUTHFUL APPETITE;
HIS GOBLETS BRIMM'D WITH EVERY COSTLY WINE,
AND ALL THAT MOTE TO LUXURY INVITE,
WITHOUT A SIGH HE LEFT,——
                                    CHILDE HAROLD.

Figure 29.8   Frederick Bacon, illustration to Childe Harold, *from* The Byron Gallery, *1838, engraving, Bodleian Library, University of Oxford (shelfmark 38.695 engr. pp.P.7).*

Figure 29.9   Charles West Cope, Plate III from Thirty Illustrations of Childe Harold, *1855, engraving by John Thompson, Bodleian Library, University of Oxford (shelfmark 1708 d. 389).*

poet-narrator who is close to the foreground of the poem, framing it with his address to Ada, and who is filled with the required nostalgia and a sense of uselessness. The poem's structure is indeed 'broken', most spectacularly by the footnotes, which are written in an entirely different voice, which has the effect of setting the main narrative of the poem into an ironic frame.

But, all this apart, I imagine that viewing the poem as a romance seemed rather unsatisfactory. Although we move from the opening apostrophe (stanzas 1–7) into what looks like a core-narrative about Harold (stanzas 8–16) in a way that conforms to the rules of romance, Harold, far from acting in some story set in the past, turns out to be thoroughly embedded in contemporary modern Europe. The first place we spot him is, after all, the field of Waterloo. Harold himself becomes phantasmal and eventually vanishes altogether, and altogether without explanation, after the simple lyrics, supposedly composed as a letter home by him, at the central point of the poem. As the hero of a quest-romance, he is distinctly unsatisfactory; even more problematic is the fact that Harold doesn't seem to *have* a quest – he doesn't have a story to be a character in (Curran, 1986, p.151). Neither Harold nor the narrator is searching for something that will confer meaning (like, say, Malory's knights search for the Holy Grail in the romance of King Arthur). Instead, they are in flight *away* from what the poem characterizes as the stable centre of existence – love, home, family, nation: they are in a state of restless directionlessness dramatized in the poem's very first stanza: 'I depart,/ Whither I know not'. The (always frustrated and never to be resolved) quest of this poem seems to be to find a quest now worth embarking upon at all, a quest to give meaning to randomness. As the disappointed reviewer for *The Anti-Jacobin* protested in August 1812, remarking on Cantos I and II:

> 'A Romaunt,' without interesting incidents, daring enterprizes, or heroic achievements; and above all, without a hero, endowed with a soul and spirit, capable of great actions, and ardent to engage in them, is a perfect anomaly in the annals of chivalry, or in the history of romance.

(*The Anti-Jacobin Review*, August 1812, vol.42, p.344)

The reviewer was especially scathing about the lack of purpose evinced by the hero 'wandering over the world, without any fixed object' (p.344).

Yet, looked at from another angle, Harold (and the narrator) do embark on a 'quest' and on a 'pilgrimage'. It's just that instead of arriving at one holy shrine, they arrive at a dozen or so, and they do so in a modern, and debased, guise – as mere tourists. As the reviewer for the *British Review* noted, the poem was not so much romance, as travelogue:

> ... our puzzle is now to account for those portentous titles of a poem, the subject of which is certainly neither chastity, nor valour, nor truth; nor fairies, nor damsels, nor deliverers; nor heroes baptized, or infidel, but the narrative of a modern tourist, passing from place to place, with little or no incident, but with local descriptions most poetically dressed, and reflections which might occur to a mind like Lord Byron's without the pain or peril of travel.

(*The British Review*, June 1812, vol.3, p.278)

Travelogue

One way of making sense of *Childe Harold's Pilgrimage* is to say that Byron takes one mode, romance, with noble, archaic, epic and escapist connotations, and crosses it with another, modern travel-writing. In fact, the two genres have a great deal in common. Swallow the change from past to present, from fiction to documentary, and from poetry to prose, and the two modes look not unlike one another: both are structured as travels through strange territory, both are desultory, digressive and episodic. Neither knight nor tourist quite knows what he may find or what adventures may befall him, and both are not quite sure of the ultimate significance of their adventures. In romance, it is the mysterious lady fleeing from out of a wood that may embroil the knight in some quarrel that he doesn't understand; in travel-writing, the writer gazes on scenes, people, and artefacts that s/he has to decipher and interpret.

This said, we don't usually take a tourist as seriously as a pilgrim or a romance hero. All set out from home, but both the pilgrim and the romance hero know, or at any rate think they know, what they are looking for (and that it is worth looking for), and set off full of pith and purpose. By comparison, Harold is aimless and desultory; he sets off out of an ill-defined but addictive restlessness and anomie at no particular time: 'Self-exiled Harold wanders forth again,/With nought of hope left, but with less of gloom' (stanza 16). His 'shrines' and 'adventures' find him, and take their shape and meaning from his sensibility. Byron's modern wanderers trail without much purpose down the usual route to Switzerland (because to get to Italy you had to go through one of the Swiss passes) and beguile their anomie along the way with the local 'sights'. Turning quest-romance into travel-writing in this way is a sort of black joke on the degeneracy and aimlessness of the modern, post-war world.

Byron's reinvention of travel-writing at this juncture was particularly shrewd as a commercial decision. Bear in mind that the English had been debarred from travelling on the Continent for some 20 years, more or less ever since war had been declared on Britain and the Netherlands by revolutionary France in February 1793, with a short break in 1802 as a result of the peace of Amiens. Gibraltar, Malta, Albania and Greece remained open throughout, but France, and most especially Italy, which came early under the thumb of the French empire, were not. It is this confinement that partially accounts for the growing popularity of native picturesque spots, most especially the Lake District, as you've already learned, but also the Wye Valley and the north Devon coastline. Travel-writing had always been popular, often regarded as ladies' reading because it was informative and educational, but supposedly light and entertaining; it often came lavishly illustrated. By a commercially happy coincidence, Byron's disgrace and exile from Britain coincided with the first moment that it was possible to travel in much of mainland Europe after Napoleon's second fall. As the Hon. Richard Boyle Bernard MP put it rather stuffily in his *A Tour through some parts of France, Switzerland, Savoy, Germany and Belgium* (1815):

> I had long been desirous of visiting the Continent, but the long
> continuance of the war, and the little prospect which lately

appeared of its termination, seemed to afford no chance for the
accomplishment of my wish ...

These great and glorious changes, the reality of which it was at
first difficult to believe, having opened to the subjects and
commerce of Britain, countries from which they had been for so
many successive years proscribed, it was not long before
numbers of British repaired to the Continent to indulge that love
of roving for which they had always been distinguished ...

(Bernard, 1815, p.2)

They went in numbers, and wrote about it too. In 1815 and 1816
something like eleven travel books about the Continent appeared, and
there would be many more to come.

The travelogue aspects of Byron's poem tap the phenomenon of the
Grand Tour, which largely determined the way in which travel in Europe
had been conceived of and managed over the preceding century (Chard,
1999, p.11). The Grand Tour was essentially an eighteenth-century
aristocratic phenomenon. Armed with letters of introduction to all the
best families, and accompanied by a tutor (often known as a 'bear-
leader'), aristocratic young men were sent away to the Continent for
some two or three years – Paris first and then Venice and Rome. They
went to acquire a cosmopolitan polish around the *salons* of the great,
some experience of the world (including of women), and a fair amount
of valuable bric-à-brac in the shape of classical statuary and the like to
do up the garden with, and, for the drawing room, a portfolio of
sketches of classical ruins, perhaps even a portrait of themselves leaning
negligently against such ruins executed by one of the many society
portraitists that milked that market in Rome, Angelica Kauffmann among
them. The Tour was also structured quite rigidly as a prescribed
sequence of noteworthy places and objects designed to improve the
mind, working up in scale to the great climax of Rome as source of
western culture. It was designed as 'maker and marker of the elite'
(Redford, 1996, p.15).

In some ways, then, Cantos III and IV of *Childe Harold's Pilgrimage*,
together with Byron's own travels in Europe, ending as they do in Rome,
are recognizably part and parcel of the idea of travel associated with the
Grand Tour. The poem's itinerary underscores Byron's own membership
of the aristocracy. There, admittedly vestigially, is the tutor–pupil
partnership in the relationship between Harold and the surely older
narrator. There, too, is the value set upon cosmopolitanism. However,
there are three unusual elements to Byron's take on the Grand Tour. The
first is the way in which these 'tourists' do not intend to return to Britain.
Unlike the stereotypical aristocratic youth, Harold/the narrator have
apparently no inheritance to return to, no estate to cultivate and
embellish with the odd obelisk, no woman to marry, no dynasty to
breed, no responsibilities to fulfil. Far from it – they are running away

from all these things. Second, and related to this, the sort of 'improvement' the narrator imagines is oddly irresponsible. Measured against Jean-Jacques Rousseau's evocation of the stern purpose of Enlightenment travel in his educational tract *Émile* (1762), the Byronic sensibility looks downright *déclassé*: 'Travelling for its own sake is wandering, being a vagabond ... I should like to impart to the young man embarking on his travels a lively interest in educating himself' (Rousseau, quoted in Chard, 1999, p.29). Third, and following from the other two, Byron's aristocratic cosmopolitanism looks at this historical moment actively unpatriotic in its rejection of Britishness. Travel-writing at the turn of the century was by contrast characteristically structured in part as a meditation upon the relative values of the foreign and the values and institutions of English society, and, on the whole, came down in favour of the comforts and freedoms of England. Thomas Love Peacock's hilarious satire on the contemporary literary scene, *Nightmare Abbey* (1818), rolls these points up into one devastatingly funny phrase put into the mouth of the Byronic Mr Cypress: 'Sir, I have quarrelled with my wife; and a man who has quarrelled with his wife is absolved from duty to his country' (Peacock, 1924, vol.3, p.103).

Although Byron travelled over the Alps and down into Italy, the vast majority of his middle-class readers could not afford to, whether for want of money or for want of leisure. Instead, they read *Childe Harold*. Part of the reason for its immense success was the poem's ability to repackage the benefits of the Grand Tour for this audience. In place of actual travel, it offered virtual travel at a fraction of the price. The charm of travel-writing for a middle-class audience lay partly in educating readers in how to make what they see their own – if not by buying it, then by acquiring it as cultural capital. If you could through your refined sensibility (honed by identifying with Byron's, for example) make what you 'see' your 'own', then the fact that you've neither seen it nor will ever own it is usefully obscured. As one anonymous travel-writer put it, 'The landscape was transferred to the paper with a strict adherence as possible to nature and to truth. The reader will thus be probably enabled to travel with the Author, and to have all the prominent features of the country vividly imprinted upon his mind' (*A Picturesque Tour,* 1817).

Travel-writing of the period was not homogeneous, but there are certain features that these many publications tend to have in common:

- They are in prose.
- They are almost invariably couched in first-person narrative, which, as Chard notes, helpfully 'allows the subject of commentary to move easily between one domain of objects and another, to shift back and forth at will between specific objects of commentary, and to pause in the account of a particular place, in order to reflect at length on some idea that springs to mind' (1999, pp.6–7).
- In fact, they are typically couched in what was called 'familiar' prose, often taking the form of a journal or of letters supposedly sent home.

Letters in particular concentrate the virtue of this sort of writing – they are written to illuminate and entertain someone 'back home', a surrogate for the reader, they have a quality of 'on-the-spotness' and spontaneity, and they can glide by virtue of their rather loose generic structure across a wide range of tones and modes, including comic/ sentimental anecdote, observations, sentimental effusion over landscape, and quasi-anthropological comment. All of this material is aligned within a personal relationship between writer and imagined reader, which is often rooted in the reason for travelling at all. Sometimes this might be invalidism (as in the Revd John Gardnor's *A Journey down the Rhine*, 1791), sometimes a broken heart (this is the premise of Mary Wollstonecraft's celebrated *Letters Written During a Short Residence in Sweden, Norway, and Denmark*, 1796). The relation between letter-writer and imagined letter-reader is typically extended in the reading process to include the actual reader; this is the implication of the remark of Wollstonecraft's husband William Godwin about her *Letters* that 'they would make anyone fall in love with the writer.'

- They are eclectic – half the fun of reading them is to discover the adventures with inns and inn-keepers, the petty discomforts and disasters, mingled with accurate and strongly-felt description of, say, Mont Blanc. Their structural premise is the adventure, and therefore the unexpected. They are compounded variously of anecdote, complaints of discomfort, tips to other travellers, bits of history, remarks on galleries and museums, sketches of picturesque scenery, anthropological observations on the physiognomy of the people; they may deal with economics, agriculture, politics, architecture. James Mitchell's *A Tour through Belgium, Holland, Along the Rhine, And through the North of France, in the summer of 1816* is subtitled 'In which is given an account of the civil and ecclesiastical polity, and the system of education of the kingdom of the Netherlands; with remarks on the Fine Arts, Commerce, and Manufactures'. A typical 'letter' ranges over the following subjects:

> *Road to Brussels. – Amusements by the Way. – Tenderness towards the horses. – Advantages of the Public Conveyances. – Behaviour of a Young Lady of Quality. – Brussels, its Elegance, and Accommodations. – College. – Pictures. – Botanical Garden, etc. – Hospital of St Jean. – Visit to Waterloo. – Monuments there. – Mount St Jean. – Hougomond. – La Belle Alliance. – La Haye Saintes. – Appearance of the Field. – Kindness of the people of Brussels to the English. – English church there.*

From this summary, it should be clear what sort of opportunities travel-writing offered Byron. What must have appealed, I think, was its pleasurable disorderliness. Its eclectic and episodic nature afforded Byron plenty of room for manoeuvring within a first-person narrative. Its Wollstonecraftian precursor suggested a landscape brimming with the sentiments of a broken heart, and realized a personal relation with the reader close to seduction, which Byron raised to unprecedented and unrivalled heights of potency by casting it within impassioned poetic language.

However, Byron's travel-writing is distinctive. Something of this can be gauged from looking at a couple of extracts from travelogues published in the period which cover some of the same sights. Byron's choice of *which* sights he writes about isn't especially startling; many who went exploring on the Continent before or after Waterloo, for example, tended to travel along the Rhine, though usually on their way back home. The pleasure that travellers principally promised themselves in their route down or up river was to admire the 'picturesque' effect of the Rhine castles, which stand high above the river on impregnable crags. Such was the purpose of the Revd John Gardnor who, in 1791 or so, travelled down the Rhine, sketching as he went. He remarked of nearby Coblenz:

> The view from the citadel is extensive and delightful. The palace, at the foot of the mountain, and on the shore of the Rhine; – the confluence of two magnificent streams; a bird's e'e [eye] view of the whole town, occupying the peninsula at its extremities; – the little islands which seem dropped into the rivers; the convents embosomed in woods; – the villages, castles, etc. which invite the eye to the distant hills, and give an uncommon interest to the horizon – these are subjects for a poet; or for a journalist [here, meaning a diarist] who could combine historical knowledge with emotions excited by the contemplation of a grand, varied, and beautiful landscape.

(Gardnor, 1791, pp.102–3)

In some ways, this reads like a proposal for *Childe Harold's* later treatment of the scene, in the post-Napoleonic era when history seemed to have decisively inhabited the picturesque. Some 30 years later the anonymous author of *A Picturesque Tour through France, Switzerland, on the Banks of the Rhine and through part of the Netherlands in the year MDCCCXVI* (1817) also travelled through this part of the world. What he has to say of these Rhine castles throws into high relief Byron's own characteristic take on them.

EXERCISE   Read the following short extract from *A Picturesque Tour* and compare it with Byron's stanzas on the Rhine, especially stanzas 46–51 (Anthology II, pp.275–7). What differences strike you?

> Small villages, ruined towers perched on steep rocks, with the verdant vine trailed along the sides of the mountains, while their tops are crested with dark wood, constitute an assemblage of objects which follow in continual succession ...

The numerous castles which are scattered on the banks of the Rhine, erected in times of personal insecurity, were principally designed as places of predatory resort, by which the navigation of the river was rendered insecure, and the merchant was liable to the perpetual depredations of restless marauders ... And hence it became an important object with the Hanseatic league[11] to protect the commerce of the Rhine from the rapacity of the robbers who dwelt upon its banks, and to demolish the numerous fortresses by which they protected both their rapine and themselves. The robbers selected the most inaccessible situations which could be discovered; and their castles are often seen perched upon such lofty rocks as the eagle would select for its nest.

(*A Picturesque Tour*, 1817, p.367)

DISCUSSION   The author of *A Picturesque Tour* offers a resolutely unromantic and depersonalized account of the castles. He may be susceptible to them as a picturesque 'assemblage of objects', but he makes it pretty clear that he's on the side of the merchants and law and order. His historical overview clearly suggests that the situation of law-abiding modernity is vastly preferable to 'personal insecurity'. In some ways, Byron follows the same structure; here too are the picturesque views, here too the history lesson. For him, like the other two writers, the Rhine scenery takes its charm from 'a blending' of 'streams and dells,/Fruit, foliage, crag, wood, cornfield, mountain, vine,/And chiefless castles ...', and the castles are initially assimilated to natural picturesque beauty – the walls are overgrown with leaves (stanza 46, lines 411–13). Like this anonymous writer, Byron notes that the castles were tenanted by robber chiefs, but he draws quite a different set of conclusions, investing the scene with a new affect (stanzas 48 and 49). On the one hand, the chiefs of the past are the very stuff of romance. On the other, in a move which should begin to seem familiar, Byron fills the scene he describes with his own state of mind, describing the ruins as like 'a lofty mind/Worn, but unstooping to the baser crowd' (stanza 47, lines 415–16).

Our comparative reading suggests two ways in which Byron supplements the genre of the travelogue: the first, hybridizing travelogue with romance, and the second, suffusing the scene that he views with a theatrical performance of his own sensibility. In this he was adapting and updating the genre of eighteenth-century topographical poetry, in which

[11] The Hanseatic league was a confederation of northern German towns set up in the twelfth century for their mutual prosperity and protection. At the height of its power it comprised 85 towns, but it fell into decline in the late seventeenth century. (Author's note.)

the poet either walks through a landscape or muses on a place. Wordsworth's *An Evening Walk*, which you studied in the units on the Lake District, is a conventional exercise in this sort of poetry.

Now that we have some sense of the two or three main genres within which Byron is working, let's revisit the poem.

EXERCISE   I'd like you to start by making a list of places and people mentioned in the poem. Try to answer the following questions:

1   What, if anything, do the locations that the poem describes have in common? Can you organize them thematically into groups?

2   What, if anything, do the people that the poem discusses have in common?

DISCUSSION   The sites the poet deals with before his arrival in Geneva seem to me to have one important and powerful thing in common – the fact that they are all in ruins as the result of war. In this poem, the bloody ruin that Byron sees in the field of Waterloo isn't qualitatively different from that dramatized by the ruins of the Rhine castles or the scant remains of the Roman capital of Helvetia, Aventicum, sacked by the barbarians. They are all shrines, places sacred to violent death and lost causes – stops on an ironic pilgrimage. These shrines are universally plundered or perverted from their original function, the holiness of 'relics' is downgraded in modern life to the desirability of souvenirs and museum collectables, the adventurers are hopelessly belated (all the chivalric dying is long done). This point is powerfully made by Byron's footnote on the battlefield of Morat:

> The chapel is destroyed, and the pyramid of bones diminished to a small number ... A few still remain ... Of these relics I ventured to bring away as much as may have made a quarter of a hero, for which the sole excuse is, that if I had not, the next passer by might have perverted them to worse uses than the careful preservation which I intend for them.

(Footnote to stanza 63, Anthology II, p.283)

The places are associated strongly with the fall of empires and cultures in the shape of recent Napoleonic history and older histories (Waterloo and Brussels, but also the Rhine castles) or with the failure of ideals of freedom (the heroic victory of the free Swiss at Morat in the fifteenth century has been reversed by the French invasion of 1798). Around Geneva, on the other hand, locations have important (modern) literary associations with the three Enlightenment philosophers whose thought at the time was felt to have instigated revolutionary thought: Voltaire, Edward Gibbon, and Jean-Jacques Rousseau. (As it happens, Gibbon sympathized with the conservative Edmund Burke in his horror at the

French Revolution, but his critique of Christianity aligned him in radical minds with the revolutionaries.) Lastly, Byron evokes natural locations: the Rhine, up to a point, but also and especially Lake Geneva and the Alps.

The people have one thing in common, too; they're mostly dead – did you notice? If they're not dead, like the important exception Napoleon, they ought to be. One largish category is of warriors, who are mostly dead in the cause of 'liberty', a word, which, as you know from your reading of Unit 6 on the French Revolution, is strongly charged with revolutionary ideology. This is what links the otherwise rather oddly assorted figures of Harmodius who attacked 'Athens' tyrant lord' (stanza 20), the Camerons who rebelled in 1745 (stanza 26), Major Howard, and General Marceau (stanza 56). The other category is that of the Enlightenment thinkers: Rousseau, Voltaire and Gibbon. These three are also associated in complicated ways with liberty, empire, ruin and destruction. Voltaire's wit was sufficient to 'shake a throne' (stanza 106); Gibbon was the expert upon the decline and fall of the Roman Empire. Rousseau releases France 'which lay before/Bow'd to the inborn tyranny of years' (stanza 81), but the result is that France lies in ruins (stanza 82). The last category is small, but important: it contains four women – Ada, Julia Alpinula, Julie (heroine of Rousseau's *La Nouvelle Héloïse*) and Madame de Warens, one of the women with whom Rousseau was in love, as he describes in his *Confessions* (1782). The first two are both daddy's girls: Julia dies for her father in a style that appeals to the errant father Byron. The last two represent forbidden love: Julie because she falls in love with her tutor, St Preux, against the prohibition first of her father and then of her husband, the divorced Madame de Warens because she first seduced and then lived with Rousseau outside wedlock for some years. What links the two pairs, then, is love outside accepted social structures. The second pair, then, may well have appealed to Byron as types of his forbidden love for Augusta.

To sum up, then, this tour of modern Europe is preoccupied with the idea of ruins, monuments, and destruction, with the sense of the end of an era and with the failure of Enlightenment optimism and purpose. In this it is quintessentially Romantic. But if wartime British Romantic writers are until 1815 centrally preoccupied by the failure of the French Revolution and the ideals associated with it, after Waterloo they become preoccupied additionally with the failure of heroism, as typified by Napoleon, and are beset by a paralyzing sense of belatedness. In this way the figure of the tourist, who always (by definition) arrives after the event, is the perfect figure for post-war *ennui* and post-heroic modernity. Byron's defensive fabrication of a myth of personal grandeur or enlightenment in this poem is one of the poetic strategies that emerge from this impasse – and its enormous success across Europe testifies to how much this was a general state of mind.

Private confessions

Earlier, I suggested that Rousseau's autobiography was an important model for *Childe Harold III*. This is particularly evident in the poem's efforts to come to a (necessarily makeshift) conclusion. In its last stanzas the poem achieves some sort of summation and poise, endeavouring to view and define itself as it enters the public domain. The poet reflects upon the status of the poem in the world: are the verses a 'harmless wile' designed to 'beguile/My breast, or that of others, for a while'? (stanza 112, lines 1041, 1043–4). Put another way, are they personal therapy or public entertainment? He conspicuously renounces as motives for the poem's composition (and publication) public fame, personal reputation and, presumably, commercial success. Instead he turns the poem towards his daughter, Ada, and makes her the addressee: 'with thy name this song begun' and 'with thy name thus much shall end' (stanza 115, lines 1067–8). Making the poem private (supposedly) in this way means that it claims the function of the making of a fantasy both on his part and on hers of a father–child relationship; it is to be a sort of love-letter to her future self from his dead self:

> Albeit my brow thou never should'st behold,
> My voice shall with thy future visions blend,
> And reach into thy heart, – when mine is cold, –
> A token and a tone, even from thy father's mould.

(Stanza 115, lines 1072–5)

As befits the poet and the reader only tied together by the reading of 'words', both will be only 'names' to each other, despite their status as bodies tied by blood (stanza 117). Yet the poem still may have power as a blessing over the child's 'cradled slumbers' (stanza 118, line 1099); and it closes with a hope, significant in light of the poem's dominating metaphorics of fire, that her fire 'shall be more tempered' than her father's (stanza 118, line 1098).

How far did this concluding fantasy of the poem's function in the world as a parent–daughter love-letter match up with its reception? So far we have concentrated on unravelling the composition of the poem within its many and varied cultural contexts: of Byron's own life, writings, and reputation; of other figures and writings that lie behind Byron's itinerary and intellectual agenda, most especially Napoleon and Rousseau; of allied genres such as romance, travelogue, topographical poetry, and autobiographical confession. But if a poem does not come into existence without an author, nor does it sustain its existence without readers. This poem has had a long line of readers that stretches from its first readers all the way down to you. Those successive readers have determined the poem's changeable meaning just as much as Byron ever did, and so we're now going to turn our attention to what contemporary readers made of *Childe Harold III* and, accordingly, of its author.

5 Byron and the Byronic

It would be hard to overstate the impact of *Childe Harold* when it was first published. It made available a whole new state of mind. Even the worldly and thoroughly unsentimental Princess Lieven, wife of the Russian ambassador, was deeply affected, as she described in a letter dated 14 March 1822 to her lover Prince Metternich:

> Did I ever tell you what happened to me on this same Brighton beach? I was here in the summer of '18. My husband had brought me for my health. I was quite well in myself, but I was desperately depressed. My mind was so vacant that I could think of no reason for going on living. The third canto of *Childe Harold* had just come out; I had taken it with me; and to give myself something to do, I had begun to translate it. I worked at it enthusiastically in my room, and I always took the poem with me when I went to sit on a certain rocky point, which is quite dry at low tide, but completely submerged at high. Lord Byron says terrible and sublime things about death by drowning, and I had always thought that passage particularly fine. I was reading it one day on the rock; and I felt that nothing could be simpler than to stay on the point until the sea had covered it. I conceived the idea quite dispassionately ... I experienced no distress of any kind, nothing but a great unconcern in my heart and in my head. I waited on the rock a good half-hour, my mind made up; but the tide did not rise. When at last it did, my madness ebbed as the water advanced. In short, I did not wait long enough even to get my feet wet, and I did right. I laughed at myself as I went home; for, at that moment, nothing seemed so delightful as the small details of life, and nothing so stupid as the desire to die ...

(Quennell, 1937, pp.162–3)

Though the Princess concludes by laughing at her temporary folly, she had fallen victim to a melancholy that became instantly and supremely fashionable.

As I remarked at the outset, the publication of the first two cantos of *Childe Harold* in 1812 made Byron instantly famous, shot him to bestsellerdom, and would come to define his poetic identity within the literary marketplace. At the same time as achieving this unparalleled success, the poem was accounted as markedly original, not usually a ticket to wild and instant popularity. Peter Manning accounts for this seeming paradox by observing that the form – the chivalric romance in the mould of Scott – was already popular in the marketplace and so a market was ready-made to hand, but that Byron's satiric take on the chivalric changed the politics of the form. Chivalry had hitherto been associated via Edmund Burke's famous *Reflections on the Revolution in France* (1790) with nostalgia for the *ancien régime*. Of the various humiliations heaped upon the Queen of France, Marie Antoinette, in late 1789 and early 1790, he famously wrote:

> Little did I dream that I should have lived to see such disasters fallen upon her in a nation of gallant men, in a nation of men of honour and of cavaliers. I thought ten thousand swords must have leaped from their scabbards to avenge even a look that threatened her with insult. – But the age of chivalry is gone. – That of sophisters, oeconomists, and calculators has succeeded; and the glory of Europe is extinguished for ever.

> (Burke, 1982, pp.169–70)

Byron freshened up, inverted, and ironized by juxtaposition with other familiar but jarringly modern modes the usual politics of chivalric romance. In so doing, Byron put into play the conflict between patriotic heroism and contemporary sense of *ennui* dramatized by works such as Stendhal's *Scarlet and Black* (1830) and outraged most of the reviews' political sensibilities (Manning, 1991, pp.170, 171, 173). The poem was therefore familiar, yet with a daringly different edge of political devil-may-careness. Yet though the politics of *Childe Harold III* throughout are deliberately controversial in their anti-patriotism, this was not on the whole what contemporary reviewers concentrated upon. What they were struck by was the way that *Childe Harold III* generated public fascination in Byron himself.

What interested commentators about the poem, and sold product, was the way in which *Childe Harold III* had made Byron fully 'Byronic'. Byron the author became Byron the 'celebrity'. When I describe Byron as a 'celebrity', I don't simply mean that he was famous. Writers had been famous before. Rather, I am registering that for the first time a writer was more famous and more desirable than any of their works. This amounts to the invention of a new idea and practice of authorship, one that we are now so familiar with that we take it for granted. As the editor of the *London Magazine* put it in slight bewilderment, '[Byron] has awakened, by literary exertion, a more intense interest in his person than ever before resulted from literature' (Scott, 1821, p.50).

You may have noticed that throughout our discussion I've avoided calling any of the voices of the poem 'Byron', though the closeness of the poet-narrator's journey to Byron's own well-documented journey makes it hard not to conflate the travelling aristocrat and his poetic persona. It is undoubtedly a temptation to assume that Byron was entirely 'Byronic' through and through, so I have included among the extracts in Anthology II the letters that we still possess which he was writing as he was travelling through Europe around the time of the composition of *Childe Harold III*. They are written during May and June 1816, during which the poem was composed. One of the things that they help to make plain is Byron's rather haphazard method of composition. He dashes off a few stanzas here and there as something about the scenes around him catches his imagination. The letters also show him thinking he's finished the poem before he has added the stanzas on Rousseau, Voltaire and Gibbon. It seems that he did very little revision to blend the individual stanzas into the poem as a whole. The letters show Byron working out some of his reactions and ideas *at the same time* as he is composing *Childe Harold III.*

EXERCISE   Now read through the letters that Byron wrote over this period (Anthology II, pp.309–17). How do they compare with the effect of the poem?

DISCUSSION   Byron's a bit of a chameleon, and his self-presentation depends very much on to whom he's writing. It's a slight surprise after the refined glooms and sexual *ennui* of the poem to find that his spirits are high enough to fall upon the chambermaid 'carnally', that, having abandoned England in this dramatic way, he is chattily interested in the theatrical gossip of Drury Lane, and calls for red tooth-powder only available in London. The tone generally to Hobhouse is reminiscent of the voice of the footnotes, though more irreverent.

The letters to Hobhouse are couched in a different tone from those to Augusta, which are more sentimental and more confessional. Even these are not exactly 'Byronic'; a comment in a letter to Augusta of 8 September on his separation from his wife is both heartfelt and flippant:

> As for me I am in good health – & fair – though very unequal – spirits – but for all that – she – or rather the Separation – has broken my heart – I feel as though an Elephant had trodden on it ...
>
> (Quoted in Marchand, 1976, vol.V, p.91)

We've been looking at these letters so that we have a sense of the difference between Byron the man and Byron as he portrays himself in the poem. The very different rhetoric of these letters underscores that the rhetoric of the poem is not itself natural or unmediated autobiographical confession. Mind you, the letters are just as much a construction of Byron as *Childe Harold* itself – none of these documents gives access to the 'real' Byron, but the variety of them does help us to see that all these versions of 'Byron', though bearing a family resemblance, are fictions.

Armed with this proviso, we can now look at why it was that readers at the time (without access to Byron's private letters) found it so easy to conflate Byron with Harold and with the voice of the minstrel. This conflation was made possible by the singular coincidence in 1816 of Byron's fictional characters with Byron's own life, something that hadn't happened before. Byron's early fractured verse narratives, unlike their source, Sir Walter Scott's *Marmion,* never revealed the secret that the gloomy and misanthropic hero is concealing with such visible and sexy suffering. Consequently, with their curiosity whipped up but unsatisfied within the narrative, readers looked outside the frame of the poem to the author himself for the explanation and source of this mystery. This effect was only strengthened every time Byron published another in the series of his obscure narratives featuring essentially the same hero. Byron therefore was a site of extreme interest even before the explosion of rumour, accusation, counter-accusation and newspaper scandal-mongering that marked the breakdown of his marriage, which provided an explicit extra-poetic event to anchor Byronic guilt. A real-life event (the separation) turned into a widely-circulated story about Byron's shocking secrets. That story, especially the story of incest, supplied the missing 'key' to Byron's already established narrative vocabulary of dark heroes tormented by fatal secrets and mysterious crimes never to be forgiven (Elfenbein, 1995, p.28). Compounding this development, *Childe Harold III* changed Byron's poetic stance by putting the 'I' squarely at the centre of the poem. The poem thus appeared to contemporaries as unique, because daringly personal; as Isaac d'Israeli was to put it in his essay on *The Literary Character,* it was 'sublime selfism'. The hero who conceals his secret by forever talking about how silently he is bearing his suffering is now explicitly 'Lord Byron' himself, dramatizing himself on a scale of heroic grandeur. The Byron effect of profound, unplumbable subjectivity was produced by his language of inexpressibility: the more the poem confessed, the less it actually gave away. The effect is of a 'deep' source generating visible effects but not itself representable. Because it is not representable, it seems more authentic (Elfenbein, 1995, p.19). The result is to generate (perpetually baffled) desire in the reader, and it is this that produces the effect of private seduction memorably described by John Wilson Croker in the *Edinburgh Review*:

> Each of us must have been aware in himself of a singular illusion, by which these disclosures, when read with that high and tender interest which attaches to poetry, seem to have something of the nature of private and confidential communications. They are not felt, while we read, as declarations published to the world, – but almost as secrets whispered to chosen ears. Who is there that feels, for a moment, that the voice which reaches the inmost recesses of his heart is speaking to the careless multitudes around him? Or, if we do so remember, the words seem to pass by others like air, and to find their way to the hearts for whom they were intended, – kindred and sympathizing spirits, who discern and own that secret language of which the privacy is not violated, though spoken in the hearing of the uninitiated, – because it is not understood. There is an unobserved beauty that smiles on us alone; and the more

beautiful to us, because we feel as if chosen out from a crowd of lovers.

(Quoted in Reiman, 1972, vol.2, p.895)

Byronic alienation produces an intensely personal relation with the reader, who feels him/herself to be a special soul, even a lover, by appreciating the poem's 'secret language'. As the ravished novelist Susan Ferrier wrote to a friend in 1816: 'Did you ever read anything as exquisite as the new canto of *Childe Harold*? It is enough to make a woman fly into the arms of a tiger ...' (quoted in Elfenbein, 1995, p.60).

Each successive poem then bolted on to this Byronic **mythos** (a body of anecdotes, feelings and imaginings clustered around a central story or figure). After his death, Byron could be conflated even more readily with his hero: 'Ten years have passed away since the mortal pilgrimage of *Childe Harold* closed, and he bequeathed to the world his undying name' (quoted in the introduction to Finden, 1833, vol.1). So successful was this drama of subjectivity in seizing the public imagination that Byron himself was in danger of being trapped by it; as his friend and biographer Moore remarked in his *Letters and Journals of Lord Byron*:

> Even the strange, perverse pleasure which he felt in painting himself unamiably to the world did not prevent him from being both startled and pained when the world took him at his word; and, like a child in a mask before a looking-glass, the dark semblance which he had, half in sport, put on, when reflected back upon him from the mirror of public opinion, shocked even himself.

(Moore, 1830, vol.2, pp.1–2)

This power of the Byronic to constitute itself as 'unique' was undoubtedly enlarged by Byron's status as an aristocrat and his power to display, while withholding, a desirable mode of subjectivity to his aspirational middle-class readership. If reading his poetry allowed the reader to identify with a culturally privileged vantage point, so too and perhaps even more importantly did the display of reading the poetry. An entire industry grew up which taught the consumer how to read Byron and how to show everyone else that they knew how to read Byron (Elfenbein, 1995, p.51). The quarterly literary reviews, newly emerged to shape the taste of a new mass readership, explained how to read Byron's 'beauties', typically identified Byron with his heroes, and regularly offered the poet psychological and even marriage counselling, thus binding the poetry ever closer to the author. Murray's brilliant entrepreneurship fostered an extraordinary culture of adaptation and extraction in plays, tour books, schoolbooks, elocution anthologies, parlour-songs, portraits, illustrations, even a dinner-plate set.

Although Byron's influence, political and poetic, upon subsequent generations throughout the nineteenth century was extraordinary and wide-ranging – his fans included the Italian and Polish freedom-fighters Mazzini and Mickiewicz, the working-class Chartist agitators, the French and Russian poets Lamartine and Pushkin, and the labouring poet John Clare who, confined in a lunatic asylum, began to write poems entitled *Childe Harold* and *Don Juan* – still, his influence may in the end have been strongest upon the respectable middle-class reader, male and female. 'What a change he has created, not only in our poetry, but in our dramas, novels, and almost national character! ... He quite sublimated the quiet English out of their natures, and open shirt-collars, and melancholy features, and a certain *dash* of romance, were as indispensable to young men, and are so still, as tenderness, and endurance, and intense feeling of passion among the fair sex', wrote a novelist looking back from the vantage point of 1829 (quoted in Reade, 1829, pp.3–4). In many ways, this serves as a perfect gloss on the characters of both the melancholy young Captain Benwick in Jane Austen's *Persuasion* (1818), who has been overdosing on Byronic affliction in the wake of his young wife's death, and the heroine Anne Elliott, despite her impeccably Enlightenment and anti-Romantic advice to the Captain to read less Byron, recommending 'a larger allowance of prose in his daily study' (Austen, 1988, p.101).

Austen depicts the melancholy and impassioned Benwick reading extracts from Byron to Anne, repeating his favourite lines and falling more than a little in love with her in the process; although he doesn't, apparently, quote *Childe Harold*, this is substantially the way in which this poem in particular was appropriated by its readers. It was an operation much facilitated by the meditative nature of the poem, which swiftly became a measure of sensibility. Thus the charming provincial Maria Jackson, writing to her cousin and fiancé John Torr in 1839, mentions her favourite passages:

> They are; in Canto I. verses 42, 42 [*sic*], & 'Song to Inez' at the end of 84. stanza. – In Canto II. Stanza 3. In Canto III. Stanza's [*sic*] 6.7.12.17 & following, 21 & following, 36 & the four following – 113 to the end ... I shall resume *Childe Harold* with a double pleasure now that I know you are daily reading it.

(Carritt, 1933, p.83)

If you look up these stanzas in *Childe Harold III*, I think you'll find that they are those that describe states of mind; this is a shorthand advertisement for her sensibility. The poem also became a mine of cultivated sentiments useful for all emotional occasions: Thomas Parry's *The Beauties of Lord Byron* (1823) arranges extracts under useful titles such as 'The Misery of Living Unbeloved' and boasts additionally of the convenience of his appended index to Byronic sentiments in making them into a 'practicable' handbook (Manning, 1991, p.188n). The poem would also become a way of authenticating touristic sensibilities, 'an ennobling repertoire of poetical attitudes which tourists could strike' (Buzard, 1993, p.115): Murray would subsequently put out tour-guides with bits of *Childe Harold* inserted so that you knew what you were supposed to think and feel at any given sight, but *Childe Harold III*, as we've already seen, might equally well be taken along as a tour-guide in its own right. John Torr, writing to Maria Jackson from Geneva in 1840, wrote:

> On Monday I rowed on the lake for some 7 hours – it was a lovely mode of spending time – the blue clearness of the water, the situation, and the mountains around appeared enchanting. – I read *Childe Harold* there, and as I anticipated, found Byron's description of the spot correct even to a word.

> (Carritt, 1933, p.176)

For the early Victorians, Lake Leman now looked Byronic rather than Rousseauesque. *Childe Harold* saturated the Continent with 'poetical evocations' providing 'a full-dress travelling persona that could be momentarily appropriated ... with the smallest gesture or quotation' (Buzard, 1993, p.117). 'Every Englishman [abroad] carries a Murray for information, and a Byron for sentiment, and finds out by them what he is to know and feel at every step' (William Wetmore Story in 1863, quoted in Buzard, 1993, p.120).

The effect of this practice of extraction was very much to depoliticize the poem. Thomas Raffles, whom we've already met, for all his fulminations about the perniciousness of the thought of Rousseau, Voltaire and Gibbon, for all his heartfelt sense that everything about Britain was better than on the Continent, still happily extracted many stanzas on sublime scenery from Byron to decorate his letters home when he felt himself to be lost for words. Murray, extracting Byron for his tourist handbooks, made his selection for pathos and passion and excised the political grounds for much of the sentiment (Buzard, 1993, p.123).

For nineteenth-century culture, Byron thus became many things; if through his life and politics he served as a role model for those who wished to fight for freedom, his poetry could equally well, and especially to readers of *Childe Harold,* be seen as sentimental and cultural capital and, as such, a ticket to cultivated respectability. So it was that the quintessential Romantic aristocratic rebel and gentleman amateur could underwrite capitalist, commercial, aspirational and thoroughly middle-class Victorian culture. Something of the magical ability of Byron's celebrity in life and death to unify these disparate impulses is registered in Joseph-Denis von Odevaere's depiction of the dead poet, in which his body is stretched across a plinth bearing the titles of his most-loved poems; most prominent of all is the title, *Childe Harold.*

6   Conclusion

What I have been describing in the preceding section is the way in which Byron came to be the quintessential Romantic author through a confluence of his life and writings in the minds of his readers. This is a profoundly post-Romantic way of thinking about Byron as a Romantic artist. Instead of going along with the idea that the artist has privileged access to the ideal and the divine, and therefore is special, original, and originating, I have suggested that it was in many ways Byron's *audience* that made him Romantic. But perhaps it would be more useful at this stage to finish a little more conventionally, and a little less controversially, by making a short list of what makes *Childe Harold III* a 'Romantic' poem within the aesthetic terms laid out at the beginning of this block.

EXERCISE   Try to do this now, looking back across your work in these two units and back to the beginning of the block.

DISCUSSION   My list runs like this:

1   Byron's poem deliberately disorients its reader, through its multiple personae, through its skips and jumps at the will of the poet-narrator, and through the way that it imagines itself merely as part of an unfinished sequence – a fragment, albeit a longish one.

2   The poem privileges the subjective over the empirical – history is not something that simply happened, but something that needs interpretation; landscape is not simply unproblematically there, but gains its power, even its form, from the subjective gaze that rests upon it.

3   The poem privileges the unplumbable, unknowable, and inexpressible (associated generally with the Romantic notion of the imagination's access to the divine) rather than the rational.

4   The poem characteristically envisages the human condition as hung precariously between the antitheses of body and spirit, reason and desire – neither Napoleon, nor Rousseau, nor the poet-narrator is actuated by reason or motivated towards the reasonable or attainable but rather blown about by irrational, half-comprehended urges and guilts – ambitions that cannot be fulfilled, sins that have no name or origin, and affections that are insatiable.

Appendix: Chronology, 1816

April 21	Signs deed of separation from his wife.
April 23	Leaves London for Dover.
April 25	Sails for Ostend.
May 1–6	At Brussels, begins third canto of *Childe Harold.*
May 4	Visits field of Waterloo.
May 8	At Cologne.
May 10–16	Journey up the Rhine – Bonn, Coblenz, Drachenfels, Mannheim.
May 20	At Basle.
May 25	Arrives Sécheron, near Geneva, and subsequently books in to the Hôtel d'Angleterre at Ouchy, where he meets Shelley.
June 10	Moves into the Villa Diodati, at Cologny.
June 22	Begins tour of Lake Geneva with Shelley, following Rousseau's geography in *La Nouvelle Héloïse* – Meillerie, Clarens, Vevey. Visits castle of Chillon, setting for the climax of Rousseau's novel.
June 27–8	Visits Gibbon's house at Lausanne – completes *Childe Harold III.*
July 1	Returns to the Villa Diodati.
July 10	Finishes fair copy of *Childe Harold III* and sends to John Murray in London.

References

The Anti-Jacobin Review, August 1812, vol.42, p.344.

Ashton, J. (1884) *English Caricature and Satire on Napoleon I*, 2 vols, London, Chatto & Windus.

Austen, J. (1988) *Persuasion,* ed. R.W. Chapman, vol. V, Oxford, Oxford University Press.

Bainbridge, S. (1995) *Napoleon and English Romanticism*, Cambridge, Cambridge University Press.

The Battle of Waterloo, A Poem, with Notes, by a gentleman, late of Queen's College, Oxford, London, 1817.

Bernard, Hon. R.B. (1815) *A Tour through some parts of France, Switzerland, Savoy, Germany and Belgium*, London.

The British Review, June 1812, vol.3, p.278.

Broadley, A.M. (1905) *Napoleon ... with many thousands of contemporary Autograph letters, state documents, Portraits, Water-colour drawings, Views, Maps, Plans, Broadsides, Musical Compositions, Popular Songs, and Caricatures, in 28 volumes*, London.

Burke, E. (1982) *Reflections on the Revolution in France*, ed. C.C. O'Brien, Harmondsworth, Penguin.

Butler, M. (1981) *Romantics, Rebels, and Reactionaries: English Literature and its Background 1760–1830*, Oxford, Oxford University Press.

Buzard, J. (1993) *The Beaten Track: European Tourism, Literature, and the Ways to 'Culture', 1800–1918*, Oxford, Clarendon Press.

Carritt, E.F. (1933) *Letters of Courtship between John Torr and Maria Jackson, 1838–43*, London, Oxford University Press.

Catalogue of the Waterloo Museum, 97, Pall Mall, Established in the year 1815, (1815) London.

Chard, C. (1999) *Pleasure and Guilt on the Grand Tour: Travel Writing and Imaginative Geography 1600–1830*, Manchester, Manchester University Press.

Christensen, J. (1993) *Lord Byron's Strength: Romantic Writing and Commercial Society*, Baltimore and London, Johns Hopkins University Press.

Curran, S. (1986) *Poetic Form and British Romanticism*, New York and Oxford, Oxford University Press.

Description of Messrs. Marshall's Grand Historical Peristrephic Painting of the Ever Memorable Battles of Ligny and Waterloo, illustrative of the most interesting events of those Tremendous Engagements ... Now Exhibiting, In which the Figures are the Size of Life, 7th edn, Liverpool, *c*.1817.

Elfenbein, A. (1995) *Byron and the Victorians*, Cambridge, Cambridge University Press.

'Finden's illustrations to the life and work of Lord Byron, with information by W. Brockedon' (1833–4) 3 vols, London, John Murray.

Fitzgerald, W.T. (1815) *Wellington's Triumph: or, The Battle of Waterloo*, London.

Gardnor, Revd J. (1791) *Views Taken on the Rhine ...*, London.

Godwin, W. (1798) *Memoirs of the Author of a Vindication of the Rights of Woman*, London.

Guide to the Grand Improved Model of the Battle of Waterloo, Now Exhibiting at the Cosmorama Rooms, 209 Regent Street, London, *c*.1815.

Lockhart, J.G. (1893) *The Life of Sir Walter Scott*, London, Adam & Charles Black.

Lovell, E.J. (ed.) (1966) *Medwin's Conversations with Lord Byron*, Princeton, Princeton University Press.

Manning, P.J. 'Childe Harold in the Marketplace: From Romaunt to Handbook', *Modern Language Quarterly*, 1991 (June), vol.52 (2), pp.170–90.

Manning, P.J. and Wolfson, S. (eds) (1996) *Lord Byron: Selected Poems*, Harmondsworth, Penguin.

Marchand, L.A. (ed.) (1976) *Byron's Letters and Journals,* vol.V, London, John Murray.

Mitchell, J. (1817) *A Tour through Belgium, Holland, along the Rhine, and through the North of France, in the summer of 1816*, London.

Moore, T. (1830) *Letters and Journals of Lord Byron with notices of his life*, 2 vols, London, John Murray.

Moore, T. (ed.) (1832–3) *Works of Lord Byron*, 17 vols, London.

Peacock, T.L. (1924) *The Works of Thomas Love Peacock*, 10 vols, London, Constable.

A Picturesque Tour through France, Switzerland, on the Banks of the Rhine ..., London, 1817.

Quennell, P. (ed.) (1937) *The Private Letters of Princess Lieven to Prince Metternich, 1820–26*, London, John Murray.

Raffles, T. (1818) *Letters, during a Tour through Some Parts of France, Savoy, Switzerland, Germany, and the Netherlands, in the summer of 1817*, Liverpool.

Reade, J.E. (1829) *Cain the Wanderer*, London.

Redford, B. (1996) *Venice and the Grand Tour*, New Haven and London, Yale University Press.

Reiman, D.H. (ed.) (1972) *The Romantics Reviewed*, Part B: *Byron and Regency Society Reviewers*, 5 vols, New York, Garland.

Root, C. (1990) 'History as character: Byron and the myth of Napoleon', in *History and Myth: Essays on English Romantic Literature,* ed. S.C. Behrendt, Detroit, Wayne State University Press, pp.149–65.

Schama, S. (1995) *Landscape and Memory*, London, HarperCollins.

Scott, J. 'Living Authors, No. IV: Lord Byron,' *London Magazine 3*, (1821) pp.50–61.

Scott, Sir Walter, 'Review of *Childe Harold's Pilgrimage*' in *The Quarterly Review,* 16 (October 1816), pp.172–208.

Scott, Sir Walter (1951) *Poetical Works*, ed. J. Logie Robertson, London, Oxford University Press.

Smithers, H. (*c.*1817) *Observations made during a Tour in 1816 and 1817 ... To which is added Several Original Anecdotes relative to the Battle of Waterloo ...*, Brussels.

Southey, R. (1816) *The Poet's Pilgrimage to the Field of Waterloo*, London.

Ward, J. (1821) *The Battle of Waterloo, in an Allegory, Painted for the Directors of the British Institution, founded June 1805, for the express purpose of encouraging the Fine Arts ...*, London.

Warton, T. (1762) *Observations on the Fairy Queen of Spenser*, 2nd edn, London.

Williams, H.M. (1798) *A Tour in Switzerland; or, A View of the Present State of the Governments and Manners of those Cantons: with comparative Sketches of the Present State of Paris*, 2 vols, 2nd edn, London.

Williams, H. (1983) *Rousseau and Romantic Autobiography*, Oxford, Oxford University Press.

Further reading

Bainbridge, S. (1995) *Napoleon and English Romanticism*, Cambridge, Cambridge University Press. Deals with Romantic writers' longstanding fascination with the figure of Napoleon.

Buzard, J. (1993) *The Beaten Track: European Tourism, Literature, and the Ways to 'Culture', 1800–1918*, Oxford, Clarendon Press, especially pp.114–30 on the ways the Byron industry inflected nineteenth-century tourism.

Elfenbein, A. (1995) *Byron and the Victorians*, Cambridge, Cambridge University Press, especially chapters 1 and 2 on the poetic and cultural mechanisms whereby Byron became a celebrity.

Gordon, G., Lord Byron, *Childe Harold's Pilgrimage* (Cantos I, II, and IV).

Hibbert, C. (1987) *The Grand Tour*, London, Methuen. A general and entertaining overview of the phenomenon, with interesting illustrations.

Redford, B. (1996) *Venice and the Grand Tour*, New Haven and London, Yale University Press, especially chapter 1, 'Perspectives'.

Scott, Sir Walter, *Marmion*. The important verse-romance for the period.

Conclusion to Block 6

Prepared for the course team by Robert Wilkinson

After this encounter with Romantic works and ideas it will be clear, I hope, why in the Block Introduction I stressed the idea that Romanticism is not easy to sum up or define. We have seen in the aesthetic theory of the early German Romantics an extensively elaborated set of beliefs about art, resting typically on the metaphysical assertion that reality is spiritual in nature, a constantly evolving will knowable only via imaginative insights somehow embodied in works of art with mythic, symbolic dimensions, yet which are always inadequate to their task of conveying the insights concerned. These ideas are consonant with the typically Romantic moral belief that the good consists in striving constantly for an ideal that we know will always elude us. This ideal appears to be embodied in the character of Faust, who knows that if he bids the moment stay (if he ceases to strive) he is doomed. Yet the relationship of Faust to Goethe, and of Goethe to the Romantic movement of which these early theorists were leading members, is, as we have seen, not straightforward.

Music was held (in contrast to its relatively lowly status in the Enlightenment) to be the art par excellence capable of embodying the Romantic ideal. As the philosopher Arthur Schopenhauer (1788–1860) put it:

> ... we must attribute to music a far more serious and profound significance that refers to the innermost being of the world and of our own self ... For this reason the effect of music is so very much more powerful and penetrating than is that of the other arts, for these others speak only of the shadow, but music of the essence.

(1969, vol.1, pp.256–7)

The extraordinary change in the way music was conceived in the light of such ideas we have seen exemplified in the songs of Schubert you have been studying, so different in their method and goal from the music of Mozart. Again, Byron (who was to become almost synonymous with Romanticism across Europe in the first half of the nineteenth century) would have accepted very few of the doctrines so passionately advanced by the Germans, coming closest to them in his belief in the power of the will, though shorn of its metaphysical complexities. It would be difficult to mistake any of these ideas or works for ideas or works of the Enlightenment; but it would be equally difficult to pick out some feature or set of features that they all have in common.

However, I hope it is also clear why I said that the situation is not hopeless. It is, I hope, now evident what is meant by some of the ideas most commonly advanced in primers of the history of thought as characteristic of the Romantic movement and which have been mentioned at various points in this course. Romantic works are often said to exhibit a special concern with or to presuppose a special value for the *individual* self, by contrast to the typical stress of the Enlightenment, which is to see individuals as the manifestations of universal principles and having a *common* human nature. The inner life of individuals is said to have become a central theme in art, in contrast to the goal of producing somewhat generalized and perfected imitations of nature as in the preceding period. The thoughts and emotions of both artists and portrayed characters are taken to be of self-evident interest in a way that is new in Europe. Again, the complementary belief that the expression of feeling is of value for its own sake and worthy of aesthetic contemplation comes to be taken very seriously. Moreover, it becomes legitimate to take an interest in the remote in time and the remote in place, in folk legends and fairytales, in other cultures, and these manifestations of human imagination are held to be of special value to us, and again worth contemplation. This is a consequence of the important belief that the imagination itself is a faculty which can bring us to special forms of knowledge beyond the grasp of reason. In the Enlightenment, progress had been viewed, as is appropriate in the framework of the rationalism of the time, as the accumulation of true propositions which allow us ever greater understanding of and mastery over nature. It followed that past ages were ignorant of important truths and consequently to be viewed merely as steps on the way to the glorious present (and the even more glorious future). For the Romantics, past ages were as endowed with imagination as the present, and their productions consequently of still current interest and value. Again, certain modes of feeling, from pantheistic intuitions to dissipated, world-weary Byronic disillusion, the doomed loneliness of the exceptional individual in a philistine world, come to the centre of cultural awareness and become highly fashionable.

Now there is no *logical* link between the belief that the imagination gives us access to truth (for example) and the belief that the whole inner life of human beings and its expression is of self-evident interest and value: you can believe either of these ideas without being logically committed to believing the other. Nor is there a *logical* link between either of these beliefs and (for example) the belief that Byronic disillusion is an appropriate response to the human condition. Again, the belief that reality is not a rationally decodable mechanism but a constantly evolving manifestation of some form of will is equally logically independent of all these other beliefs. The links between ideas such as these are more psychological than logical. Once you begin to take inwardness seriously, once you begin to regard detailed introspection as a centrally valuable human activity (as the Pietist tradition did), and once you come to believe that the enlightened view of things leaves out of account some precious aspects of the emotional life of individuals, then the predisposition to accept sets of beliefs like these is readily understandable. The will, the imagination and the emotions are important aspects of our inner life which come to be concentrated on in a view of the world where the detailed workings of consciousness are taken to be of the greatest interest. Even if these ideas are not logically tightly linked, they do have, as it were, a common flavour, and they do have the weaker logical relation of consistency: they can all be true together. The consequence is that the Romantic movement produced works that can display quite a variety of properties which need not be tightly logically related. Works that are called Romantic, I would suggest, are better regarded as having a family resemblance than a common essence (a shared property or small set of properties), though they cannot be mistaken for works informed by the ideas of the Enlightenment. Instead, they have complex and individual relations of similarity and difference. At least, I would suggest that this is a reasonable hypothesis you might like to test as you turn to further examples of Romanticism in the final block of the course.

References

Schopenhauer, A. (1969) *The World as Will and Representation*, 2 vols, trans. E.F.J. Payne, New York, Dover Books (first published 1819).

Glossary

Units 24–25

Cult of sensibility: one of a number of aspects of pre-Romanticism in European culture, a reaction to the strict rationalism of the Enlightenment. It manifests itself in the later decades of the eighteenth century in a new value being given to emotion, both in life and art. Emotional sensitivity became admirable in a way it had not been before.

Idealism: the view that ultimate reality is mental or spiritual in nature and none of it physical or material.

Mimetic theory: the theory that art is an imitation of nature. Additionally, the adjective 'mimetic' can be used now in a different but related sense as a synonym for 'representational' – as opposed to abstract – in the description of works of art.

Pantheism: the view that God is not transcendent (that is, logically independent of the creation) but immanent (that is, in some way present in all things in the world: not distinct from the creation).

Rationalism: the belief that human reason is capable of discovering the ultimate truth about what there is.

Symbolism: in the context of Romantic aesthetics, symbolism is a key technique used by Romantic artists. A symbol is a device used to convey obliquely, by suggestion rather than direct statement or depiction, a deep, inexhaustible aspect of experience which cannot be directly stated or depicted.

Units 26–27

Dramatic irony: the theatrical device which opens up a contrast between the knowledge to which the audience, listener or reader has access and the different knowledge available to the stage character(s), reflecting a contrast between appearance and reality.

Pathos: the literary device which draws on emotions of tenderness and sympathy from the audience, listener or reader.

Unit 28

Arpeggio: a chord of which the notes are played in succession, rather than simultaneously.

Strophic song: a song in which the same music is repeated at each verse.

Through-composed song: a song in which each verse has different music, or in which there are no distinct verses.

Units 29–30

Alliteration: the practice of starting a string of words with the same consonant or consonantal sound.

Anti-hero: a central but unheroic figure who occupies the conventional place of the hero in a story to comic or ironic effect.

Antithesis: a counter-example or argument to the 'thesis', the initial statement.

Apostrophe: opening address to a person or persons.

First-person narration: the story is told in the first person ('I').

Frame-narrative: a narrative within which another story is set, a frame-narrative usually provides an opening and a conclusion, and more rarely intrudes upon the inset narrative.

Genre: the set of inherited artistic conventions within which a particular text is working or to which it is alluding.

Imagery: any language which implicitly or explicitly compares one thing to another.

Implied author: the author whose presence and character are inferred by the reader from the text itself. Not to be confused with the biographically-verifiable author.

Metaphor: a linguistic figure by which one thing is implicitly compared to another.

Metaphorics: an interconnected system of related metaphors.

Mythos: a body of anecdotes, feelings and imaginings clustered around a single figure.

Persona: the character in which a first-person narrator tells his or her story.

Personification: the practice of writing about inanimate objects as though they were human beings.

Psychodrama: a drama or story that takes as its subject the play of inward emotions.

Quest-romance: a genre of romance that typically sends a hero on a journey seeking something sacred or divine, dwells upon his adventures upon the way, and is invested in the hero's ultimate spiritual enlightenment.

Sensibility: a loaded term in the late eighteenth and early nineteenth centuries, meaning something like a capacity for refined feeling.

Unreliable narrator: a narrator who cannot always be trusted to tell the whole truth to the reader in so many words, and whose self-interested stance must be taken into account by the alert reader.

Voice: a term which allows us as readers to distinguish between the implied author and the many voices s/he may adopt.

Index